THE BOY
WITH THE
PERPETUAL
NERVOUSNESS

A Memoir

GRAHAM CAVENEY

Simon & Schuster
New York   London   Toronto   Sydney   New Delhi

Simon & Schuster
1230 Avenue of the Americas
New York, NY 10020

Copyright © 2017 by Graham Caveney
Originally published in Great Britain in 2017 by Picador

First Simon & Schuster hardcover edition July 2018

SIMON & SCHUSTER and colophon are registered trademarks of Simon & Schuster, Inc.

For information about special discounts for bulk purchases, please contact Simon &
Schuster Special Sales at 1-866-506-1949 or business@simonandschuster.com.

The Simon & Schuster Speakers Bureau can bring authors to your live event. For
more information or to book an event, contact the Simon & Schuster Speakers
Bureau at 1-866-248-3049 or visit our website at www.simonspeakers.com.

Interior design by Carly Loman

Manufactured in the United States of America

1   3   5   7   9   10   8   6   4   2

Library of Congress Cataloging-in-Publication Data is available.

ISBN 978-1-5011-6598-6
ISBN 978-1-5011-6597-9 (ebook)

To Anja Rutten, with thanks

How dangerous is the acquirement of knowledge and how much happier that man is who believes his native town to be the world, than he who aspires to become greater than his nature will allow.

—Mary Shelley, *Frankenstein*

When my pen leaks, I think awry. And who will give me back the good ink of my school days?

—Gaston Bachelard, *The Poetics of Reverie*

She says things like Neural Pathways, and Emotional Processing, and Some Success with Veterans from the Vietnam War. She says things get frozen, shelved, not properly digested. There is a bagatelle behind my eyeballs. She says follow my finger. I follow her finger. It is pulling back the spring on the pinball machine in my frontal lobe. Recall the scenes, she says. Recall them as though they are on a video loop. Got that? Video. You can control what happens. You can pause or fast-forward or rewind. It's a black-and-white movie, loosely auto-biographical: "based on actual events," as the blurbs always put it.

I am playing Me: typecasting, you might say. I am fifteen and I have bad skin. I have bad skin and I have long hair. My hero at the time was Jim Morrison from the Doors and I reckoned that on a dark night, in a fog, at fifty paces, I might be able to pass for him. This was 1980. Punk had already happened, but not in that ground-zero, road-to-Damascus way that is so often attributed to the arrival of the Clash's/the Pistols'/ the Damned's first album. Not for intense and bookish young boys from Accrington, anyway. For us, for me, punk was still partly a rumor, even after its demise. We caught it as it was leaving the building. The memory of the Sex Pistols' Manchester Free Trade Hall gig was mythic, not singular. It was like the Kennedy assassination or the moon landings, both ancient and crushingly modern. (One day, technology will enable us to prove conclusively just who did attend this event, and that day will be a day of terrible reckoning. Names will be broadcast on loudspeakers throughout the city, and grown men will weep.)

Where was I? That's right, following her finger. "Her," by the way, is Julie, my therapist. It is 2012 and I am having postrehab therapy for the issues that led to my addictions. There used to be scare quotes around both these words—"issues" and "addictions"—but not anymore. Now they just trip off the tongue with all the sincerity we can muster. She carries on with the finger stuff, the one next to her thumb, right hand, fully extended. As it moves back and forth she is asking me to remember details—the more detailed the details the better. The name for this treatment is EMDR—eye movement desensitization and reprocessing therapy. The idea—and there is an impressive amount of evidence to back this up—is that traumatic and distressing events are not processed properly at the point of trauma (it is, if you like, precisely what is traumatic about them). The event(s) thus become buried, only to surface later as neurosis, pathology, disorder. It has an almost tactile specificity to it, this EMDR stuff, as though my brain is Play-Doh and needs to be remolded. It's also had some remarkable success, particularly in the States, and that always makes me suspicious. I may have PTSD, it's my most recent diagnosis. It would make sense, from what I've read. I am, as they say, textbook. And if you have PTSD then you need EMDR—treat one acronym with another. What we're doing is time-travel. My mind is a TARDIS and somehow my experiences can be unlocked and reprocessed through this side-to-side eye-movement recall.

And it is true that something is shifting. I am remembering one specific incident within an incident—the feel of bristles on my face. The movie starts to seep into color. There is a dissolve, a rearrangement of dimensions and perspective. That bit looks sharper, the angle on the bed. There is a softer focus on the lens. Something about it strikes me as ludicrous, it reminds me briefly of a *Carry On* film, one of the bawdy British movies of the '60s and '70s. I start to laugh. Julie smiles at my laughter, encouraging me: This is your film now, you can make it into a comedy if you like, it's yours to view however you want. . . .

I am laughing hard now; a contained hysteria that I can feel at the back of my throat. This is absurd. There is a man, look at him! He has hair on his back . . . he's grunting . . . He's . . . There's a boy . . . Underneath him . . . The mise-en-scène is off. The set is made of cardboard.

Julie is staying with me, calm, alert. I'm changing my tenses: "It was . . ." becomes "It is. . . ." I switch pronouns, "I" to "he" to "it." Projections onto the back of my closed eyelids, faster and slower at the same time. It's like old newsreel clips: Pathé, home movies. Clips of people from the silent era walking and waving in that disjointed flickering motion. For some reason I associate old celluloid footage with baseball (Babe Ruth?), although I am not an American and have never seen baseball. The images slow down. There's an overdub with the kind of hallucinatory soundtrack that gets used in sixties acid indie films, the kind with Peter Fonda, maybe directed by Monte Hellman. And . . . action!

His hand is on my cock, his cock is on my stomach, his mouth is on my mouth. He is masturbating. There's a boy who looks like me. He's lying on his back. I'm looking down at him from the ceiling. And cut.

"Dissociation" is one of those terms that has entered our collective wisdom in ways that I am both thankful for and irritated by. Thankful in that it gives legitimacy to the experience of sexual trauma. Irritated that the experience can be reduced to a one-word tick box. The ambivalence about being diagnosed speaks to the condition itself. Who doesn't want their experience to have a description? Yet who doesn't want to be more than their diagnosis? "Dissociated" it is then, for the moment, and amongst other things.

It is certainly my experience that when reality is overwhelming, unprocessable, noncomputable, our minds simply take us somewhere else. We replace unacceptable truths with fantasies—fantasies which may have a truth of their own, yet which place us at odds with the cold unforgiving empiricism of the-world-as-it-is. Thanks to genre fiction, Hollywood, and popular psychology, we now expect the Mad and the Dangerous to have rationales of their own. The fucked-up kid is our new femme fatale. The kid locked in a stranger's basement. The kid who witnesses his mother's murder. The kid forced to participate in genocide. We love our fucked-up kids nearly as much as we despise the adults they become.

What we know is that trauma is never something that is simply left behind, like blood at the scene of a car crash. Rather it is something that the survivor, the sufferer, carries within them; the wreckage that is part of their self. The first time that I heard the term "dissociation" was in relation to chemistry, whereby it describes the process of ionic compounds being broken down into smaller particles and ions. I remember sitting in chemistry labs as a kid watching obscure-sounding acids or salts being dissolved in water, and watching this kaleidoscopic process of crystallization as each constituent part . . . what? retreated? was liberated? got banished from? all the others. I remember asking the teacher, a disappointed man named Mr. Stokes, if these dissociated parts could be reunited or reintegrated. He assured me that, with a few exceptions, they could.

Of course, this idea of a traumatized childhood carries with it the implication that there could be such a thing as a nontraumatized childhood. Readers of Freud will know that, for him, childhood was itself a kind of trauma—a time when the infant has to relinquish his tyranny over his parents and be coerced into the dreaded disillusion of the reality principle. According to this model, no one emerges unscathed. We become who we are by abandoning our most primal desires, being born again into the laws of our Father (societal norms, nonincestuous desire, relationships with bodies other than our own). The "traumatized child" then is nothing more than a tautology, a description of an inevitable process of disenchantment.

To which I want to add: if growing up is traumatic enough in itself, then getting fucked as well kind of adds injury to insult. I didn't get a free pass on all the other horrors of adolescence on the basis that I was busy dealing with the specific horror of an unwanted cock.

It seems to me now profoundly unfair that I still had to contend with wet dreams as well as abuse; romantic rejection *and* sexual assault. Abused children often talk about having their childhood stolen from them, and for good reason. What is harder to describe is the feeling of having been robbed of a childhood that you didn't have—the childhood you imagined you might have had had it not been for the being-fucked stuff. Put another way, the question becomes something like: If I was being abused during a period of my life that I know to be experienced by people who weren't abused as still volatile, traumatic, and confusing, then to what extent are those feelings specific to my abuse? How could I ever know? Only a nonabused me would be able to solve this fucking riddle, and a nonabused me would not be me. Answers, please, on a postcard.

NEXT

When a Person From Accrington (PFA) meets a Person Not From Accrington (PNFA), there will, at some point, be the following exchange:

PNFA: So where are you from . . . ?

PFA: Er . . . (either sheepishly or defiantly, embarrassed or proud) Accrington.

PNFA: Oh . . . (delighted by their perspicacity) . . . Stanley . . . !

Accrington Stanley FC was indeed the only claim to fame that my hometown had when I lived there. Years later we would be able to add Jeanette Winterson and the actress Julie Hesmondhalgh to our roll call of Accrington's great and good, but in the seventies and early eighties, the folk memory of a founding first-division football team was as close to recognizable as Accrington got.

When I first left home and went to university, I probably had a dozen such exchanges within the first day. Such was my annoyance that I tried to fudge it with a vague "Lancashire way," which only served to make me seem either evasive and furtive, as though I was on the run from the police, or dim and uncertain, like I'd just had a course of ECT. I tried amending my answer to "Manchester" for a while, mainly on the basis I had a northern accent and a record collection that contained the Buzzcocks, Joy Division, and Magazine. This would work until I actually met someone from Manchester, or anyone who had been to Manchester, or anyone who knew anything at all about Manchester. Within minutes I would be forced into mumbling something about "a town near to . . . er . . . cotton mills . . . close to Blackburn." Eventually I would blurt out "Accrington," they would say "Stanley" and another little bit of me would die.

Quite why I took so vehemently against my hometown's football club I don't quite know. It's partly the name. Could we not have been a robust United or a stoical Town? "Stanley" made us sound as though the team consisted of one man, or, worse, eleven men all with the same name. It added to my sense that I wasn't from a place so much as a punch line to some unimaginative southern scriptwriter's joke.[1] Where you from? Accrington? Sorry to hear it. I did try on the football thing as a kid for a while. I decided that if supporting a football team was compulsory (and it felt as though it was), I would at least give it a perverse twist and support Burnley Football Club. My dad dutifully took me to Turf Moor (Burnley's Stadium). I still remember the chant—"Leighton James, Alan West, Martin Dobson, and the rest . . . na, na, na, na, na, na, na, ana"—sung by the Longside (Burnley's Football Club's supporters' end) with boozy exhilaration. I remember getting a hot pie and Bovril at halftime and scalding fat oozing out of the crust onto my paws. I remember thinking, as we stood behind the goal, how unfair it was that we had paid full price but only really got to see half a game, and wouldn't it be better if they used one end of the pitch rather than both. I remember the fence being charged, the one that separated the Away fans from the Home fans, and a chant going through the ground "A-G-R-O / A-G-R-O / Hello" to the sound of Gary Glitter's "Hello, Hello, I'm Back Again." I remember feeling sick and grabbing hold of my dad's hand and him telling me not to worry. I remember the chants getting louder—"You're gonna get your fucking head kicked in"; "You're goin' home in a fuckin' ambulance"—and sharpened coins and empty crisp bags filled with piss and crushed beer cans and darts all being thrown from one side of the railings to the next. Ah, the beautiful game.

---

1 Not just southerners, actually. There was a time when *Coronation Street* used Accrington as shorthand for a certain kind of existential dread. "A face like a wet Wednesday in Accrington" was one I remember.

NEXT

Her legs, pumping up and down the cold street, had the
regularity and power of pistons.

—Pat Barker, *Union Street*

I was born in Roughlee Hospital on November 26, 1964. It's just a few
miles from Pendle Hill, a place famous for its witches, one of whom,
Alice Nutter, has been memorialized with a statue near the hospital.
I am looking at my birth certificate now. It's my mother's writing, no
doubt about it. Name and Surname of father: john CAVENEY. That's
how my mum has written it; lower, then upper case. No middle name,
like me. The family joke that we couldn't afford one.

Under "Occupation of father": "maker, lorry driver." "Maker"? I
suspect that my mum meant laborer, but she is clearly emphasizing
that there is a Skilled element to her husband's labor. I don't remember
him being a lorry driver. For most of my life, he was the groundsman
at the local comprehensive (the UK equivalent of a US public high
school)—a job that suited him fine; solitary, outdoors, practical. "Sig-
nature, description, and residence of informant": k caveney, mather
[*sic*], 47 Cedar Street, Accrington.

The "k" was for Kathleen, her maiden name Smethurst. The
youngest of three daughters, she had gone with her two sisters, Mary
and Margaret, into the mills when she was fourteen. The girls had
lost their mum to breast cancer when they (and she) were still young,
and so it had fallen to them to cook and clean and generally keep
house. Her dad remarried—a textbook evil stepmother according to
my mum, although the resentment would always be tempered with a
"but it was good of her to take us all on."

One of her favorite could-have-been stories was that there was an older cousin who wanted to adopt her when her mum died, and who had made a few quid (where? how?) and would have sent her to Secretary School (you could hear the capital letters when she told this tale) but that her dad had wanted to keep the girls together. Just quite what this story was based on I could never find out, but it clearly troubled my mother, this sense of having been sold short.

NEXT

Though I have asked many of my acquaintances at what
stage in their childhood or adolescence they became class-
conscious, none has ever given me a satisfactory answer.
—Robert Graves, *Goodbye to All That*

If you turn to any sociologist's dictionary and look up the term "Respectable Working Class" (RWC), you will find a picture of John and
Kathleen Caveney. I'm told that we don't have a working class anymore, let alone a respectable one. Aspiration and ambition have em-
bourgeoised us all apparently, although I'd like to see Westminster's
finest sell that on the streets of Accrington. Yet RWC is what my parents were: unproblematically (mostly), unashamedly (on the whole),
non-class-consciously (virtually).

It was my dad's boast that he wasn't frightened of hard work. For
my mum, her house was "spotless" and she "kept a good table." Just
what constituted a "good table" we will find out later, but looking
back now I'm struck by the glaringly obvious (but never discussed)
gender divide. My mum's work in the mills was never really discussed
as work. I remember going to visit her factory once and being rooted
to the spot by the sheer noise of the machines. It is to my shame that
I can't tell you the difference between the weaving and the spinning,
the shunting and the braiding.

All I can tell you is that the place was stifling hot, deafeningly
loud, with huge machines that needed to be manually operated by a
workforce that was mostly female. They were communicating with
a mixture of sign language and lip-reading, the machines having
drowned out any hopes for speech. Here was "hard graft," as us
Brits used to call manual labor: the women's hands were getting

dirty, their bodies were clearly sweating. Yet it was to my dad's world that such language belonged. My mother "simply" went out to work.

And came home to work. It fell to her—her phrase—to do the washing, the shopping, the cleaning, the cooking, and those countless other jobs that were never called jobs. Even the verb "fell" is shot through with a sense of the accidental, the clumsy, the easily overlooked. Women used to "fall pregnant."

Which brings us to "the good table" my mum so proudly kept. The phrase meant that the meals were regular and homemade: a bacon sandwich or Ready Brek (instant oatmeal) for breakfast ("central heating for kids"), a packed lunch (meat or fish paste) for all three of us, and "a hot meal" at night, never later than six.

"A good table" meant that we never went hungry, rarely went to the fish and chip shop (the chippy), and always had Afters (dessert) after our tea. It meant that we ate around the kitchen table ("setting the table" was my one and only domestic task, carried out with martyred stoicism) and that the TV was turned off whilst we ate.

In the middle of the table is a plate of bread and butter, a salt and a pepper pot (white pepper: black pepper wouldn't hit the North for at least another decade), a bottle of Heinz tomato ketchup, a bottle of Daddies Brown Sauce, and a jar of pickled onions. The meal in front of me—this being a Tuesday—is potato pie and peas. The ingredients are: potatoes, corned beef, a carrot, and an onion. On top of this lies a suet crust. The crust is slightly burnt brown on top and a chewy wallpaper-paste white beneath. The peas are mushy, a luminous green that may have been the result of Mum soaking them overnight. It is a concoction that demands the sharp vinegary twist of Daddies Brown Sauce. It glugs from the bottle, smothering the dense gray blandness of the stew. It is almost pure carbohydrate, a rich, glutinous expanse of a meal designed to weigh you down and keep you close. No little light supper this: this is food that can still remember the workhouse, food that is designed with insulation in mind.

Mum takes away the plates, scrapes the remains back into the deep white pan. This "will keep," will be fried up later, crust and all: I prefer it this way. For dessert, a can of Heinz strawberry jam sponge pudding, steamed and served up with a trough of Bird's custard.

Our occasional meals out were obstacle courses in anxiety. My parents would fret about coordinating their appetites, having to reset their internal rhythms to the idea of food at seven thirty (even eight o'clock!). What were they meant to do between teatime and then? Starve?

The waiters and waitresses were scary; enforcers of an alien etiquette. My mum would apologize before asking a question about the menu, preempting her own ignorance, her I-know-I-shouldn't-be-here-ness. Dad would go quiet, shuffle, point to the thing that sounded as though it most closely resembled the things that we had at home.

He couldn't see what all the fuss was about; it got on his nerves, all these sauces and the funny squiggly writing that you couldn't quite make out. Food could be about pleasure for them, but it was about solitary or stolen time—ten minutes with a brew and a biscuit, a trip to the chip shop, or something you got from Accy Market just because you fancied it. It was about the satisfaction of a full belly. Northern working-class diets were about fuel, cost efficiency, and the sense of daily indulgence.

So food was good, in a nonfetishized, utilitarian kind of way. But what was really good—what was essential in fact to the lives of Jack and Kathleen—was the smoking of cigarettes.

To say that my parents smoked doesn't come close to describing the centrality of nicotine to the rhythm and meaning of their days. Time was measured in cigarettes: or rather, time was measured in the things that had to get done in between cigarettes, as though a day's activities were like words that had no meaning unless punctuated by the structuring grammar of a cigarette.

Cigarettes were the reason for drinking hot drinks; they were what you looked forward to at mealtimes. They were the afters that followed Afters. Cigarettes were necessary to watch television, to play snooker, to go to the pictures, to play bingo, to go out for a pint, to have a quiet night in. Cigarettes were necessary to talk to each other.

They smoked the same brand, Embassy during the seventies, Benson & Hedges in the eighties. I think the switch was something to do with loyalty coupons as much as taste. Certainly our house was partly furnished with items bought by fag coupons: an alarm clock, toasters, a portable radio, kettles, a set of kitchen knives. (Maybe they felt they couldn't afford to stop smoking?) They smoked in tandem, synchronized smoking, a harmony of in- and exhalation.

In the evenings, in front of the TV, the adverts would allow for a trip to the kitchen and a shout of "Tea or coffee?" Drinks would be brought through. Smoking could commence. One drink meant three cigarettes—one whilst it cooled, one to accompany it, one to signal its completion. Three fags to one brew, four brews a night. And so the nights wore on; mouths dry and then wet, cups replenished, ashtrays overflowing.

Need I say that their mouths were ruined? My old photos show Kath smiling in a way that tries to hide the browned and buckled teeth. Her lips are pursed, overstretched, hands hovering ready to cover the mouth in a gesture that foregrounds her shame.

She had been pretty as a girl and handsome as a woman, yet her confidence was undermined by her self-conscious mouth. Both of their sets of teeth had decayed by their forties, gone by their fifties, replaced by full sets of dentures.

My dad used his false teeth like a percussion instrument, expressing annoyance, approval, whatever, by clacking them together and swirling his jaw. If George Burns had his cigars, Groucho Marx his mustache, my dad had his dentures. They were the cymbal clash for his punch lines, the maracas of his routines. I can hear him now: "Look at that stupid bastard!" (Usually Prince Philip, though other members of the royal family would do.) "I've seen . . . *clack-clack* . . . better hair on a side of bacon . . . All that money and he still . . . *clack-clack* . . . can't afford a smile . . . *clack-clack* . . . a face like a smacked arse . . .

clack-clack . . ." and on he'd go, a running commentary on the state of the nation and the various bastards and bloody idiots who ran it.

I would love to say that John (Jack, as everyone called him) was left-wing, or a hard-core union man, but the truth is that he was a conservative: a conservative who voted Labour all his life, but a conservative nonetheless. He too had been an only child, a condition that I somehow associate with Toryism, with the privileging of the individual over (what I imagined to be) the collectivity of larger families.

More important, he was an only child who was even more Only from the ages of eight to fourteen. Whether my grandfather volunteered or was conscripted to fight in the Second World War I do not know, but I know that my dad relished his duty as his mother's guardian whilst he was away. "Away" seems an inadequate word for risking your life fighting Nazism for six years, but it was the word my dad grew up with: "Your dad's away." And, once he came back, it seemed he didn't want to talk about what he'd done or where he'd been. Thus did my grandfather return a stranger, to a boy who was a stranger to him.

And Jack? Was Jack glad to have his dad the hero back? Or was he resentful at the intrusion, jealous that his mother would no longer be his? Again! As if that first Oedipal trauma—the one that Freud was so keen on—wasn't enough.

I think that these formative years left Jack with self-sufficiency certainly, but also a sense that the world was bigger than he could ever imagine, certainly too big for him to change. I never heard him voice a racist opinion, but I certainly never heard him voice any antiracist sentiment either. He would refer to "the Paki shop," but this was as a genre of shop—one that stayed open late—and I'm not even sure if he had made the connection between "Paki" and "Pakistani." (The last time I was back home in Accrington, I felt strangely vindicated that the local "Paki" shop was run by white people, and yet still referred to as a Paki shop.)

I think that my grandfather's time in the army had given him a broader perspective on race and identity. Simply put, foreign voices and black skins did not faze or affront him. In the most general of senses he had a respect for the Otherness of other cultures. His army

NEXT

The only child's relative lack of opportunity for expressing the aggressive side of his nature is a serious thing.

—D. W. Winnicott,
The Child, the Family and the Outside World

Although Cedar Street was given as our address on my birth certificate, I have no memories of living there. The first house that I can recall was a council house in Oswaldtwistle. On the off chance that you've never been there, Oswaldtwistle—"Ossie" to the locals—is a suburb of Accrington. Ossie is the Brooklyn to Accy's Manhattan, the Montparnasse to its Paris—an edgier, slightly scruffier location with an identity all of its own. There was an inevitable rivalry between the two, one of those mock-epic grudges that can always turn serious with the right mixture of beer, testosterone, and unemployment. I was too young for these territorial battles, five or six, unaware that there were such things as "our end" and that "they" should therefore "get back down their own end." Not that I was ever out much in Ossie.

I seemed to be permanently sick, lurching from gastroenteritis to whooping cough in less than a year. Wiser people than me have said that we don't, maybe can't, remember illness the way it actually was. What we think about when we think about being ill is being like we are now—well, healthy—but with bits added on or taken off.

All I remember from that time is bottles of energy-boosting Lucozade wrapped in sheets of orange plastic, and pink chalk-tasting syrup being coaxed into me on a deep white spoon. Later I would find out that I had nearly died—"we thought we'd lost ya"—and that Masses had been said for me. Once I got well, I fell in love with this story, making Kath repeat it in all its gory sentiment. She would indulge me, telling me how everyone had been really worried ("really, really, really worried, Mum?") and how I had been really ("really, really?") brave.

The odd Dickensian flourish notwithstanding, my illness helped convince them that it was time to move. There was some untreated land across from our backyard which Jack became convinced was to blame and, besides, they were hoping to do something that no one in their family had ever done before.

They were going to buy a house.

Such a move had been unthinkable to both sets of my grandparents—they had rented the same houses all their lives, it had been the safest (the only) option. My parents were set to become part of a relatively new socioeconomic group: the property-owning working class.

Years later, when I was a student on the obligatory left, I would hear talk of "false consciousness" and "embourgeoisement"—the process whereby the working class was effectively bought off, assimilated into the socioeconomic power structures that had kept them oppressed. Workers of the world unite, you have nothing to lose but your chains. And mortgages, and color TVs, shag-pile carpets, stereo hi-fi systems, and central heating.

The political muscle of the working class, so it was argued, was being softened up by giving them the illusion of freedom through material comfort. To which I say: outside toilets. No heroic struggles of the left, no strikes or wars against imperialist aggressors were made easier by having to go out in the freezing cold in order to take a shit. The prospect of becoming home owners may have been fraught with all sorts of dangers, but an atrophying of class awareness wasn't one of them. There was nothing "false" about this consciousness; it was the very stuff of their lives. They had grown up pissing into chamber pots, paying money to slumlords who had thought it only fair that my parents should carry out the maintenance on their property.

And so it was that we ended up on Lister Street—number 24, opposite the chippy, next door to the corner shop. It had a vestibule, a word I always think has church-like connotations, somewhere where you might find a tabernacle. Everywhere you looked there was Catholic tat—small statues of the Sacred Heart, with his heart-shaped heart that glowed in the dark. Statues of St. Christopher—patron saint of children. Tiny bottles of holy water that "never evaporated" (want to test the science on that, Mum, every time you fill 'em up?); small cards bearing pious verses; a 3-D picture of Our Lord looking gormlessly out over some sheep; palms when they were in season, rosary beads which were always in season. We had candles with Latin inscriptions, candles with fey poems, and candles that weren't really candles but that were battery powered and doubled as lamps. The Virgin made an appearance in nearly every room. Her statue had pride of place in the living room, on the mantelpiece, the body of her recently crucified Son draped operatically across her arms. Her picture was in both bedrooms, the blue and white of her head scarf blended into the whiteness of surrounding doves, her hands locked in supplication. The Pope kept watch over what we got up to in the kitchen, the watchful eye of His Holiness gazing tenderly upon our boxes of shredded wheat and family packs of chocolate biscuits. He blessed our wall-to-wall carpeting, the three-piece sofa that kept its wrapping for years.

I have my own room—the front room, looking out at a garden that has no grass. Both backyard and garden were paved over, reassuring slabs of concrete that only needed the odd bit of weeding. Given Jack's job anything more would have been too much of what Lancastrians call a busman's holiday. His love of being outdoors never extended to gardening. Or gardens. Or even indoor plants. The natural world in general was a closed book to my parents. And to me, still. Even now, if someone mentions that their clematis is coming along nicely, I tend to think of a skin condition or venereal disease.

At the bottom of the street is a playground, nothing more than a bit of spare ground with some swings. Everyone calls it "the wreck." Later it occurs to me that what it is actually called is "the rec"—as in recreation—and I wonder if the pun is intentional. I spend summer nights swinging on the swings on this wrecked rec. It is where I first hear Diane Hacking tell me about girls' periods, though I wasn't sure if I believed her. I thought she was just saying that, the way boys say

NEXT

It is impossible to keep constant watch over your crib. In your breast—you poor little thing!—a mysterious combination is forming.

—Italo Svevo, *Zeno's Conscience*

I can't tell the kind of story that goes: "When I was seven and a half my mother bought me my first set of Legos and it was then that I knew I was destined to be an architect." Memory doesn't work that way, at least my memory doesn't. My oldest friend, Dave Hesmondhalgh, can do a version of this. Give him a year from, say, 1972 onwards, and he can pretty much give you where he was, the friends he had, and the records they were listening to. It's an impressive feat, one that I feel means that he is closer to himself, more aware of how his previous selves all connect and have developed.

My recall is more impressionistic: not so much chronology or linearity as disjointed montages of sensation. This makes for wild anachronism, as I lump together stuff from my late childhood with that of early adolescence. It is like a Godard film, full of jump cuts, a bricolage of photography and science fiction. Some of this has got to be the drugs. You cannot—as I have—live the life of a drug addict and/or alcoholic and still expect to trust your memory.

So I am ten, or I am seven or I am nine. On Saturday mornings my mum drops me off at the pictures, where a theater full of kids the same age (a bedlam of kids?) run around and watch cartoons. There is a serialized Western that always seems to be out of sequence. The goodie wears white and the baddie wears black and there is a stagecoach that is always crashing. Then there is the Emperor Ming, an imperious fellow whom I secretly wish well, urging him on to victory as though him defeating Flash Gordon would also represent my own triumph over these other kids—such childish children—who are all screaming for their hero.

The shrieking of the kids is piercing, hysterical; toffee and pop fly through the air. The soft spring-back seats are being kicked and pummeled, a sort of percussion to accompany the soundtrack. My ten- or whatever-year-old self is on edge: I want to cry but know I can't. What I want is for the other kids to shut up and watch the film, for them to do it properly and silently. What I want is queues and rules and orderly adults ordering them to hush. I hadn't then read *Lord of the Flies*, but when I did I recognized Piggy as my earlier self, insisting on the civilizing power of the conch whilst all around him boys were unleashing their murderous boyhood.

Was I really such a precious little bastard? It would seem so. Little Lord Fauntleroy, as my dad used to tease. The world of boys was a mystery to me (as was the world of girls). Their sheer physicality—all that rough 'n' tumble—seemed an assault on my only child's autonomy. It blurred the borders between me and them, between this loved and sickly child and the anonymous mass that is Children.

In an attempt to save me from those Saturday morning picture shows, my granddad teaches me to play chess. And cribbage. And poker. It's the miners' strike of 1974, and I have never been happier. When, ten years later, I spent time as an undergraduate campaigning for the miners, I am now convinced that it was partly out of gratitude for the favor they had done me in bringing about the three-day week and the blackouts. It can't be true, but it seemed that the whole of the country, or the whole of Accrington (same thing), was bathed in candlelight.

I finish school early (no lamplights), go up Dill Hall Lane, past the newsagents on the corner who wouldn't sell me a copy of a magazine with glam rocker Marc Bolan on the cover because "you do know it's for girls" and knock-and-only-me my way into my grandparents' tiny terraced house. Sally, my grandma, makes me a milky coffee to go with the shortbread, and my granddad mock-spits into his hands and says, "Now then, I'll stop you farting in church." And we play.

Fifteen two fifteen four fifteen six, two is eight and one for his nob makes nine. We do this night after night. We're hypnotized by numbers, lost in the rhythm of those precious fifteens and the possibilities of those discarded cards known as "the box." We are warriors in combat.

During these battles my grandfather seemed to me the kind of man that men should be. Here—across a makeshift card table—I was able to see how a man could be both daft and noble, delightfully playful and deadly serious. I was learning that the value of my own hand was dependent on the opportunities afforded to it by the other's hand, and that both hands were at the mercy of chance. He taught me the value of play.

About poker he taught me that I should never play poker. Or at least not against retired sergeant majors who had fleeced half the East Lancashire regiment. We played for Monopoly money, equally distributed at the start of each session. He would tease me to distraction, punctuating the examination of his cards with an array of "Ooo, would you look at thats?" and "That'll do nicelys" aimed—and succeeding—at instilling a fatal uncertainty into whatever hand I held. He would bankrupt me within half an hour, lend me some more, and then bankrupt me again. At the end of the session he would faithfully tot up my debt—often in the millions—and then offer me the chance to win it back the next night.

Was Dad jealous of the time I spent at his parents, of my closeness to a man he had never really known? There was, as we say, little love lost between them. They seemed so physically different: Dad small and compact, sinewy, his strength in his forearms and torso. Jack Senior was over six feet, his body broad in the shoulders, his chest wide and expansive.

There had been a huge fallout when I was still an infant, one of those stories that has reached mythic status by the time you encounter it as an adult. Firstly, Jack Senior had wanted me to be called Patrick—the name of his own father, a giant of an Irish patriarch who had sired eleven children back in County Mayo. Jack Junior would have none of it: I was his boy and would carry a name of his (i.e., my mum's) choosing. Besides, was it not time to leave behind the Irish association? Patrick Caveney for Christ's sake! How bloody Oirish do you want the little sod to sound? Why not call him O'Kavanagh and have done with it? No: Patrick would mean Paddy, and this boy was not going to be anybody's Paddy. And not another bloody John-Jack either. "Graham" was just that little bit different, not one you hear a lot, not common.

There had never been a St. Graham either; a fact that, as Mum used to point out, meant that I would get to be the first.

On top of that my grandparents had had a dog—a small yappy corgi called Reena (and, yes, I can hear every syllable of displaced Irish romance in that name as well). Reena had bitten someone—a neighbor I think—when I was still a toddler. It was Dad who gave the ultimatum: if you want your grandchild to come visit, get rid of the dangerous dog.

The feud went on for months apparently, the two men walking past each other in the street. Quite how it was resolved, history doesn't relate, except to say that all my memories of my grandparents are steadfastly corgi free.

After the war my granddad worked at Blythes Chemicals—a major employer situated on the canal on the road to Blackburn. The factory was there to dye the cotton, though to me its powers extended to alchemy. The water around it would turn into colors I had never seen before, or since; a kind of orangey turquoise overlaid with sickly viscous greens and yellows. We would have called them psychedelic, except we didn't know what psychedelic was. Instead whenever we passed that part of the canal—Bridge Street—Mum would joke, "Granddad's been cooking again." This probably wasn't far from the truth, now I come to think about it. At some point there had been a spillage and he had received burns to his face, so he must have been directly involved with the processing. He even got some compensation, though it can't have been much. I remember a Christmas food package arriving each year at their house, and my grandma's bitter verdict, "Not enough to make up for his looks, is it?"

Over my summer holidays we walk: me, my granddad, and a non-corgi black Labrador that is also called Reena. We walk for miles: over Jackson's farm, through the park, out to Rishton, over Ribbesdale, down into Clayton. We walk and we talk, or rather I pester him to tell me war stories and he torments me about Diane Hacking, who may or may not have sent me a Valentine's card.

He evades the war, I evade Diane Hacking. We settle on the subject of my "big daft" great-uncle Clifford, a bland lumbering cartoon of a man who communicates solely in monosyllabic grunts. Go round and see my great-aunt Florrie—my granddad's sister, wife to Clifford— and it is him, the dreaded Cliff, who will invariably open the door. "Who's out," he will say when I ask "Who's in?" "Dunno when who's back," he continues, the already unfunny joke becoming unfunnier by the second. I tell my granddad this and he is torn between not wanting me to talk badly of my elders and wanting me to talk badly of this particular elder. He laughs and tells me a funny story about Cliff going for a packet of fags and coming home three days later, shamefaced, sans fags. We walk farther on.

Everybody knows my granddad, the big fellow with the beret and the dog. A couple of people even salute. I am his lad's lad: "our Graham," soon to be "Our-Graham-Who-Goes-to-St. Marys," said in one breath, another name.

NEXT

From the *Accrington Observer*, cutting clipped and glued into album; date missing, but I'm guessing August 1974: "Eleven-year-old Graham Caveney, 24 Lister Street, Accrington, is this year's winner of a knockout putting competition held in Gatty Park by Hyndburn's Recreation and Amenities Department. . . . His efforts earned him the first prize of a £1 book token, a 50p record token, and a set of book plates. Said Graham who is due to start at St. Mary's College, Blackburn, next month: 'I'm going to buy the Fivepenny Piece's record but I don't know what book I'll buy. I shall defend my title next year. The competition is a good idea because you can get bored during the summer holidays.'"

Need I say more?

Here it is: my very own *Aspern Papers*, the Key to All Mythologies. All future character traits are to be found—the annoying pedantry, the self-aggrandizement ("I shall defend my title," for God's sake), the pious didacticism. And can we detect the spectral hand of Kathleen Caveney? Yes, we can. For the bit about me being "due to start at St. Mary's College" was her handiwork, her contribution to my entry into fame and fortune. She actually went into the offices of the *Accrington Observer* and demanded that they insert this vital piece of information, as though no Gatty Park Putting Contest Victory story could be complete without the knowledge of whether or not the winner was headed for the nearest grammar school.

It was the last year of the eleven-plus—1974—and a whole host of stories around social mobility and working-class education were being circulated and contested. For my parents there was no contest: this was my ticket out of having to do the kinds of jobs they had had to do themselves. It was as simple as that. It was only years later that I realized how complicated such simple stories are.

My passing the eleven-plus was not unrelated to my having become an altar boy a few years before, but I'm not sure how. The priest from my local parish—a scary jowly Irishman called Father McAvoy—had come to our school and told four boys to ask our parents if they would like us to "serve on the altar." They had said yes—all four sets of them. They had said yes the same way they said yes when the same priest asked them if they could keep a missionary box for the starving children of Africa ("just your spare copper," which spare copper?) and yes when he asked them if they were truly sorry for their sins when they went to confession.

So an altar boy I became. And I loved it. I would be called out of school to serve at a christening or to a funeral, slipped some silver for the former, a pound note for the latter. I remember saying how weird I thought it was that leaving this world merited a bigger tip than arriving into it, and Father Mac joking that, unlike the dearly departed, the newly arrived needed to be more prudent. I loved the long red cassock with its missing buttons, the white surplice, getting to bang the gong and checking that there was enough host and wine before the service.

I was confirmed whilst still "on the altar," chosen name John (what else?). Confirmation is one of the three sacraments of initiation (along with baptism and Communion). It was, I was told, the proudest moment of my life.

A sweet-smelling oil called chrism has been consecrated by the bishop, the arrival of whom is itself one notch down from the Second Coming of Christ. We kneel before him and kiss his ring. Acts of the Apostles is read. This will be a second baptism, one fitting the age of reason, a commitment between the confirmand and the Holy Spirit. We have been practicing for weeks, rehearsing our lines, kissing Father Mac's pretend-ring finger (which smells of tobacco). Photographers have been hired for the day, suits pressed. Mothers are spitting into their hankies and wiping clean their children's faces. I look, in the words of my mum, like an angel. My hair is a mixture of buttercup yellow and sugar-stealer white. I am podgy cute, with the kind of chubby cheeks that make grown-ups want to squeeze them. The bishop doesn't squeeze them. What he does is slap me on the face. It's a gentle slap and I knew it was coming. In fact the slap had been eagerly anticipated, symbol as it was of the hardship I would endure as a follower of Christ. And as he slaps me—me and hundreds of other boys who are all lining the aisles of the Sacred Heart Holy Roman Catholic Church, all waiting to be slapped—he says, "Peace be with you."

NEXT

Preacher in the pulpit roars with all his might
Sing Glory Halleluia with the folks all in a fright
— Lonnie Donegan, "Putting on the Style"

I am a devout child. I want to be good. Each night I kneel by my bed and pray, eyes squeezed tight: "Gentle Jesus, meek and mild, look down on me, thy little child. And if I die before I wake, I pray my Lord my soul to take. . . ." Then I remember that it's selfish just to pray for myself and so I think of my family. I linger purposefully over the ones I don't like, my way of doing penance for not liking them. I think of my fat cousin Simon and his fat face. I ask Jesus to make me be nicer to him, to stop me from hating his half-opened mouth and the way he says "You what?" I line up the people I love in my head and think warm thoughts to each of them. I then slot the people I don't love into the lineup of the people I do. Father Mac has told me the best way to pray for people I don't like. He tells me to try and think of them when they were babies, to remind myself that they weren't always bullying idiots or annoying arseholes. This works for a while: I replace fat Simon the stupid grown-up with fat Simon the gurgling baby, and I almost like him. Then the picture changes to a grown-up with a baby's head, and that doesn't work at all. Besides, babies aren't so innocent; they aren't innocent at all. They're born with original sin. It's why they need to be baptized.

I become obsessed with the Stations of the Cross—a retelling of the various falls and encounters Jesus underwent on his way to being crucified. We—the priest, one other boy, and me—walk one way down the nave of the church and stop beside a hung wooden carving, "Jesus Falls for the First Time" or "Meets His Mother," and my job is to wave incense whilst a prayer or contemplation is offered. Then we go back up the other side, dutifully stopping and thinking how awful it must have been when Jesus was "Stripped of His Garments" (No. 10) and "Nailed to the Cross" (No. 11) but thanking God that he is "Taken Down from the Cross" (No. 13) and finally "Laid in the Tomb" (No. 14). The incense ensures that the prayers get wafted up to heaven, although Father Mac also told us it was because people used to smell.

This story, the cross story, has a happy ending; but this isn't happiness I'm feeling. It is something close to rapture, both ecstatic and absurd. My young boy ears hear the reality of suffering, not the finale of everlasting life. I cannot imagine eternity, but I can imagine a tortured body. Or at least I can try. If I stare hard at the nails and then dig my fingernails into my palm, then (scrunched face) nearly, but (scrunch even harder) not really. It is unimaginable. The pain and suffering that Our Lord went through is beyond my imagination, and yet that mustn't stop me trying. It's the least I can do to repay him for his agonized Passion.

It is why—it's one of the whys—I go to confession. Once a fortnight, usually a Saturday morning, I go to the Sacred Heart. It is the church for which I'm an altar boy, the church into which I was baptized. Which means that the Sacred Heart is also *the* Church, a synecdoche of the "one holy Catholic and apostolic church" in the words of the Nicene Creed.

On the left-hand side is a row of confessional booths, maybe three or four of them. There is a small light over each one, a bare green bulb. Each confessional booth is divided into two parts, one half where the priest sits, the other half for the penitent. There is a priest in each. Father Mac will be one of them, the others will have come over from the surrounding parishes, or the schools, especially to hear confession. If the light is on it means that there is someone making their confession. I sit in the pew and wait my turn. A light goes out, a door opens, and a woman hurries out from the penitent's side of the booth. She keeps her head bowed. She is in a state of grace, or soon will be once she has made her act of contrition. She goes to the side altar—our Lady of Compassion's altar—and lights a candle. She kneels, bows her head, and prays. I know her. She is Mary Watson's mother. I remember Mum saying that she suffers from arthritis and that this is somehow connected in my mum's eyes with her house having had central heating installed. She's mouthing her Hail Marys, counting each one off on the beads that she threads between her fingers. My turn. I step inside the booth, close the door, and begin. "In the name of the Father, the Son, and the Holy Ghost . . ." The priest is sitting on the other side, wooden paneling separating us. We communicate through a square latticed grille that slides shut when not in use. The voice says something like, "May the Lord in your heart help you to confess your sins with sorrow. . . ." It's Father Mac, I'd know his voice anywhere, as sure as he knows mine. "Bless me, Father, for I have sinned. It has been two weeks since my last confession. During this time I have sworn . . . I have not honored my mum and dad . . . I have placed other things above my love of God . . . I have had impure thoughts . . . I have not been as charitable as I should have been . . . and that is all I can remember, Father." "And for these sins, are you truly sorry?" "Yes, Father, I am truly sorry and will try not to sin in the future. . . ." Father Mac—it is definitely him—tells me to say ten Hail Marys and ten Our Fathers before absolving me in Latin, which I don't understand but which finishes, ". . . *in nomine Patris et Filii et Spiritus Sancti.*"

Quite what the relationship was between all this and my impending grammar school education I was too young to know. Something to do with homework, conversations between teachers and priests, the guarantees of respectability, and Good Catholic Families. I do know that the same four who got into St. Mary's were the same four who had been chosen as altar boys.

NEXT

How can they see with sequins in their eyes?
—"Razzle Dazzle," *Chicago*

Julie encourages me to do a relaxation exercise. I sit quietly, and focus on my body: aware of my feet on the floor, my arms by my side, my buttocks on the chair. I concentrate on my breath: slightly chilled at the tip of the nostrils as it goes in, warmer on its way out. She asks me to remember a time when I felt perfectly safe and happy.

And I think of Blackpool. Not the Lake or the Peak District, not the Yorkshire Dales or even the Ribble Valley, but the brash and trashy glamour of kiss-me-quick Blackpool.

Throughout the nineteenth century, Blackpool had been *the* destination for Lancashire's textile workers, a pretty much en masse vacation organized by the mill owners, trade unions, and schools. We went there with a sense of contained exploration, an excitement that was as much about familiarity as it was about novelty. And when I say "we" I mean the whole of Accrington, not just me and my parents.

This was still (just) the time of the Wakes, a whole fortnight when the town would close down and vacate. Going to Blackpool was not so much an escape from Accrington as an extension of it. We would travel with people we knew, lodge with them, and meet up with them in the town's various working men's clubs. My dad seemed to know more people on the Golden Mile than he did on Accy Market, or maybe it was just that he had the leisure to stop and talk with them. No wonder Kathleen's assessment of the place was that "it was just like home," although crucially for her it was a home in which she didn't have to cook or clean.

They were both united in the belief that sea air—Blackpool Sea

Air in particular—possessed medicinal, quasi-miraculous properties. "Get a lungful of that," Mum would say as I inhaled the mixed aromas of doughnut fat, burger grease, and candy floss, "you'll sleep tonight." Thus were the restorative properties of "a fortnight away" announced, safe in the knowledge that we weren't really Away.

I love being in Blackpool, and I love my mum, and I love being with my mum in Blackpool. We play telly bingo in the amusements arcade and win a crappy fluffy-toy prize. We call it Walter and bury him in the sand. We eat toffee apples at the Pleasure Beach, at the entrance to which is a glass case containing a mechanical clown who rocks back and forth, laughing maniacally. It is like he is a prisoner inside his box but a tyrant in waiting to everyone outside it, a demon howling at jokes only he can hear.

I cry and my mum buys me an ice cream. We go on the Ghost Train. There are signs saying No Petting, but I don't know what petting is. We go to the Winter Gardens to see the Irish Crooner Val Doonican. My mum loves Val Doonican. I think he's a bit soppy but laugh at the one that he does about a goat.

There is a pitch-and-putt course near our hotel and the three of us go and play a round that I call a tournament. My dad wins, but I'm annoyed with my mum for not taking it seriously, not doing it properly. She leaves me to what she calls "have a paddy."

My mum says I should sit on a bench on the pier and wait for the performers ("the turns") to walk down to the theater. That way I'll be guaranteed an autograph. I wait for hours to see the comedian Jimmy Clitheroe, but don't see him until we see him that night on the North Pier stage. My mum watches me whilst I go on the trampolines. She won't let me buy a hat with a "suggestive" slogan, says I'm too young, that there'll be plenty of time for that.

Why do I cringe, shuffle with discomfort, as I recall these golden (mile) years of my youth? Is it the genre that is inherently self-satirizing, all those poor-but-honest, grim-up-north parodies coming home to roost in the inside of my skull? Or the memories themselves, tainted with time, co-opted by a million compilations of BBC nostalgia fests? Maybe: but there's something more. It is something about class, something about working-class memory having been scripted by someone else (novelists, documentary film makers, sociologists).

Writing about my working-class childhood feels like slipping on hand-me-down clothes. The cut and the cloth are nonnegotiable, neatly tailored. It is my story, my body in history, that doesn't quite fit. My memories are tight across the chest, their sleeves hang down over the fingers. In her book *Landscape for a Good Woman*, Carolyn Steedman writes about how working-class childhoods are denied any complex subjectivity or unconscious conflict, and made instead to carry the weight of other people's interpretations, metaphors, analyses. She makes the point that "It would not be possible, in fact, to write a book called 'Middle Class Childhood' (even though) the shelves groan with psychoanalytical, developmental, and literary accounts of such childhoods." She's right. Childhood is middle class unless specifically stated otherwise.

NEXT

No improper books have come my way. And I am too young to read anything suitable for me. If I don't have to hide my books from my mother, I can't take any interest in them.

—Ivy Compton-Burnett, *Men and Wives*

I didn't know I was working class until I met people who weren't, and I met people who weren't when I went to grammar school. When a mate sneered that I was going to become a "St. Mary's Bum Boy," I reacted in a very bum-boyish way, I cried. It had never occurred to me before that Being Clever and Doing Well were anything other than laudable and wonderful things. Isn't this what you were supposed to do? If going to school wasn't going to make you clever, then why go to school? And if St. Mary's RC grammar school was the best school, then why didn't me going there make me the Best Boy, not a Bum Boy? It was all very confusing.

My dad bought me a dictionary (I still have it: I used it to check the spelling of the word "laudable") and joked that I had to be careful not to swallow it. My grandfather bought me a fountain pen, a Parker, silver nibbed. Mum took me shopping for the regulation school blazer. I remember there being a debate about whether they could buy the school badge separately and sew it onto an ordinary blazer, and whether or not this would mark me out as different (poor) or get me (them) in trouble.

Then came the day, my first day as a stuck-up-think-I'm-clever-too-good-for-the-rest-of-us-St.-Mary's-College bum boy. And I was terrified. It was the school equivalent of the Saturday morning pictures: a mob (a "berserk"?) of children, all of whom seemed to have internalized a manual labeled Boisterousness 101. And me. They play-fought and scuffled and made fart noises with their armpits; they had nailed bits of metal to the bottom of their shoes, making them sound like hooligan tap dancers. They all seemed to know one another too, a series of Venn diagrams consisting of older brothers, sporting fraternities, and the mysterious allegiances to be found in the school playground.

Need I say that it was in books that I took refuge? I certainly had all the symptoms: introversion, solitude, hypersensitivity. And so bookish boy it would be.

Not that being recognized as a Type in any way deadens the pain; quite the opposite. I now work in a bookshop and deal with them daily, my heart never ceasing to bleed a little for every awkward one of them who comes through its door. Intense young men—of all ages and genders—who can't quite make eye contact, in search of the troubled poets whose troubles will liberate them from their own. I love them as only a bibliophile can love the similarly afflicted—homeopathically. "Try this," I say, offering a volume of Sam Riviere to a gothy girl clutching her collection of Anne Sexton. Or—for the kid with holes in his jumper who is just coming down from a Burroughs binge—"You need the new Ben Marcus." Somehow we get through the transaction, less seller to buyer than reader to reader, facilitating each other's progress through a day that will somehow have been saved by the books that have populated it.

I don't remember the earliest books I read. It was Kathleen's boast that she had taught me to read before I started school. I do remember the pride in her voice when she would mock-scold me for always having my nose in a book, and the brief flurry of panic about what all this reading must be doing to my eyes. I never saw her read a book, not even one that Her-Graham-Who-Went-to-St.-Mary's-College wrote. Maybe there was the sense that, much though she was enthralled by the world of books and grammar school ("He does Latin!"), it was certainly not a world for her (Latin?). She had, as we say, done her bit. She had taught me: she had sacrificed for me; she had helped to get me there. Now it was up to them, the teachers and the priests. And the priests who were also teachers.

My dad, on the other hand, read like a demon. His weekly trips to Accrington Library saw him return with four, sometimes six books a time. I guess that the northern weather left its groundsmen with time to kill, time that could be spent with James Hadley Chase, countless histories of the Wild West, and biographies of American movie stars. He managed to read whilst watching TV—a feat which I remember being half impressed by and half suspicious of (and still am). He read *Titbits* magazine and *Reader's Digest*, how-to manuals and novels by the Jameses Herriot and Herbert. He read in the same way he watched David Attenborough documentaries—a mixture of curiosity and mild self-improvement.

Like many an autodidact, it was inconceivable to him that any book could be wrong. When I was older, I would try to get him to see that historians (say) had disagreed with each other, that one book might directly contradict another book, and that what we thought of as being "facts" were often only opinions—politically charged opinions—that had been handed down to us in such a way as to make them seem forever true. He didn't like that. Books had served him well and he didn't want to be told that their foundations were anything other than solid. Or maybe he just didn't want to be told this by his son.

It was thought that I "got" my bibliophilia from my dad, as though pleasure in books was a genetic predisposition, like diabetes. I can't remember any of the fairy tales or monster stuff that I'm sure there must have been. It was only really with the discovery of Enid Blyton that I received my diagnosis as a Reader.

I would love to report that my experience of Blyton was tempered by suspicion of her relentless class prejudice and racial stereotyping. Not a bit of it: I adored them. The Famous Five books explored peer-group friendships in a way that seemed exhilarating and liberating to me. Here were kids forging identities outside of the adult realm, semi-grown-ups (growing-ups?) who not only found ways of standing apart from the authority of their elders but often talked back to that authority. I found in these books a group of people who were exploring the world on their own terms. The fact that these terms were not those of my class or background mattered not a ginger-beered belch compared with the fact that they were doing it at all.

I am not unaware that these books were underpinned with what we might call ideological difficulties. Did she really throw the term "golliwog" around as though it was just some harmless Brexiteer banter? Yes, she did. And was the school that the Five attended an exemplary model of comprehensive meritocratic inclusion? No, it was not. On the other hand, the "tomboyish" Georgina famously bent a bit of gender, making her if not the Lady Gaga of children's fiction, then certainly its k.d. lang. And, reactionary bluestocking or not, Blyton's books showed me that reading was about forging emotional connections with other worlds, not just having your own reflected back to you.

They did something else as well. In the library and local bookshop Wardleworths they would be filed next to other books, books that were similar but different, a combination which suggested that even when these particular alternative realities had been exhausted, there was a possibly infinite number of others just waiting to be explored. Books led to other books: they came in droves.

Is it overstretching the point (overcressing the egg sandwiches?) to say it was thanks to Ms. Blyton—snob, purveyor of privilege, and xenophobe extraordinaire—that I ended up reading the books which would enable me to take these cheap shots at her? Probably. But it is certainly true to say that it is thanks to Enid Blyton that I discovered Books, and for this I take off my non-PC Noddy hat to her, racial epithets and all.

There may not have been a connection, but my first English teacher got nicknamed Enid. A quiet, bearded lay teacher, Mr. Lawrence always seemed to be apologizing for himself. Head down, he would enter the room and swallow his first hesitant instructions, which meant that they weren't instructions at all, they were requests. "Er . . . okay . . . um . . . if you . . . no . . . could you? Right. Stop it." But it was too late. We already smelt blood. "Enid clap-clap-clap . . . Enid clap-clap-clap . . . Enid . . ." and on it went, a brooding relentless monotone. "Enid clap-clap-clap . . . Enid clap-clap-clap." He is, in that brilliant phrase, beside himself. He is almost literally hopping mad. "Enid/Enid/Enid," faster now, building to a frenzied climax.

"Please. Stop . . . No, please." Don't beg, Mr. Lawrence, you will only make it worse. "EnidEnidEnid"—a full-blown chant, no pause between each taunt, as though we are the possessed, intent on conjuring up the devil. He starts to cry and we stop. Mission accomplished: the sound of a grown man's sobbing, thirty guilty bottoms shuffling.

Mr. Lawrence wanted us to be equals in a situation that could never be one of equality, to befriend us in a world where we could never be friends. I felt sorry for him, although my pity never stopped me from joining in his torment.

His successor, John "Jock" Roland, changed my life. He was the first man I can recall making a conscious attempt to emulate. He had Mediterranean good looks, a gliding graceful walk, and—my first encounter of this—a southern accent. A lay teacher, there were even rumors that he was an atheist, a Catholic atheist of course. His gift to me was in making me see that books were not (only) an escape from the world, they were an enrichment of it.

He used to run his own small bookshop at the back of the prefabs and it was there that I spent every lunchtime. When I told him—red-faced at my childish taste—that I was reading Frank Richards' Greyfriars books, he gave me a copy of Orwell's essay "Boys' Weeklies." That a writer could write seriously on such topics seemed to me daring, even scandalous.

Orwell was a fully-fledged Penguin-published Author, and yet here he was writing about the kind of books I was reading. He was taking them—and therefore me—seriously. I've just reread that essay, and I'm struck by its audacity, by Orwell's ability to combine lit. crit. and political journalism twenty, even thirty, years before such things became norms of cultural studies.

I'm not sure if I knew the word "iconoclasm" when I was thirteen and standing gobsmacked in Jock Roland's bookshop, but it is what I experienced, in all its genre-shifting frisson. Not only were there stories, but there were stories about those stories. There were even stories hidden away in those stories that they didn't seem to know about, stories that got told despite themselves, stories waiting to be uncovered. I was discovering that writers read other writers, that they were also readers. There seemed to be much more at stake in this business of world making than an imaginary school or a fat boy's postal order. "Everything is safe, solid and unquestionable," wrote Orwell about the world of Frank Richards' fiction. "Everything will be the same for ever and ever."

John also taught poetry. One of his party pieces was to recite Hilaire Belloc's "Tarantella" from memory, no small feat for anyone who has come across the feverish meter and rhyme schemes of its "Do you remember an inn, Miranda? Do you remember an inn?" He gave us the inevitable Wilfred Owen, the inescapable Ted Hughes, and the predictable Philip Larkin.

Yet he also gave us e. e. cummings ("to reassure those of you who can't spell proper") and Dylan Thomas. He read us Adrian Mitchell's "Tell Me Lies About Vietnam" and I remember wishing that we were still at war so I could protest against it. He gave us W. H. Auden and T. S. Eliot, Emily Dickinson and William Blake. He could do a po-faced William McGonagall and a straight-faced Robbie Burns. He gave us Shakespeare ("My mistress' eyes are nothing like the sun") without telling us it was Shakespeare and teased us for liking it before we'd found out who it was by. He gave us D. H. Lawrence and told us that the mucky bits weren't always where you'd expect.

NEXT

I say shame, shame, shame, shame, shame, shame, shame
Shame on you.
> —Shirley & Co., "Shame, Shame, Shame"

I'm in the locker room with a boy my own age and he has me in a headlock. His name is Sean. He wears his blue-black hair in a feather cut, his tie fashionably thin, top button undone. His forearms are strong and lightly cushioned by a soft pubescent down. He has me in a headlock and I am slowly being forced to my knees. He has black brogue shoes and red cotton socks, even though the latter are banned by the school dress code. His eyes are an intense brown that borders on yellow. They are victorious eyes, cruel eyes.

He will win this fight as he has won every fight we've had. He will win it because I want him to win it. I must never speak of this—these "fights"—to anyone else, him included. Him especially. Those are the rules.

Is "love" the right word for an adolescent same-sex crush? Probably not. Though "crush" seems right for everything else about it—demolished, compressed, reduced to a pulpy mass. I've found my very own David Watts, the eponymous hero of a Kinks song, soon to be covered by the Jam.

I watch him in lessons: he's not too bright. He struggles with Latin, with declensions and the placing of the verb. I can see his pretty-boy face blanch with fear when Father Stuart calls on him to translate some archaic nonsense. "'This is the agreement' . . . You, boy." "*Hec* . . . er . . . *est* . . ." (C'mon, Sean, *concordia*. You can do it. Say it. *Concordia*.) ". . . *concordium* . . ." No. Fuck. Next. "We bequeathe by this charter these manors to the lord." "'You, boy, again.'" "*Confirma* . . . ah . . . *hec manerium* . . . gulp . . . ah . . ." Wrong again. The class laughs as though it has never heard this joke before. Caveney: *"Confirmamus hac carta hec maneria domino."* Correct.

Such were the reasons that swots got placed in headlocks by boys with eggshell-colored eyes.

What seems strange to me now is that I never considered this mania as even vaguely homosexual. In my mind there was nothing same-sexual about my attraction to him, partly because we were so obviously not of the same sex. Look at him: Captain of the team, of pure and noble creed. Now look at me: *Dominus et domina terram Deo et ecclesie confirmant.* Exactly.

NEXT

Jesus loves you more than you will know.
　　　　　—Simon and Garfunkel, "Mrs. Robinson"

I put the disc onto the spindle in the middle of the turntable. It is a satisfying ritual, one that rewards you with a click. I lift up the arm, it is like a dragon's head with one sharp tooth. I put the needle on the vinyl's thicker, raised, outermost edge. The inner circle is the color of mustard. I have to be precise, delicate. There is a *ccrrrrssssrrrssscc* and then it starts, a gently insistent bassline: de-dum-de-dum-de-dum-de-dum-de-dum-de-dum melting into my abdomen.

What sounds like cellos but are probably synths surge up through my stomach and gently waltz around in the lining . . . "Well she's my woman of gold / And she's not very old / huh / Well she's my woman of gold / And she's not very old / huh huh . . ." It is 1974 or 1975. My cousin Helen is becoming a Tartan Roller, as fans of the Bay City Rollers were known. She wears white Oxford bags with a tartan scarf stitched down the side of each leg plus a scarf tied around her wrist.

Her undying love for Marc Bolan has proved to be not so undying after all, and so, three, four years after it first became number one, I become the default owner of T. Rex's "Hot Love." At a conservative estimate I probably play the song fifteen, twenty times a day. My dad buys me a pair of headphones to stop himself from killing me (or himself). I can't quite work out everything that he's singing, and I don't understand the bits that I can work out. Who is this woman who twitches even though she's not a witch? Is she the same one who lives by the coast? Is that why she's faster than most? Why does he say "and" as though the two things naturally follow, as though it makes sense when it so obviously doesn't?

And then there's those noises, the grunted sighs, the slurry whispers, the girlish squeal which doesn't sound like any girl I've met. I think he must be American, that would explain (some of) it. Kathleen quite likes him, buys me some of his other records. They come with pictures of him on them—blue and red not-quite drawings, not-quite photos which emphasize his hair and eyes. He wears makeup and a top hat, a combination that makes him seem both shy and arrogant at the same time.

There's one called "Jeepster"; it has these raucous angular guitars which sound exactly how he looks. They strut and throw their head back, pout, and do that thing with their shoulders. Did he just say something about "the universe reclining in your hair?" He did. The universe!—a place bigger than the world—reclining?—just sort of lying in a hammock, or on a settee. In your hair! I must have a girlfriend. If I have a girlfriend, I'll tell her that she has the universe reclining in her hair and I'll feel like Marc Bolan. I ask my mum how to get a girlfriend and she tells me to ask my dad. Jack Caveney has a question of his own: "What the bloody hell is a jeepster when it's at home?" It's a good question, Dad, I don't know, "I'm just a vampire for your lo oo oo ve . . . ah ah ah . . ."

What strikes me now (apart from just how tolerant they were) is just how absent music was from my parents' own lives. If they were courting in the mid to late fifties, where was the rock 'n' roll? Photographs of them from their early marriage show my dad sporting a tame version of a teddy boy quiff: more Johnnie Ray than Presley. His lapels were thin, trousers wide and tapered.

Kathleen was a looker, but her style aped that of Hollywood, presumably a much richer source of inspiration than any of the (few) visible female singers of the time. Did they jive, do the twist, go to the hop? Where were they when they heard of Eddie Cochran's death on his British tour of 1960: Was it their Kurt Cobain moment? Who did Kathleen have a crush on? What music did they choose to snog to?

I suspect that their music was that of the dance halls, and as such was regulated and regimented; something that happened on weekends. They would always get up to dance at family weddings. It was always the same dance, the one where the man gently pulls the woman by the hand and she spins around under his arm, leans back, spins round the other way. Jack would always look as though he was on guard duty on the dance floor, never catching his wife's eye but looking around at the buffet, the bar, the queue for the Gents.

My friend Dave Hesmondhalgh has written a wonderful book called *Why Music Matters*. In it he documents the myriad ways that music connects our inner lives to the world at large, how it helps us to negotiate the relationship between private experience and public identity. The title has been running through my head as I have been thinking about Jack and Kath, and whether it held true for them. My generation takes it as an article of faith that music matters, nothing could be more certain (sometimes that belief is that it's the only thing).

For my parents music was Entertainment, the soundtrack to a Night Out—a pair of slippery double-edged terms if ever I heard them. Can you not hear the class sneer echoing in these words? (The defendants were headed for/on their way back from a Night Out, m'lord.) Is it even possible to use the word "entertainment" without the raising of an upper lip, a tacit admission that there is always the presence of the "so-called" lurking there somewhere, a judgment which must prefix the pleasures of the feckless masses?

Like my books, records are becoming A Thing. They're starting to breed. My cousin John—Helen's brother—has given me his copy of a single that has been obsessing me for months. It couldn't be less like T. Rex whilst still sounding sort of exactly like T. Rex. But whereas Marc was smoldering and impish, fey and Byronic, this lot look like debt collectors. Me and John are watching them on telly—*The Old Grey Whistle Test* it must have been. No glitter or feather boas are in evidence here. They're called Dr. Feelgood and they look like they want to have sex with your mum. Or maybe just have.

The lead singer is wearing a white suit jacket over a black button-down shirt and dark straight-legged jeans. The bassist is walking up and down the stage as though he is measuring up for a fitted carpet, whilst the drummer—who I would later learn is called simply (and wonderfully) the Big Figure—is as inscrutable as Buddha. And the lead guitarist? The lead guitarist is called Wilko Johnson and looks like no human being I have seen before. There is something Frankenstein's monsterish about him, as though he is being constantly surprised—affronted even—by the way in which the various parts of his body have been assembled. Someone somewhere is sending jolts of electrical current throughout his body, causing him to pace the stage in manic pursuit of whichever bastard is responsible. His neck sends his head bolting out in these spasms—convulsions—which seem to punctuate the gaps between each chord.

On the sofa we sit, staring at these men possessed. The singer and harmonica player Lee Brilleaux is doing that thing with his fist, battering out the time, punch-conducting the rhythm of the band. His vocals cut in: "If there's som'ing 'at Ah like / It's tha way tha woman walks / An' if it's som'in' Ah like bedder / Is the way she baby talks . . ." What happened to all that reclining in your hair stuff? This isn't that. This is She doing Something, and Doing It Right, whatever that means.

Records breed records, like all that begating stuff in the Bible: the difference being that in music the genealogy often works the other way. "If you like the Feelgoods, you gotta like Howlin' Wolf," says the man at the Disc and Tape Exchange, Accrington's premier music shop, "or Muddy Waters . . . or Eric Clapton." I have just bought *Stupidity*, Dr. Feelgood's live album, which has a blistering version of a song called "I'm a Man." ("I spell M-Aaaaaa-N," which, as my dad points out, isn't really how you spell "Man" at all.) The man—spelt properly this one—tells me that there is another version, a better version, by the Yardbirds from the sixties, and that if you like this, then you'll definitely like that. He plays it to me. It sounds horrible. It sounds horrible because it isn't Wilko Johnson singing or Lee Brilleaux harmonicaing or the Big Figure being a Big Figure. It isn't in fact Dr. Feelgood, and what I like about this song is precisely that it is by Dr. Feelgood.

There was nothing like buying records for reminding you that it wasn't just records you were buying. Purchasing a piece of vinyl was a way of announcing your identity. It was a pledge of allegiance.

So the man in the record shop is into the blues, and I am into Dr. Feelgood, ragged-arsed exponents of the blues. In a few months I'll be into ELO, Supertramp, and Fleetwood Mac. Soon I'll discover that 10cc is the cleverest band in the world, with songs stuffed full of irony and pastiche, punning their way through the charts with a wink that only Graham-Who-Is-Doing-Very-Well-at-St.-Mary's-College can see.

NEXT

A tiger is a tiger, not a lamb.
Mein Herr.

—"Mein Herr," *Cabaret*

The homework was simple enough. Write about how you understand the word "God"—"god" even. A couple of pages, nothing more. I write something like:

> God is everywhere and God is nowhere. He exists in the world and in me, and He is the bridge between those two things. He is my conscience and He is the feeling of wholeness. When I think or feel that He is not with me, I go to a place that some people call "hell," but is really just the absence of God's love and Truth. . . .

And on it went; the quasi-mystic, half-baked theology that only a fourteen-year-old boy who takes his Catholicism seriously could come up with. I remember thinking that I could nick a bit from Gerard Manley Hopkins ("The world is charged with the grandeur of God") but that the priests would probably know. Jock Roland would certainly know and, besides, it's probably not a good idea to combine plagiarism with religious piety. It won the form prize and ended up being published in the school magazine.

It is the daily school assembly. There are the usual announcements (list of candidates for detention, sports stuff) followed by the usual prayers. This not-quite-Mass tends to be rounded off by a not-quite-sermon, a kind of thought for the day delivered by our headmaster.

He is already a legend, a hip youngish gunslinger of a priest by the name of Father Kevin O'Neill. Everyone calls him the Rev. Kev, a name that nicely captures his brand of vocation and cool. He wears thick glasses, the kind that used to be called jam jar and that make him look a bit like Buddy Holly. His hair is black and wiry, worn combed back, as though in homage to a teddy boy past that he never quite had. He clears his throat, his voice is well-spoken without being posh. "I would like to thank everyone who submitted articles and poems and drawings to the school magazine. . . . It's been the best year ever." (Laughter; he says this every year.) "My attention was particularly taken by a piece about a young man's relationship to God." (Fuck!) "I won't name him because I don't want to embarrass him but I'm sure he won't mind if I read . . ."

And read he does. Every fucking word. I am no longer just a quiet and reflective poet, I am now a visionary. Not just Gerard Manley Hopkins, but Moses: Jesus even. After all, he was an only child too (wasn't he?). Of course I want to melt between the cracks of the assembly room floor, but I also feel myself floating above them. All clichés apply: grounds were summoned up for swallowing, hearts were proudly inflated, faces did indeed color.

He doesn't know me yet, the Rev. Kev, though I want him to. He has only been the head for a couple of years, taking over from Father Cassidy, a man about whom people used the word "kindly" partly because they didn't know what else to say about him.

Father O'Neill wasn't anybody's idea of kindly: he was a rock star. It was said that he smoked "pot." He was into Stevie Wonder—not like Enid's pretense of being into David Bowie (setting us "Space Oddity" for Prac. Crit. only works if you have heard the record, Mr. Lawrence)—but properly into him, concertgoing and all. He rarely wore his dog collar, but when he did it served to remind you/me that being a priest was both nothing special and yet something extraordinary. It said, Here is a man who is devoting his life to Life, that banal, troubled, and troubling thing. It said, It couldn't be easier, this priest thing: you just have to listen to people and do what's right, maybe offer them guidance when they're stuck or compassion when they're in trouble. Yet it also announced, This priest thing is a thing like no other. You are willing to embrace people in all their pettiness and spite, love them precisely at their most unlovable, forgive them at their most unforgivable.

And he teaches English. I love Jock Roland—I want to be Jock Roland—but he's not going to forgive me all my trespasses. And besides, he's got a wife and child. I look at their pictures as I stand in his bookshop asking what to buy next. I'm jealous of his kid. I quite fancy his wife.

Apparently Father O'Neill teaches Beckett! Beckett! I have tried three or four times to read *Molloy*, and each time I seem to get further away from it. I tell this to Jock Roland—I bought the bloody thing from his shop after all—and he tells me that this experience (the desire to read, the failure to understand, the going back to read) is a very Beckettian way of reading Beckett. I should carry on, learn to fail better, listen to the language.

I wait for the Rev. Kev outside his office. It's on a school corridor and I know the other kids walking past assume I'm in trouble. I quite like this, the thought that they think I'm in trouble. Even though I'm not. I've never really been in trouble.

He is walking along now, heading for his office, key in hand. "Are you waiting for me?" "I'm . . . I wrote . . . I'm Graham Caveney." (I hate my stupid name. It always sounds as though I'm swallowing the last bit.) "I wrote that thing about God." (That thing! About God! Those two things shouldn't go together: I've made the Divinity sound like a shopping list.) "Ah, yes. Come in . . ."

We drink coffee and talk about books. He is relaxed in a way that makes me feel relaxed, interesting in a way that makes me feel interesting. He was delighted to read my meditation (a meditation, that's what it was!) on God and he thinks that, yes, I'm right, it isn't just that God is in the details but that God is, as it were, the Details. Transcendence isn't something magical: it is something verging on the banal, the everyday certainly. And that's what makes it magical.

Have I tried D. H. Lawrence? He was saying something similar although from a very different position of course. (Of course!) I tell him about Beckett and he makes the same point as Jock Roland, except that he says that the next time there is a performance—*Godot* or *Krapp*—we (the school?) should go. You've never been to the theater? I hadn't. You must. That's where Beckett comes into his own. (But isn't it weird being a . . . well . . . a . . . priest and liking Beckett, who didn't . . . you know . . . believe in . . . ?) Not at all. The God that Beckett didn't believe in doesn't exist; that's why he didn't believe in him. (I haven't a clue what this means but I love it. It is the cleverest thing anyone has ever said to me.) Besides, he, Samuel Beckett, believed in words and we all know that . . . ("In the beginning was the Word?") . . . laughs . . . Correct. He knew that I'd been an altar boy and we have a moment about Father Mac. He, the Rev. Kev, is reading Philip Roth. Had I? I should. What was I working on (working on!) next? Yes, writing. He'd be happy to.

Julie wants to talk about how reading and writing are important to me. Or the ways in which they are important, and how words can conceal as much as they reveal. She says they can help us to hide from ourselves as well as understand ourselves. And that this often looks like the same thing.

NEXT

To me education is a leading out of what is already there in the pupil's soul.

—Muriel Spark, *The Prime of Miss Jean Brodie*

Kathleen was worried about my eyes, all this reading can't be good for them. It's not the only thing she was worried about, mind you. Along with thousands of others, she had lost her job at the mill. She did a couple of jobs now. In the mornings she worked as a cleaner at the local bingo hall. I would help her out during my school holidays, sweeping up mounds of disused sheets, their random patterns of numbers all punctuated with felt-tip pens like some unseemly trace of lipstick. There were three of them—my mum, my aunty Margaret, and a woman called Theresa. I remember them making me coffee with Carnation Milk and joking that they needed to have a fag with theirs because "a drink's too wet without one."

At lunchtimes Kath worked in a factory canteen, up near Clayton, past Accrington Victoria Hospital, and down towards the Stanley ground. She would heat up cans of soup ("something hot," a phrase in which the something being hot always seems more important than what that something is) or make them doorstop sandwiches with gooey white bread that held your fingerprints. At night it was back to the bingo hall: selling the sheets of numbers that she would sweep up the next day, serving tea and biscuits, checking the numbers of "another lucky winner."

Before my book habit became terminal, I would go with her in the evenings, awed by the theatricality of the place. Like so many bingo halls, it had been a picture house in a previous life. The customers were virtually all women (men were tolerated so long as they were accompanied, like dogs in the park) and would vary from those who got "all dolled up" to those who didn't really see bingo as going out at all, for whom it was an extension of their living room. The latter would arrive in their slippers, their hair in curlers (but under a head scarf). Next to them would sit women whom Jack would describe as "all fur coat and no knickers"—a category which I didn't understand but was keen to know more about.

The caller was invariably a man, a failed club-comic type in an overstarched white shirt who wore too much cheap aftershave. "All the sixes, clickety-click . . . One little duck number two . . . unlucky for some thirteen . . . two fat ladies eighty-eight. And those luuuurrvely legs eleven . . ."

The place would go mental, wolf whistles and catcalls, a scary mixture of parody and Pavlov. "Here" signaled that we had a winner and it fell to Kath or one of the other women to read out the numbers on the card back to the caller. Winning numbers verified, the winnings would be paid out according to a Line or a Full House. Drama over, a new one begins; eyes down, look in.

But I'm not going with her to work anymore. In fact, I'm not really going anywhere anymore. What I am doing is sitting in my room and reading, and it's starting to worry my mother. We're sitting in a café in Accy Market. We are eating meat pie, chips, and peas (mushy, naturally). It is a Friday. I remember this because we usually ate fish on Friday—a mini-Lent Catholic abstention—but today we are eating meat, and we are eating out.

She asks me about school and how if there's ever anything wrong I can always talk to her or Dad about it, and that I'm not to think that they won't understand, because even though she knows I don't believe them but they were young too and she does know how hard it can be, especially being an only one, and that she and Dad love me and only want what's best and want me to be happy but that you don't seem happy and is it something at school and the work—the work, is it that you can't keep up with the work . . . ?

What I want to tell her is that I love the work and I love the school. I love John Roland and I love the Rev. Kev. I love Beckett because I don't understand it and Harper Lee because I do. I love Eric Stewart for singing that he's not in love in a way that suggests the exact opposite and I love Noosha Fox for telling me how sorry she is that she's only got a s-s-s-single bed.

I don't say any of this. Of course I don't. I'm a teenage boy, a teenage boy with grammar school ambitions, raging hormones, and a crushing overestimation of my literary sensitivity. I think I know what she thinks. I think she thinks that she's spoiled me, that this is the only-child moment that people (I am sure) warned her of. I don't reassure her on that score either.

What I do do is mumble something about Blackpool, how I don't want to go, getting too old, would rather stay at home. She doesn't kiss me, not in public, not since I told her not to. What she does is that thing where she puts both of her hands on the sides of my face, brushing my hair from my forehead with her thumb, almost as though she's taking my temperature.

NEXT

Cheap holiday in other people's misery . . .
    —Sex Pistols, "Holidays in the Sun"

And so I don't go to Blackpool that year, and neither do my parents.
We go instead to Fleetwood, to a caravan (a UK trailer) that is won-
drous just to sit in and listen to the rain. Aunty Mary and her family
are in one they bought a few years back, an investment that was dar-
ingly aspirational at the time. She's done quite well for herself, my
aunty Mary. Her husband—my uncle Jack—is a painter and decora-
tor, a job that was a real trade before we all became convinced that we
could do it ourselves. She no longer "has to work"—a phrase always
used with an equal mix of awe and resentment—although she cooks
Jack's meals, does his bookkeeping, orders his supplies, raises my two
cousins, and helps to raise me.

During primary school I would go there for my lunch—"dippy
eggs and toast," her speciality. Now at secondary school I still go for
the occasional Friday night sleepover. I don't want Mary to be my
mum, but I do want John to be my brother, just as I want Helen and
her tartan-stitched Oxford bags to be my sister (with a Girlfriend option, once I figure out what girlfriends are for).

On Fridays we gorge on crisps and pop, take turns playing records,
except that I never seem to get a turn. Helen plays George McCrae's
"Rock Your Baby," Hot Chocolate, and Showaddywaddy. There's an
insane thing by Darts—"Daddy Cool"—and the middle bit has almost a separate song built into it. When this bit happens—the "girl
can't help it" bit—I do my impression of a demonic Den Hegarty,
the one with the pantomime quiff, and roll around on the rug that
is my stage holding the hairbrush that is my microphone. John plays

"Denis" by his new favorite band even though Helen says he only likes the song because he luuurrrves the singer. John says that she—Helen—luuurrrrrves the lead singer in Showaddywaddy even though he looks like someone from *The Planet of the Apes*.

There's a song called "Baby Stop Crying"—Bob Dylan (I don't yet think of him as one-word-only-needed Dylan). When it comes to the chorus, we all start to shout at Dylan's imaginary "baby," singing along in the manner of the harassed mums we hear in Accy Market: "Stop crying . . . Shut it! I'll give you something to cry about!!" (Dylan pleading his heart out . . . "Baby, please stop crying . . ."). "Will you stop that bloody racket, I've had it up to here . . ." (chorus again: "stop crying") . . . "Straighten your face, you miserable cow . . ." (we're becoming hysterical now . . . upping each other's ante). "I'll give you such a pasting when we get home . . ." (do de do de do . . . "stop crying / stop crying / stop crying" sung in that iconic whine). "Stop! Bloody! Crying! Stop it! For God's sake . . . Will you give it a rest? . . . Stop it! Stop that crying . . . I hate you!" (Helpless with laughter now, the earnestness of Dylan's plea seems to be blending with our own crass parodies.) . . . StoooOOOOP Blooooody Cryyyying.

Aunty Mary comes through and tells us to stop shouting. John tells her that it's not us she should be telling to stop, it's Bob Dylan's bloody girlfriend and her stupid bloody crying.

I can't remember when I knew that Aunt Mary was an alcoholic, perhaps only when I became one myself. The line was that "she liked a drink"—a phrase that was elastic enough to cover a multitude of sins whilst hinting at redemptive pleasures. Aunt Mary fell down the stairs? Well, she does like a drink. But she seems all right and is having a laugh about it? She's a bugger is that one, she likes a drink. Occasionally she "liked *her* drink," a slightly harsher judgment, the implication being that she was more possessive of her drink, or that the drink was more possessive of her.

I remember her sitting at the Formica table in her kitchen, fixing what she called a pick-me-up. Years later she would fix them for me, although by then we no longer called them pick-me-ups. Add one large brandy to an equally large Benedictine, mix with hot water, and sip as though it is Communion wine itself. There was a belief that Benedictine was medicinal. You would hear it all the time in the pubs and clubs: "a benny and hot" to settle your stomach/warm you through/ward off a chill. It has the sickly sweet taste of cough syrup, the warmth of the hot water colluding in the myth that what you are really drinking is a slightly more social version of Lemsip cold medicine, not really drinking at all. More of an unprescribed tonic, in fact. Like the Guinness when pregnant, the Mackeson's stout to build your strength up, the barley wine to sharpen the appetite, the couple of pints to relax you, and the drop of whisky to help you to sleep.

It never occurs to me to ask, when my mum tells me to go and run a few errands for Aunty Mary, why she can't do them herself. Just as it never occurs to me that the pills she takes for her headache are anything more than pills she takes for her headache. And it doesn't seem peculiar that before she leaves the house to go to her caravan in Fleetwood, she has to have a few of her pick-me-ups, any more than it seems peculiar that the only time she does leave the house is to go to her caravan in Fleetwood.

I remember Jack mumbling a few things about her, about how she would test the patience of a bloody saint, or he'd sigh his exasperated sigh when Kath came back after one of her visits, teary and troubled. Still no one used the term "alcoholic," let alone the word "agoraphobic." The wisdom was that Aunty Mary "took after her father," a diagnosis which suggested that nothing more needed to be said. (Occasionally there would be expansions on this: "a bad 'un," "a wrong 'un," and, intriguingly, "an eye for the women," as though his drinking was a symptom of the more serious charge of promiscuity.)

In Fleetwood there are bottles scattered throughout the caravan. Not ours, of course: me and Jack and Kath are in the next one over. But Aunty Mary's is awash with home brew. She began brewing her own a few months before, part of a new fad whereby she could make her addiction respectable by making it her hobby. It became "something to keep her busy," something to occupy her mind. She spoke of it as though it were some wholesome rustic pursuit, like mountaineering or hang gliding. "All my own work," she proudly announces, forcing on visitors a bottle of her homemade mild, which probably kicks in at around a not-so-mild 12 or 13 percent: "It's all good stuff. I made it mi'self." Thus did Aunty Mary rid herself of the stigma of drinking at home.

The caravan is part of a site—there are hundreds of them, row upon uniform row, each white and seeming to perch on its allotted patch. There is an amusement arcade which consists of a pinball machine, a telly bingo, and one of those machines that threatens to send its whole load of 2p coins cascading over the edge if you could just get your own 2p to drop at the back and give them a nudge. There is a clubhouse, its promise that there will be entertainment every night of the week, something for everyone. We plan our week: one day in Blackpool (for old times' sake), a day in Fleetwood itself (Kath wants to buy some fish), a round of pitch and putt, the rest of the time our own.

At night we go to the clubhouse. If I say there was a Beauty Contest—an actual "c'mon girls it's all a bit of fun who's gonna be the first to volunteer?" beauty contest—it will sound the stuff of cliché. But there was a beauty contest. To follow this up by saying that there was also a "knobbly knees contest" feels like I'm mistaking some god-awful sixties kitchen-sink realism for my actual life. But there was a knobbly knees contest. Music: Middle of the Road hearing their mama singing some chirpy-chirpy-cheep-cheep song and then finding said mama gone. Repeat ad infinitum. Drinks: halves of lager and black, or lager and lime, or port and lemon; all "fizzy women's drinks," for women who want to be drunk but who don't like the taste of their drink. For the men, mild or bitter, punctuated by the occasional virile rum.

And jokes: lots and lots of jokes: Pakis and mothers-in-law and husbands who can't get it up and women who are begging for it and poofs and Paddies being stupid and the black fella who lives next door with the funny accent and the Chinks and then yet another Paki along with some bird with big knockers-tits-melons-baps-gazungas-mammaries-anything-in-fact-except-breasts and the Germans (said with another funny voice) and still more Paddies and Murphies who seem to be simultaneously forever on building sites but also perpetually on the dole (how does that work?) except, that is, when they're not blowing themselves up with their homemade bombs and here's an impression of an Indian-Paki which is much the same if not exactly the same as a Paki-Paki because they're both the bloody same in that they're not us and we're not them and that's the way it is and that's the way it should be and that's the way we like it and don't worry about it 'cos it's all a-bit-of-fun-can't-take-a-joke-just-having-a-laugh-what's-the-matter-with-you?

I drink lemonade and eat crisps and I hate these people: these people who are no longer my own people. It is the kind of hate that is flat and heavy and weighed down with shame; a resentment that pushes my chin into my chest and keeps my shoulders stooped.

I hate their parochiality, their lack of imagination posing as virtue, their fear of others posing as pride in themselves. I am a sulky teenager who takes his sulking seriously. I didn't have an epiphany, no "I saw the Pistols/the Clash and knew that life would never be the same" grand awakening. What I had was seven nights on a caravan site, a week of corrosive disenchantment.

I have a friend who is convinced that when she heard Patti Smith sing "Jesus died for somebody's sins but not mine," the words irrevocably altered the structure of her DNA. I envy her her certainty, her precision. I don't remember that, but I do remember hearing her interpretation of Springsteen's "Because the Night." It was on that caravan site—the amusement arcade next to the clubhouse.

I would escape there to play pinball and for some reason (a jukebox? a radio?) the song seemed to be permanently playing. I remember getting not quite an erection but a warm caress around my balls listening to that opening piano, the way it manages to be both teasing and ominous, the kind of minuet you might hear just before the scary bit in a black-and-white movie. And then she wailed, wailed from a place deep inside herself. "Take me now baby here as I am . . ." It is a place whose contours are those of willful and aggressive surrender, a place where we are both tyrannized and liberated by . . . what? Bodies? Ours? Other people's? Something that's in between them? Soon after I saw Patti Smith on *The Old Grey Whistle Test*. She was reciting poetry and singing about horses, singing as though she were at a séance, possessed. She was dressed in a man's jacket, pantaloons, and a wide-brimmed hat which she wore pulled down over heavy-eye-shadowed eyes. I loved the fact that she spelled her name with an *i*. It seemed to explain why she sounded a bit like a boy. And also why she looked like one. I'd seen androgynous men before—seventies glam rock consisted of nothing but. But androgynous women? Patti Smith looked like a cross between Joan of Arc and Charlie Chaplin. I stare at the TV screen, at this woman who is like no woman I've ever seen. And life gets bigger.

It was the same summer I read Kafka, a Rev. Kev Recommends that is my shelter from the world of the clubhouse. I sit in the caravan and read about a man who wakes up to discover that he has been transformed into a giant insect. When he tells his boss that he can't come into work (or—wonderful touch—that he might be late) because of the whole insect thing, his boss doesn't get it. He gets that he's an insect: he does, after all, come round to Gregor's house to look at him. What he doesn't get is Gregor's explanation of how this state of affairs—this metamorphosis—is going to impact his career prospects. And the reason he doesn't get Gregor's explanation is that Gregor's words are no longer words. They are, as befits a giant insect, the noises of a giant insect. I am enraptured.

NEXT

My condition is not unhappiness, but it is also not happiness, not indifference, not weakness, not fatigue, not another interest—so what is it then?

—Franz Kafka, *Diaries*

I sit in his office and I pour out the whole sorry bitter saga. About stupid bloody Fleetwood and the bloody stupid people. About how I hate the small-souled, petty-minded white working class and how I hate myself for hating them. I am possessed of an adolescent's outrage, terminally in despair at the world's ignorance and lack of ambition. Possessed also by a Catholic sense of fallibility, that what is wrong with the world is what is wrong in us. People are lacking, are simply not good enough: it's why we need the story of Christ. He nods his head, crosses his legs, a wise and patient man-priest.

I had stopped going to confession a few years before, the "forgive me Father for I have sinned" recitation of my weekly transgressions managing to be both inadequate and overly dramatic. Yet this is what this was, a therapeutic face-to-face with someone who understood the enormity of what it meant to want to be good. He didn't give me a penance or offer me absolution. He sat and he listened and together we tried to make sense of my world. He called Jack "a man of the soil," a phrase which elevated him from being a groundsman into a Lawrentian hero.

It wasn't just my dad who was changed by redescription; it was Kevin as well. He was showing me that the way in which we name someone transforms the way we see them. Is this the reason I stopped calling him "Father," because I didn't want to put him in competition with my actual father, or because you don't call your friends "father?"

Yet "Kevin" never seemed quite right either—way too informal, like calling the queen "Liz." "The Rev. Kev" worked as description but not as a form of address. In private it was "you," in public "Father." I still haven't worked out what to call you.

We agreed that Kafka could well have been writing about adolescence (as well as about old age/illness/the human condition) and that—ha-ha-ha—my acne had given me a unique insight into Gregor's condition. We kind of quite liked the sister, Grete, and the way she fussed over him and his food. He used the word "arthropodic." It's the first time I'd heard the word and I vowed to use it in the future. And, yes, it was like a parable but also not at all like a parable.

What made it so perplexing was that Kafka played it straight, didn't go for allegory. It was like he wrote this most unnatural of stories in the most natural way possible, and that everything about the metamorphosis made perfect sense within its own terms, was a . . . yes, a closed circuit. So it wasn't really that I hated my mum and dad; it was more that they were part of a closed circuit—this total bloody thing—which meant that they weren't able to talk my language any more than Gregor's parents could talk insect. Which was sort of funny, if you thought about it. As well as all the other things—sad, infuriating, boring. And these things can—do—coexist. More than we think. That's it: our emotional responses conflict more than we think about more things than we think and books can help us to hold these conflicts in some kind of balance.

Perhaps, he suggests, Fleetwood had been invaluable in showing me how different worlds coexist in me as well as the one we live in. I'm to remember how many other worlds there are. Next year I should maybe come with him to Crete. Every year he took two or three boys to Crete and next year it would be great if I could be one of them. I would be slightly younger than the other two—they were already in the sixth form—but I was old beyond my years and would get so much from it. Of course he would ask my parents. He was the headmaster.

And so my question to you, now that I am no longer in danger of having to ask it, and you are incapable—what with the being dead and everything—of having to answer, is this: When did you decide to fuck me?

Is that too coarse? Doesn't take into account the various mixed motives and conflicting emotions of our lit.-crit. conversations? I apologize. Try again: Was there a point at which you thought that this precocious adolescent boy, with the bad skin and bookish pretensions, might be someone who could ease your loneliness, perhaps even share your bed? After all, he/me awakened something in you, didn't I/he? Was I a younger you? A reminder of the kind of curiosity and intensity that had once fueled your own boyhood, maybe even made you want to be a priest? Had there been someone who understood you in the same way you understood me? A priest of your own, perhaps? Who listened intently to your ambitions and dissatisfactions? Did he lend you books? Did you ease his pain in a way that brought its own not unproblematic rewards, a way that made you think, this is the way pain ought to be eased? And passed on?

NEXT

You are at once both the quiet and confusion of my heart;
imagine my heartbeat when you are in this state.
—Franz Kafka, *Letters to Felice*

I buy a copy of Patti Smith's *Easter*—it has *that* song on it and I skip
all the other tracks in my haste to hear her tell me to take me now
baby here as she is. Ask me what else is on the album (people did,
people do) and I draw a complete blank. There's a sweary one, a hymny
one, and a punk rocky one with a bad word in it. And then there is
track three, side one.

She is the reason I buy Mink DeVille—"Spanish Stroll"—slick and
camp, the backing vocals suggesting that all these strange figures—
Mr. Jim, Brother Johnny—had much more complex relationships
with the singer than he was letting on.

She's the reason I get into Springsteen. Who would have thought
that *that* song was written by a man, and not any man but the man
who everyone said only wrote about cars and being born to run?

Patti Smith is the reason I buy an album called *New Wave*—a com-
pilation with a red cover and a photograph of a punk spitting beer
into the camera. Her track was called "Piss Factory," a four-and-a-half-
minute jive poem about a job she'd had "inspecting pipe" (what?).
I remember thinking that crappy jobs in America sound like cool-
crappy jobs, whereas crappy jobs in Accrington were just crappy.

And she is the reason I fall in love with Chrissie Hynde. Because
Patti had many things, but what she didn't have was a behind cased in
tight leather trousers, one that's "gonna make you . . . make you . . .
make you notice."

I'm watching *Top of the Pops*. (Again! Did my TV week really revolve around that half hour every Thursday, those last two minutes of *Tomorrow's World* seeming to last the length of the longest chemistry lesson ever, Led Zep's "Whole Lotta Love" announcing the start of a long weekend?) I'm watching and waiting for the one good record that must surely come. There is a band fronted by a woman who is neither blond nor decorative, neither a dolly bird, a backing vocalist, nor a dancer (1980: the available options for women in pop).

She is both playing and wearing her guitar. She could be Suzi Quatro's older sister. The tune is sharp and soulful, an insistent rhythm neatly counterpointing a melody that always seems to want to veer off somewhere else. The woman is singing about the things that she's got and how she's going to use them. Which is fine: except that these things, the things that she's got, are not the usual things that women who sing songs have got. She's got "brass" and "bottle" and "intention." And the way she's going to use these things are not at all like the way you might expect her to use them either.

Chrissie Hynde didn't seem to mind being a rock star, in fact she seemed quite comfortable with the fact. She wasn't a capitalized-*P* Poet and she certainly didn't seem intent on gobbing into your living room, dismantling international capitalism, or annoying your parents. What she did seem to want was my attention, for me to join her in celebrating her glorious physicality.

When she says "Gonna use my arms" does she consciously swallow the *m*—inviting and threatening me with the knowledge that she knows where my sick soul can be found? And what about those "fingers," the fricative first syllable savored as though she is spitting you out at precisely the moment she's inviting you in. I'm in love. It's terrible—a bit like having stomach flu.

I buy the first Pretenders album and it becomes the soundtrack to my new discovery: heterosexuality. She swears. Not a "bloody" or a "bugger," but a full-blown double whammy of "shitting bricks" followed soon after by a "not me baby I'm too precious, fuck off." I'd heard Patti Smith swear (she'd told me that she didn't fuck much with the past, but she fucked plenty with the future), but that was poetry, and so didn't count.

Chrissie Hynde's swearing counted. As did the rest of her. Her arms, her legs, her fingers, her her her imagination . . .

He says that he missed me, the fortnight that I was away in Fleetwood, and that it's unusual because he doesn't usually miss people. It's an occupational hazard—this not missing people, not getting too attached to an individual person, because you are meant to be attached to all people.

On the album cover she's wearing a red leather jacket, with black lace peeking through the sleeves. On the back there's an address where you can write to her, somewhere in Covent Garden, London. Beneath this: "To achieve maximum effect / PLAY THIS RECORD LOUD."

The northeast, near Sutherland, though he lost the accent a long time ago. Yes, he still goes back. Not as much as he should. He'll take me with him sometime. Think you'll find it interesting.

Track two is simply called "The Phone Call" and is utterly incomprehensible. It was something about "a message" that she both did and didn't want to receive, and that was causing her all sorts of problems. Me too. We didn't have a phone, and I didn't have a girl to phone even if we did. It dawns on me that the two things—girls and phones—might be connected: promises of intimacy.

He tells me that he read English at Cambridge. Not "did" or even "studied": "read." He made it sound both leisurely and life changing, as though there was nothing else that could be done: at Cambridge or anywhere.

This isn't about fancying her. Or not just about fancying her. It is about hunger.

He needs his books to be arranged, sorted out alphabetically, by genre, by author. He'll pay me the going rate, whatever that is.

"I was a good time . . . I got pretty good" she sings on "Tattooed Love Boys." Not she "had" a good time, but she "was" a good time. I close my eyes. Open them. I write her name in capital letters.

He had been—still was, ha-ha—a bit of a teddy boy, had seen Chuck Berry way back when. Never got Presley though—funny that—too many theatrics maybe or was it God help us those bloody films? Elvis in Hawaii feigning romance with some dolly in a frilly skirt. Bogus. Not his idea of rock 'n' roll. Pretenders? Never heard of them. Good name for a band though, all the right registers—the Platters, genuine heartache, reminded him for some reason of Oscar Wilde.

There's an instrumental track which I want to skip but never do because it feels like being unfaithful to her: to Her.

Blackburn has a film club, not the local Odeon, but a society where people who are really into films go and discuss them, hire a projector, and introduce them. Films that they never show on the telly or screen at the flicks, films by "auteurs" (auteurs? what a word), stuff from Italy, the French New Wave, stuff you'd really like. (He's thought about what I'd really like, and he's right. I do really like it.)

In 1995 I read the following words by the music critic Simon Reynolds: "Her voice—a slurred, sensual alloy of neediness and nastiness, vulnerability and viciousness—is one of the first, and best, examples of a female equivalent to the classic rock 'n' roll snarl/swagger. On songs like 'The Wait' . . . she lets rip a strafing stream of syllables that's a weird mix of speed-rap, jive-talk, and baby-babble. It's punk-scat. All hiccoughs, vocal tics, gasps, and feral growls, weirdly poised between love and hate, oral sensuality and staccato, stabbing aggression." Good, isn't it? Exactly the right mix of descriptive swagger and analytic precision, the kind of music journalism I always wanted to write but never did. It would have been even better if I had read it in 1980, because if I'd read it in 1980 it would have prevented me from writing the Poem to Chrissie Hynde that I did write in 1980. It began: "I want to die beneath your ass." Originally the line had been wanting to die beneath her "arse," but that seemed wrong, vulgar somehow.

NEXT

There is nothing bad to fear; once you have crossed that threshold, all is well. Another world, and you do not have to speak.

—Franz Kafka, *Letter to My Father*

And meanwhile my granddad died. Not quite suddenly, but neither after a long etcetera. The collective family wisdom was that he'd never been right ever since falling in the canal—a verdict which owes more to Alan Bennett than I (or surely he) would like, but which was probably close to the mark. The word "chill" became the defining motif of his monthlong illness: chilled to his bones, his very marrow, all the way through. Nobody mentioned the fact that the canal was probably full of semilethal toxic crap, the very same semilethal toxic crap with which he'd worked most of his working life.

It saddens me that my granddad's death was bound up with an element of the vaudevillian, that he survived Dunkirk only to have his fate sealed by the greasy broth of the Leeds and Liverpool Canal. It saddens me even more that I'd been out of his life for the last few years, had opted for my hormonal adolescent angst over our sessions of crib and nonsense and laughter.

His last days had been spent in hospital—Queen's Park, a place whispered with a reverential dread. It had been a workhouse in a previous life, its history seeping with the mixture of ill health and poverty.

Both my parents had been with him at his deathbed. I remember thinking that there was just one such bed—a Death Bed—and that the patient would be moved there just at the moment when they were about to die and that it would be awful when they were about to move you there because that's when you knew you were going to die. The nurses wouldn't tell you that they were moving you there; they probably had another name for it, a kind of nurse code name, but that you'd know anyway, and that maybe if they stopped putting people on deathbeds, then maybe people would stop dying.

Kath says that on this bed, even though he was fighting for breath, he was trying to take off the oxygen mask and tell them something. She was and remained convinced that he was trying to tell them that he had lent someone some money—a substantial amount—a long while ago. And: This is the person, This was the amount. When they cleared out his things a few days later, they found a couple of hundred pounds wrapped in bundles at the bottom of his wardrobe. As far as Kath was concerned this wasn't what he had been trying to tell her, but it was proof that she was right. There had been money, and we would never see it.

I don't go to the funeral. I'm deemed to be too upset. I'm grateful for the get-out, for not having to face all those crying grown-ups or my own guilt at having abandoned him. Kath tells me about her dad—my other granddad—and about how they "brought him home," laid his body to rest in the front room of their old house. She would go in and sit with him, this body that both was and was not her father. She even kissed him on the cheek; his skin was waxy.

She is glad they don't do that anymore. It was morbid. They still draw all the curtains though, a mark of respect, and if any man was respected in Accrington, it was John Caveney. He and your dad didn't get on, but he loved you. He loved your dad too in his own way, but it was difficult. The war and all that. And men, bloody-minded bloody men, stubborn to the bloody end. He adored your grandma, spoiled her, made her so she can't do anything for herself. We'll have to look after her now; keep an eye on her, make sure she's eating properly. It's what happens love, it's just what happens. It's sad, but it's not the end of the world.

And my dad? My dad sheds not one tear. Jack Caveney—son of Sergeant Major John Caveney—shakes everyone's hand and says the usual "kind of yous." He sees that everyone has a glass of something, all those aunties I never knew he had (did he know he had?), robust strong women with dim Irish ancestry. They ease themselves into funereal mode, shuffling forward as each takes their turn at passing on condolences, the wisdom of widows (collective noun: an invulnerability? a veil? a release?): "The thing about him was . . ." ". . . never one for . . ." "I'll say this about him . . ."

And when he sees that everyone's glass is full, that his mother is not just holding up but positively flourishing amongst this sisterhood of bereaved old women, he puts his arm around my shoulders and we slip out.

We slip out and go to a snooker club called the Elite, a place which could not have been more inappropriately named. He racks up the balls, the overhead light capturing the dust mites and the scuffed green baize. And we play. We play for hours, our concentration given over to the reds and the blacks and the colors. The sounds of a snooker table should be used by an avant-garde composer—a John Cage or La Monte Young score made up of the thuds of a ball hitting the back of a pocket, the kiss-collision of the white opening up the pack, the clatter of the wooden rest returning to its cradle at the table's side. I didn't think that then. What I thought then was that my dad was cooler than I sometimes thought he was.

NEXT

Nothing unites two people so completely, especially if, like you and me, all they have is words.

—Franz Kafka, *Letters to Felice*

I became friends with a boy called John Mullen. I decided to stop laughing. I wished I had a stutter. He was that kind of friend. He lived a few streets over, on the street where the school bus stopped and on which there was a secondhand bookshop that sold a different kind of secondhand book. The shop was painted green and had a wire grille and cardboard over its glass-paneled front door. In one of its windows it displayed magazines—glossy martial arts mags, bodybuilding manuals, true-crime stuff. In the other were lurid paperbacks with women on the cover, women who were called things like "Hellcat Amazons," "Divorce Bait," or "Vegas Tramp." The pictures were painted in brash Technicolor greens and reds, and yet there was a playfulness about them that spoke to even the bummiest of St. Mary's College bum boys. Do I remember or have I invented one called *Tom Cat in Tights* which showed a woman barely draped in red silk, sitting for a picture, whilst the painter sits or stands below her, gazing at the small of her back? And have I imagined that she wasn't wearing tights and so the title didn't make any sense, and wondering if it not making any sense could have been on purpose? They were chaotically priced these books, a 35¢ arguing with a 2/6 and both of them silenced by a sign saying that they were all 10p each.

The natural place for me to get my bus was at the top of my own street, but the promise of spending a few minutes with the cover of *Her Candle Burns Hot* was worth a five-minute walk. There, looking at *Coffin for a Cutie* or *Pit Stop Nympho*, wondering how come helpless women could also be threatening women, a sickly lad approached me and said: "Danish Dentists on the Job." Sorry? " 'Danish Dentists on the Job.' It's the title I've come up with for my own book. It fits the genre nicely don't you think? It's exotic—well, foreign—and it's alliterative and it has the necessary double entendre, single entendre really. Ha-ha-ha. I'm John by the way, but I'm thinking of changing it to Conrad." If he had taken a pinch of snuff I wouldn't have been surprised.

Do kids still become mates as quickly as I did with Johnny—Conrad—Mullen? I hope so. The deal was swift and solid: two straight bum boys with a shared understanding that life was sweet but organized in such a way as to be awful; that uppercase Literature and lowercase music would be the means to rectify this, and that we would be the tortured embodiment of both.

He was a few years older than me, already sitting his O levels when we met. This, I now realize, was a brave move in itself, teenagedom having its own strict codes of apartheid. He was formidably clever, the kind of lad who, according to Jock Roland's wry assessment, "gave genius a bad name." He wrote parodies of Hardy and Lawrence purely for his own (and my) amusement. He had read Chomsky by the age of sixteen and found problems with him by the age of seventeen. When asked to write a story from the point of view of the textile workers of the nineteenth century, he famously refused by saying that the textile workers of the nineteenth century were almost certainly illiterate and so it would be truer to their experience to write a ballad about the Chartists and perform it in assembly. Which he did.

He annoyed the music teacher by stating that music was not in fact a language all of its own ("it couldn't be, to describe it thus is to profoundly misunderstand the nature of language. And indeed of music") and the English teacher by announcing that Shakespeare's comedies were unfunny, and that explaining why they were funny didn't make them so.

He was from Blackpool, had transferred to Blackburn around the time of his O levels. It explains, I think, why we became such good friends—some adolescent homing instinct that allowed his physical displacement to find a mirror in my own internal misfitery. We're Sartre and Camus, we're Laurel and Hardy, we're Kafka and Brod.

I tell him about my romance with his hometown, about the pitch and putt and the pier. He tells me that this isn't his Blackpool. His hometown—his Blackpool—is one of unemployment and petty rivalries between north side and south. He tells me that there's a lot of drug problems and that he never really went to the seafront. He tells me that the locals hate the tourists, hate them because they depend on them, hate them because our leisure is their labor.

I'd only read about people like John Mullen, the semifantastical outsider savant. It felt like I'd dreamed him into being. My bus rides to school are now tutorials in the books he is doing for A level— *Hamlet* ("he really is fucking crazy, it isn't just an act"), Blake, and Lawrence's *Women in Love*. We walk from Blackburn bus station up the hill to school. The other lads (all of them, it seemed) call this trek the Khyber Pass or Paki Alley. We don't. We seem to have made an agreement to not call it that.

John seemed to have acquired a body rather than possess one. He walked both quickly and uncertainly, as though he'd borrowed someone else's legs and wasn't sure just how long he could keep them. His head had dropped onto his neck and someone had tapped his teeth into place with a small toffee hammer. His skin was the color of putty. He was arrogant, brilliant, and unpopular. Within weeks he was my best mate.

Kathleen is delighted at me having a new friend, although less so at him being a "neo-anarchist" (a "neo" what?). She resolves her ambivalence by feeding him, as though his strange opinions were more a symptom of hunger than political commitment, and that regular injections of potato pie would soon stabilize him into something more conventional. She was half right. John's home life had the kind of poverty that made my own look relatively comfortable. He was from a Catholic family, three brothers and a sister, a dad who tried to feed them all on a gasfitter's wages. Having no room of his own, going round to John's meant that we would always go out. Usually back to mine and to an avalanche of Kathleen's politically corrective cooking.

Jack's uncertainties went deeper. He called him Ratzo Rizzo after Dustin Hoffman's character in *Midnight Cowboy*, a reference to John's eternal shabbiness and jangly walk. In John he saw a different kind of cleverness to that of his son. It was verging on that dreaded thing, a clever-cleverness, which is a cleverness that is almost too clever by half. Here we were swimming in uncharted—potentially treacherous—waters. This wasn't just knowing the capital of Peru or doing sums in your head. Neither was it a matter of noses in books or even heads in clouds. What we had here was the swallowing of maps. A lad who had swallowed the map (a "bloody" usually made an appearance between the "the" and the "map") was a lad who had digested the world and therefore knew it all. It meant that knowledge had been translated into opinions and opinions into a worldview. It meant that all that thinking had gone to his head. I would watch Jack weigh up this new addition to our dinner table, see him balance being impressed by this sharp young man with being irritated at his certainties. Jack would argue with him for argument's sake, going head-to-head on issues about which I knew he was in full agreement (like capital punishment). The moment would invariably arise when Jack would fall back on: "That's just your opinion." To which John would give his infuriating response: "Whose opinions would you like me to have?"

NEXT

The mere process of learning is allied to mutiny.
—Shirley Jackson, *Hangsaman*

We're not in a band, which doesn't stop us from coming up with names for our band. Quite the opposite; thinking of band names is the music that our non-band makes. The Tranquilised Pilots, the Footnotes, Semolina Ping-Pong, ACAS, the Delinquent Gymnasts, Trotsky's Dumbbells, the Fag Ends, all were formed on the school bus to Blackburn, only to break up on the walk up the hill, usually due to ideological differences. "There's no way the Air Hostesses would release a single called 'Adolescent Breakdown,'" John would insist, "especially if we go on tour supporting the Raincoats." Thus were the Air Hostesses dissolved, their non-single unreleased, a mere two minutes after their debut nonappearance. "How about Penguin Genocide, or the Ra Ra Shirts . . . our debut single to be called 'My Donkey Jacket's at the Cleaners'?"

The second time he comes round to my house he brings with him an armful of albums and the instruction to replace my 10cc records with "these. They are important." The cover of the first record has a photograph of what looks like a skiffle band, except that the guitarist is wearing a Hawaiian shirt and the singer a white V-necked kaftan. He stands in front of his band, crazed and curly hair balancing on top of a bemused expression and a what-the-hell-do-I-know shrug. I'd heard Jonathan Richman without knowing who it was. His "Egyptian Reggae" had provided the pretext for Pan's People to dress like Cleopatra and do a shuffle dance routine on *Top of the Pops* complete with Liz Taylorish costumes and camel motifs. There were, of course, no vocals and so I hadn't realized that Richman was also, what? A Dadaist pretending to be a seven-year-old boy? Walt Whitman writing nursery songs? This was not what was meant by postpunk or New Wave, was it? It had DIY iconoclasm, the sound of having being improvised in his dad's garage. There was mischief without the mayhem. Where was the spit, the urban sneer? This boy-man was singing about leprechauns and the ice cream man, for God's sake. John-call-me-Conrad Mullen plays me "Afternoon" for the third time and now I'm starting to hear it: existentialist doo-wop. It's funny without being ironic, goofily gentle.

We work through the record, delighted, replaying key tracks. John tells me it's like Blake, the whole thing about childhood and innocence and experience, the one about flying into the mystery. I say that the Modern Lovers are like hippies, but hippies that sound like they've gone back to the fifties when music still sounded as though someone had just thought of it.

He plays me Fairport Convention—"Time Will Show the Wiser"— and does his version of a pogo dance, a scary performance that resembles someone in a straitjacket having a seizure. Next up the Chieftains, followed by Simon and Garfunkel. Then the Raincoats singing "No Side to Fall In," scratchy violins, percussions, and three-part harmonies. I suspect he secretly fancies one of the women (Gina Birch?) but that he thinks it'd be somehow wrong to admit it. He tells me that it isn't a secret, actually, and that there's nothing wrong with it and anyway it's complicated. It's like the song itself, trying to find somewhere you can fall into, and do I know about Lola? I don't know about Lola and so he tells me. I'm fascinated. I make him tell me again. So, she walks like a woman and talks like a man? Which might explain why . . . fuck! And when he gets down on his knees, they look at each other, and he wants things to stay that way. Double fuck! Suddenly 10cc's Eric Stewart pretending that he's Not in Love doesn't seem so appealingly nuanced. And Coca-Cola not transsexuality was the censor's problem? It's a mixed-up muddled-up shook-up world. . . .

A few weeks later John tells me something even more shocking. We're talking about the sheer genius of Tom Robinson Band's "Power in the Darkness"—a not unusual topic of conversation. We agree that it's a pity that he seems to be better known for the anthemic "2-4-6-8 Motorway" than for his agit-pop. We agree that it's the keyboards that make all the difference, the way that Mark Ambler's organ plays off Danny Kustow's guitar. I tell him about the sleeve notes, the ones that say politics isn't about politicians but about being on the dole, or your mate getting Paki bashed. Yet I'm a bit baffled. The bit after that says it's also about your kid sister not being able to get an abortion. What is that bit doing there with all these other noble causes, the other righteous victims? Surely politics shouldn't be about the kid sister (that I don't have) not having to have an abortion?

And so he tells me. He tells me about a woman's right to choose, the position I hold now but had never even heard about in the years I was growing up. Until that moment—halfway up Shear Brow in Blackburn, satchel in hand—it had never once occurred to me that abortion was anything other than a mother killing her baby. So deeply ingrained in me was this belief that I didn't consider it a belief. It was the natural order of things, like the blood in my veins. I didn't consider myself antiabortion in the same way I didn't consider myself antimurder. To define myself in these ways would be to imply that there was a debate to be had. And as the act was so self-evidently wrong, how could there be a rationale in its favor? Of course I was against abortion; how could anyone be otherwise?

In the lobby of our school there was a cabinet with pictures of fetuses in jars. I recognize them now as the propaganda tools of the so-called pro-life movement. At the time they were just part of the furniture, like the names of past pupils carved into wooden plaques. I once told Father O'Neill that I was having trouble sleeping, couldn't get off, or kept waking up. He told me that this meant I'd been uncomfortable in the womb. He told me this with all the authority of a doctor diagnosing eczema; no hesitation, absolute certainty. I was, according to him, already alive as me in the womb—a presocial soul awaiting its corporeal body.

NEXT

Until I learn to accept my reward . . .
—Teardrop Explodes, "Reward"

I'm fighting a running battle with my mum. About my hair, although it feels like something much bigger than that. She wants it cut, cut "nicely." She says, It makes you look ill, it's bad for your skin, your acne. I say, It's my hair, and, Other people have long hair. She says, We're not other people. It's one of my mum's recurring motifs, "we're not other people," meaning, I guess, that we are exactly like other people, just not like the other people who we don't want to be like. Respectability, it is her guiding principle. She has internalized respectability from her hair (in head scarf) to her toes (in chain-store slippers). The *Accrington Observer* carries stories about who appeared in court and why. "Drunk and Disorderly," "Shoplifting," "Non-Payment of TV License." She reads and sighs, sighs and reads. The shame. Have they none? She wouldn't be able to hold her head up. She'd rather die. Those are the people who we are not like.

I decide I am a communist—a catholic-communist with a double small *c*. I want a militant version of Christ's kindness, a sort of socialist Sermon on the Mount. I tell Mum that I'm a communist but not to be cross because I'm still a catholic. I tell her that if she thinks about it, Jesus was a communist too and she says she supposes that he was. She overhears me and John Mullen referring to our teachers by their first name or nicknames, us thrilling at our transgressive familiarity: "Tosh" Tom Kennedy, Father Simo, Jock Roland. Her chin goes up, her eyes flare, and she says in a voice that can stop a double-decker bus: "You will not refer to those men in that way, not in this house. You'll show them the respect they deserve."

I show the Rev. Kev my poem, the one that starts "Red is the colour / The color / Of life / No matter which way you spell it," and he says that poetry is about using words like musical instruments. We sit in his office and sip sherry. We are, I decide, meeting as equals. Or as equal as it's possible for two poets to be. I mean, Byron and Shelley weren't exactly equal nor Wordsworth and Coleridge. Yet he is listening to me with rapt attention. He takes books down from his shelves, a well-thumbed copy of Eliot. He reads to me. "The Love Song of J. Alfred Prufrock." He says, Listen to the gaps.

I spend the morning sorting his books, firstly by genre, then period, then alphabetically. Amongst a pile of papers on his desk I come across one of his undergraduate essays called something like "Transcendent Love or Self-deception? A Study of *Antony and Cleopatra*." I flick through it feeling voyeuristic and intrusive, as though I am rifling through his bank book or underwear drawer. I don't know the play (and still don't), which doesn't stop me from being engrossed in the essay. I don't understand it, which engrosses me all the more. So my teacher had himself been taught, had read and written and essayed just like his students. It was a thrilling discovery. He'd existed before I knew him. Before I was born.

I talk to him about it over lunch—a lunch he buys me in a fairly posh restaurant, the first time I've set foot in one. The place has deep carpets, the menu is pretending that it was written with a quill. I confess that I found his essay; read it, loved it, didn't understand it.

He tells me about the book that he should write but knows he never will. It will—won't, would—be about self-deception, the stories people tell themselves to hide from their fundamental vulnerability. As a priest he knows that it is precisely this vulnerability—our lack, our loss—that binds us together. If he's feeling mischievous he calls it original sin. Literature's power is to take this essential flaw and dramatize it. At its best, literature acknowledges what God knows: that we are our imperfections.

When the waiter asks if everything's all right, Rev. Kev says, unsniffily, that his steak was a bit fatty, but apart from that fine. I had never realized that the waiter's question—everything all right?—

could have any other answer except the one given by my parents: "Yes, smashing/lovely/beautiful." Not so much an answer as an apology, a response to an accusation. This wasn't that. This was something else. A lesson in politeness and power: "A bit fatty, but apart from that fine." This: this is how I will be.

He is wearing civvies, jeans, and a purple button-down shirt.

He tells me about his job and I thrill at hearing him describe it as a job. He tells me about his work for the Samaritans, about the man who had been held captive for years by his wife; about the heavy breathers and the perverts who demand that you listen to their fantasies.

He tells me that after the film version of *The Exorcist* came out, there was a huge upsurge in cases of possession—it became quite the thing, highly fashionable. He tells me about having to attend to a young woman who wanted him to exorcise her, and him having to read Peter Blatty's book to get himself in character. She tried to do the swearing but wasn't very good at it. She wanted the whole Latin and holy water thing. He gave her tea and digestive biscuits.

I tell him that I've asked my parents about Crete and that they're delighted, of course I can go. Actually they're worried about the cost, but they'll find the money somehow. Talking of which, he pays me for the morning's work. There's a few other jobs if I'm interested—a PTA night coming up. He could pull a few strings—get me work behind the bar. Money shouldn't be an issue. If I want to go to Crete then I—we—should go.

NEXT

. . . he knew that henceforth the entire devotion of his religion, the whole ecstatic fervor of his prayers, would be connected with, nay, inspired by, one object alone. With the same reverence and humility as he would have felt in touching the consecrated elements he laid his hands on the curl-crowned head, he touched the small pale face, and raising it slightly, he bent forward and gently touched the smooth white brow with his lips.

—John Francis Bloxam, "The Priest and the Acolyte," published in *The Chameleon*, 1894

I loved being groomed. If I had my adolescence to do all over again, not only would I want to be groomed by Kevin O'Neill I would want to be groomed by others too (collective noun for groomers? A nest, a smarm, a spoil?). I would want a spoil of groomers lending me books, talking to me about mankind's insufficiency, and gently making it known that the steak was too fatty in restaurants. Maybe I didn't have enough groomers. Maybe if my science teachers had been pedophiles I'd have done better at chemistry. Or maybe they were pedophiles but I simply wasn't to their taste. Is this sick? Not all of my past needs to be arranged along those lines, abusers and cynical groomers, the groomed and the cynically abused.

Not all of it. But some of it.

As I've said, I've got a stupid name. Before I even finish pronouncing my surname I automatically begin spelling it, swallowing the irritation that wants to say: "It's not that bloody difficult . . . C-A-V- E-N-E-Y." It is a name that seems irreducible to a nickname, that wants to resist any linguistic backslapping or semantic matiness. The "ney" means that I can't follow the rest of my peer group down the road to a democratic elongation. I can't become a Caveney-y, and so a Caveney I remain.

The "Graham" hasn't helped much either. How different would my life have been if I'd have joined the ranks of the Doms, the Matts, and the Cols? Or an abbreviation that can become its own rightful name, a Tony or an Andy, say. I could have gone for Fred or Ben, and even Jeremy can live in hope of becoming Jez. But Graham remains Graham, no matter what. My parents didn't want a name that would become something—someone—else. It is a name chosen for its self-containment, for its refusal to resurface anywhere else. It is a name of social aspiration, of gentle upward mobility. You either say (t)his name in full, or you don't say it at all. Thus announced Jack and Kathleen Caveney in choosing "Graham."

Is this why it sticks in my throat now? When I say my name I can feel the syllables protest in my trachea; they emerge reluctantly, cringing slightly as though embarrassed at having to arrange themselves in such a noneuphonic order. "Graham Caveney"—too many long vowels, those whiney *a*'s getting all tumbled up in themselves in their rush to get the fuck out of my mouth. I aspire to a bubbling stream of speech—an uninterrupted meander from throat to tongue to air. Yet what emerges is strangled and malnourished, as though the words have been deprived of oxygen and emerge pale and apologetic into the enemy territory that is just outside my mouth—the place that is no longer me but not quite you.

In my voice can be heard all the conflicts of "boy-made-good"—hidden resentment, preemptive apologies, pretensions, and uncertainties. Except that it is not just boy-made-good. It is boy-made-good-made-very-bad-trying-to-make-good-again. Say "aaaaaah": open wide.

I tell the Rev. Kev that my mum is always repeating herself, and that it gets on my nerves. He's kind. He tells me that one of the reasons my mum may feel the need to repeat herself is that, historically, she has never been listened to. He makes me relove my mum, and I love him for it.

He says an odd thing. He says that he's not got a talent for poetry—a cloth ear when it comes to his own attempts—but that he does have a feel for the aphorism. He tells me that he came up with one recently. He tells me that it goes: "If you get a friend and he's wise and true / Then fuck him before he fucks you." I remember being shocked, not by the language but by the cynicism. I think about it for a long time and decide that it's a miniparable about not idealizing your friends, about remembering that they are humans also, flawed fleshy humans, and that we are fucked if we forget it. I think about it for a long time. I am still thinking about it.

I tell him that I wish I could tell jokes, that they're a thing I just can't do. He laughs and says, "Oh, but you can."

Each morning I go to Mass. It is often only me and him. We don't acknowledge anything other than prayer and the Eucharist.

I show off. I tell him that I'd realized that Beckett's novels rely heavily on the letter M—the thirteenth letter of the alphabet, unlucky for some, and also the date of Beckett's birthday. He nods as though he knew this (did he know this?) and says, "Like Kafka's K, the eleventh. Prime numbers. Like us. We're both prime numbers."

The morning assembly, the prayers, the announcements. I think, What will we talk about later?

NEXT

Logical advice gets you in a whirl.
—Joe Jackson, "It's Different for Girls"

Quite why I didn't tell my parents that I was working behind the bar for a Parent–Teacher night, I still don't know. Maybe something to do with bars, and with Parent–Teacher nights.

I know that Kathleen would both approve and disapprove of bar work. She would be proud that I had been asked, was contributing to the Crete fund. She'd be pleased that: I'm making an effort, earning a few quid, taking some responsibility. She'd be worried that: I'm too young to be pouring drinks, that we aren't that bloody hard up, that it is too much responsibility. And: Do you need special clothes? Do they need our permission? What about your tea?

I know that Jack both approves and disapproves of Parent–Teacher nights. He liked that they talked to each other, the teachers and the parents; it was what was wrong with his schooling, the fact that they never talked to each other. They might pick up on something that the other had missed: you'd never get a full picture otherwise. And he was suspicious that they were always bloody talking to each other. "Hobnobbing" is what it was, trying to get their foot in the door, their feet beneath the table. No wonder you never got a full picture.

So, no. Best not.

NEXT

His entire existence as a priest was one long humble bow that wearied his soul. . . . As a priest, he spent his days praising, adoring and sending up incense to God, and now he too was the God of that creature who feared him and who punctually offered her devotions to him.

—Eça de Queirós, *The Crime of Father Amaro*

So I'm not working behind the bar for a PTA do. I'm going round to another lad's house. No, they don't know him. A lad my own age.

There are brandy glasses and wineglasses, chilled white wine but not chilled—definitely not chilled—red wine. There's gin and vodka which are easy to mix up but actually easy to tell apart—smell 'em if in doubt. There's what we call mixers—tonics and lemon and cordials—that some people like to pour themselves and others like to have poured for them. There's ladies' glasses, the ones with the handles. Don't—whatever you do—give a fella a drink in a ladies' glass. That'd be—ha-ha—more than your life's worth. There's pint-pot mugs and half-pint mugs, beer, obviously, barreled and bottled. Mild and bitter, and a drink called mixed, which is half mild half bitter, and even though it doesn't really matter which you pour first, you should always pour mild first. Then there's Guinness and bitter (a black and tan), but don't worry about that and just ask if you need anything. Divide your time, a spell behind the bar, walk round with the wine. Top 'em up, keep it flowing.

I'd tried and been around strong drink before. One didn't go to my aunt Mary's on a Friday night—on any night—and not try strong drink. It tasted vile. Thick and heavy, it astonished me that she was able to drink so much of it.

The parents (and some teachers) are knocking it back here as well. This isn't home brew and crisps. This is PTA drinking, drinking that wants to get drunk without it being acknowledged. These people are drinking because they like it, and they like it a lot. They are drinking "stiffeners" and "liveners" and "scoops." Jack's right, they are on the make: there's talk of sports days and prizes, school trips to the Vatican, little Offspring/Saint Name's chances of A levels and beyond.

The priests are launching a charm offensive (as we didn't say in 1980): collars and gowns and bonhomie. It's an impressive tableau, a sight for the sore eyes of the socially climbing Catholic. Kevin is not quite selling pardons but it's as near as damn it. He seems to have developed a handshake for the occasion, a two-handed clasp that seems to seal the deal on mortal souls and northern brass. It's a new side of him. I watch from behind the bar.

I still haven't decided what drink will be my drink. Beer looks promising but people seem to drink so very very much of it. Not just one pint—itself a massive measure—but pint after pint (how do they not want to pee all the time?). Imagine if it was milk. I pour some wine that looks like cranberry juice and manage not to spit it out. It's like dandelion and burdock mixed with malt vinegar and cheese. It makes the back of my teeth feel weird, like I've drunk too much strong tea. I try the white.

NEXT

My passion for iced drinks punished.

—Franz Kafka, *Diaries*

In Scorsese's film *Mean Streets*, there is a wonderful scene of Harvey Keitel getting shit-faced. The camera seems to be placed in front of him at chest height, and follows him round as though they were both strapped in to a fairground ride. The song being played—"Rubber Biscuit" by the Chips—is being played both on the screen and as a soundtrack to the action on the screen. It has the *Looking-Glass* clarity of a drunkard's logic, its nonsense lyrics ("cool water sandwich" "Sunday-go-to-meeting bun") battering their head against a saxophone. It is drinking as nursery rhyme and it is wonderful.

This—this night behind a PTA bar—is nothing like that.

Later, when I saw the film, I would try to rearrange my memories so that it tallied with those of this scene. I tried to recast my life, substituting the cool that is Keitel for the pathetic slobbering and giggling fifteen-year-old boy that is myself.

I drink the white wine, which seems to taste better the more I drink of it. I go and talk to people—these grown-up PTA people with their ties and frocks. Someone tells a joke and it is the funniest joke in the world. It's me! Me, the boy who can't tell jokes has told a joke. Well, not so much a joke, but kind of a joke. People are laughing. And I'm laughing. I say it again, I say I'd rather have a full bottle in front of me than a . . . I say, wait, I'd rather have a full frontal lobotomy. No. I'd rather have a bottle in front of me than a frontal lobotomy. Get it? A bottle in front of me. Frontal lobotomy. Listen? Shhhhh.

Julie, my therapist, wants to know: How could I have *not* gotten drunk that night? In what possible world could anyone—least of all a fifteen-year-old boy—sidestep the sheer ubiquity of drink or be immune to its all-pervasive charms? She leans forward in her chair: you were serving them drinks, and they were drinking those drinks for a reason. You were curious. There's a reason that you needed to be over eighteen to work in a bar. There's a reason you needed to be over eighteen to drink.

I don't feel well. I want to go home. Take me home. I can't go home. I'm drunk.

She says: He spiked your drink. I know he didn't actually spike your drink. But he spiked your drink. The drink was spiked. The whole evening was spiked.

NEXT

. . . in a sense, my Lo was even more scared of the law than I.
—Vladimir Nabokov, *Lolita*

A car. A car I've been in a lot recently. He's taking me home, but not to my home, to his home. We'll sit in his room and carry on talking. It's where we talk sometimes. His room with its Stevie Wonder records and the house cat and I still don't feel well. It's a big detached house—the priests' house: all of them live there, each has his own room. His is on the ground floor, on the right as you go in. It smells of furniture polish and incense, candles and cooking. They have a cleaner but I've never seen 'er . . . ha-ha-ha . . . Cleaner. Seen her. Geddit? It's like a bottle in front of me and frontal lobotomy. Still drunk. Shhh . . . My mum and dad. What about my mum and dad?

She says: Things can be preplanned without being preplanned.

I want to lie down. I need to lie down. Let me lie down.

I think: Tongues are weird. They look like they're supposed to be soft but they're really quite hard. It's their wetness that makes them deceptive. They're like olives. Except they're nothing like olives. Tongues are like . . . tongues. They're like nothing else. Are they a muscle? They kind of move around on their own, only half attached to our bodies, the root somewhere in the back of the mouth. I'm not sure where it starts. Or where it ends? Flicking a lot, searching for something, as though there's something in my mouth that it needs. Needs a lot. His, not mine. Mine recoils, it doesn't want to give his anything to work with, or against. I'd heard that people can actually swallow their tongues. Epileptics. Imagine, swallowing your tongue. Is this necking, this thing he's doing and if so why is it called necking and not tonguing? If his tongue is in my mouth then where's mine supposed to go? And how do I know it's mine, and not his? It's not licking or even slurping—it's jabbing, like in boxing.

I want to be sick. I hope I'm not sick. I feel sick.

I don't say "Stop." Not that I could say stop with his tongue in my mouth. His tongue colonizing my gums, my spittle being annexed by its insistence. I think "Stop." I think your breath is sour.

I don't kiss back. I think if I can make my tongue go limp and un-responsive, then this alien tongue, this other combative tongue, will get the message. It will know that this is not a two-tongue situation and it will somehow become embarrassed and leave. It will read the lack of resistance as resistance.

Now I see why it's called "necking." His neck has got some kind of rhythm going now. A kind of in-for-the-mouth/back-for-a-breath beat. He's making funny noises, like a cross between a whimper and a gasp, as though he's opening a present that is so surprising that it is making him want to cry. I keep my eyes closed.

I think that if we didn't have lips, our mouths would simply fray. There would be flaps of skin flapping around the hole of our mouths, like threads of cotton on a badly sewn pair of jeans. I think that lips are dry because they are on the outside, but tongues are wet because they are on the inside. Except that his tongue isn't in his inside. It's in my inside. Which makes it his outside. And yet it's still wet. Horribly wet.

I think what a weird word "kiss" is. It's one of those verbs that can be both active and passive. Like "throw" or "hit." He kisses me—active voice. The kisser is the subject, the kissing is the doing, the kissed the object. "Want," "eat," "write": Are they called transitive verbs? "I was kissed by him" would make me the subject and him the object and change kiss from active to passive. But I'm not the subject. I am most definitely the object. Then there's "cost," "read," "make," "pay," and "teach."

There's the one doing and the one having it done to, Active/Pas-sive Subject/Object, a verb determining the outcome. "Confess" and "bless," "own," "fear," and "love": there are so many verbs. His tongue and lips are the things doing the Doing and they seem to want to do more. Which would make it both past continuous as well as present perfect continuous.

Words have their own rules, their own slippery principles. He taught me that.

How come I'm naked and in bed when I don't remember getting naked? Or getting into bed? And why am I watching this whole thing from the ceiling?

His stubbled face is a thousand tacks scouring my yet-to-start-shaving face. His mustache black and oily. It's like one of those industrial cleaning brushes that we use to clean the school corridors. It is the kind of face you could strike a match on and it seems intent on taking the skin off my own.

"My private parts": that's how my parents always referred to my genitals. The phrase used to annoy me. It seemed to speak of shameful reticence, the mixture of propriety and embarrassment that character-ized their attitude to sexuality generally. Now I think that it is a good phrase—my private parts. Except they're not private anymore.

He is astride me, a knee over each of my hips, masturbating. I have my eyes half-closed. His hand is keeping up a steady rhythm. He's pacing himself. His other hand is rubbing my chest, my stomach. I can feel the palm of his hand. He fondles my cock and the fucking thing betrays me by getting hard. I lie there and think my cock is giving him the wrong message. My cock seems to be staying hard, but my mind is willing it to stay soft, even shrivel. If it stays hard, he might want to make it come. And if he makes it come then my orgasm will be his. Which wouldn't be my orgasm at all. "Don't come," "don't let him make you come," "you mustn't come": these phrases become mantras. I recite them to myself to the tempo of his masturbating hands.

He comes. The warm splodge of his semen drops on my stomach and sits there, like the stringy albumen of an egg white, like cheap shampoo. He passes me a face towel hung next to the washbasin. I wipe off and hand him back the towel. And then he says the strangest thing, a thing that will drive a thousand future therapeutic encounters, a thing that will remain in my head even as I try to drown it in vodka. He says: "Thank you."

"The whole thing is over in ten minutes tops." Discuss this statement with reference to the theme of dramatic irony.

NEXT

What are we gonna tell your mama?
What are we gonna tell your pa?
　　　　—Everly Brothers, "Wake Up Little Susie"

The drive from Blackburn back to Accrington is the longest journey that anyone has ever taken. Or will ever take. It's late at night, possibly the early hours of the morning, and I've got to face my parents. They have no phone.

Back at the house he gives me painkillers. I throw up and he gives me some more paracetamol. He tells me to chew them, get them more quickly into my system. I wash them down with water from the washbasin, water that has a metallic tang.

He says that he'll come in with me, explain what happened. Except of course that he won't explain what happened. He'll explain what he thinks could have happened. Why a couple of pupils of his had been asked to help out and how they'd probably helped themselves to a couple of drinks not knowing how strong drinks were. And how he'd let them sober up at the priests' house. And how he knows he should have found a way of letting them know but there was no way of letting them know. But at least they would know I was safe. And relieved to have me home. They would be so relieved to have me home. It would be fine. Trust me.

Whilst he's talking, talking and driving, I wonder if what really happened really happened. The man next to me, the one who is now wearing his collar, joking that it helps if he gets stopped by the police, that man is now . . . what? And what does whatever he is, and whatever it is that he did, what does that make me?

Was that sex? Was that what that was? If it was sex, then that would make me gay, and if I was gay, that would explain a lot. I could be gay. Gay's all right. Gay's cool in fact. Gay is David Bowie (wasn't it?) and Oscar Wilde. But that wasn't Gay.

We seem to hit every red light, and every red light means that Jack and Kath will be worrying that little bit more. They will be frantic, they will have talked about calling the police because that's what they always say when I come in late. But they haven't got a phone. They would have to go to Aunty Mary's to use her phone. To call the police. "We were getting ready to call the police." Which, thirty-five years later, suddenly strikes me as ironic.

Quentin Crisp was another. Now he was definitely gay. I had watched that film about him with my mum (Jack had gone for a pint, having looked in the *TV Times* and decided that it was not "his thing"). So I had sat with Kath and we had watched *The Naked Civil Servant*. Kath had felt sorry for him—a progressive form of patronization by the standards of the day. She'd said something about "a waste" and "how it couldn't be helped, you were who you were, and that was that." Of course Kath hadn't bought the Tom Robinson EP containing "Glad to be Gay," nor did she have his band's logo printed on her T-shirt. I had and did. Maybe this was all that Sean boy-crush stuff catching up with me.

Except I wasn't gay. I wasn't gay, because I had just had sex with a man (or he'd had sex with me? on me?) and I hadn't liked it. Hadn't liked it one bit. It had made me puke up bile into a handbasin and look down at things from the ceiling. It had made my tongue feel disgusting and my cock feel sore. What time is it? Another red light. Mum and Dad will be cross. They will be so, so cross.

I hadn't heard the word "pederasty" when I was molested by a pederast, or "pedophilia" as I fell victim to a pedophile. I had heard of "kiddie fiddlers." I had been told not to get into cars with "strange men."

Now I was in a car with a non-strange strange man, far stranger now than he was when the night began. And I needed him to save my stay-out-late-still-drunk skin.

I put my Yale key in my Yale lock and nervously squeeze open the front door. Kevin is behind me, his confidence trying to compensate for my dread. A part of me thinks that they will have gone to bed, that I'll be able to slip unnoticed into my tightly tucked sheets.

They haven't gone to bed.

Jack is in his chair, the chair that he always sits in, the chair that is yer dad's chair. His ashtray is overflowing more than usual, it is being kept company by an undrunk cup of coffee. Kath is in the kitchen. It's where she goes when she's upset. She can't "just sit around," "sit around doing nothing"; she's "got to do something." I'm in the doorway of the living room, Kevin still in the hallway, when the cry goes up. It is a duet: "Where the bloody hell have you been?" "What in heaven's name time do you call this?" There is a pause. All recriminations and accusations suddenly. Stop.

"Hello, Father."

He is wonderful, my molester. He listens attentively to Jack and Kath. Years later my various counselors and therapists will listen to me the same way. He listens to their worry and in it he hears their deeper fears—their fears for their only child and his precocious adolescence. He purrs the most plausible explanation for the state I'm in, both tonight and generally. It's a tough time. Lord knows he's been teaching long enough, has seen how difficult it can be for lads, bright lads especially. Often the brighter they are, the tougher it can be. And of course they're curious. It's part of growing up. Like with the drink. So when he/me and his/my friend turned up at the school tonight because his/my friend's parents were attending this boring PTA do, it was only natural that they'd want to try some of what these parents were having. It was his own fault. Should have kept an eye on me/us. Maybe it was for the best. Get it out of his system. Had to happen sooner or later. No harm done, not really. Part of growing up. And anyway, here he is. Lesson learnt, delivered safely home.

I'm sitting next to the Father who is not my father as he talks to the father who is. What do they see when they look at each other? Jack sees a man with whom he can talk man talk, yet one who poses no threat. Which makes it a different type of man talk. I remember the kind of men who were friends of my dad. They were avuncular types, warm and bighearted. Yet talkers they were not. The bonds that held their friendship together were forged on the terraces and the cricket pavilion and the factory floors. He would no more have told them his anxieties for his son than he would have talked dirty about his wife.

What Kevin's collar gave him was the right to opt out of conventional masculinity whilst still giving him access to its status. His priestly so-called celibacy didn't neuter or unman him. Rather it turned him into a comic book superhero. He was Priest-Man. Priest-Man's superpower is to be both fully present in his manhood whilst being totally removed from it. It is the power to be two things: a conduit of God and a man like any other. It is the power to do whatever he wants. Jack could no more have suspected the Reverend Father O'Neill of sexual abuse than he could have extracted his own appendix or suddenly stopped believing in God.

And Kath? Kath saw Teacher-Priest—another superhero, one who manages to be both Priest-Man and Priest-Man's double. Recalling the scene now I see her shrink into her schoolgirl self, an eager-to-please thirteen-year-old desperate to learn how to do better in this How to Be a Parent course. Earlier that night she'd become convinced that she had failed that course, failed it badly. She'd had visions of her son getting in with the wrong sort, a bad bunch, wrong 'uns. They'd fed him drugs and drink, got him to play the fool, egged him on. And at midnight when her son still wasn't home, she knew then that he was dead. They'd left him there, in the house they'd broken into/ car they'd stolen/canal he'd fallen into/his own vomit on which he'd choked, and the next knock on the door would be the police. Except it wasn't the police, it was her son, alive after all if a little bleary-eyed and dazed. And with him not quite Our Savior himself, but the next best thing. For not only was Teacher-Priest also Priest-Man, and not only had this dynamic duo rescued her son, but this pair had a third incarnation, a superheroism that would protect them, her, me, for ever: Headmaster-Priest. Thus did I present her with her own Holy Trinity, a steadfast three-in-one enigma that was as close to a divine blessing as she could ever have dreamt.

Of the various screen versions of my fifteen-year-old self that play in my fifty-year-old mind, one of them is directed by Alan Clarke. In it a young boy sits listening whilst a priest discusses the boy's future with the boy's devout parents. The camera cuts between images of adult conversations: Father talking to father, mother talking to Fathers—and the boy silently brooding. He is maybe biting his nails, chewing the inside of his cheek, looking from grown-up to grown-up as they debate the prospects that lie ahead for this child, if only he could . . . CUT . . . Flashback, the kid is being buggered by this same priest not two hours before. It is a scene that critics will call "violent and uncompromising." The boy will be seen crying, sniffling; the camera lingers on his discarded underpants . . . CUT . . . The boy is in his bedroom. He puts Josef K's "Sorry For Laughing" on the turntable and starts dancing round the room. His dance is maniacal. The music louder and louder. As Paul Haig sings "When we groove on into town / Charles Atlas starts to frown," the boy's dance punches turn into punch punches. He's hitting the walls again and again, his knuckles becoming bloody . . . "'Cause he's not made like me and you / Just can't do the things we do." The scene ends as the record ends, the boy slumped on his bed, his abject body sobbing.

This isn't an Alan Clarke film.

I clean my teeth, put on my pajamas, and get into bed. I wonder if I'm still a virgin, if it counts if you didn't want it. I start to masturbate. I think that if I masturbate it will mean that sex is something that I can still do: subject/verb/object. My cock is both too tender and not mine. There's a reason I don't show my cock to people at the bus stop, or discuss my erections in the checkout queue at the supermarket. That reason is that they're private. My private parts. The rage and the despair and the self-disgust are all there, but they are there like photocopies of themselves. Bad photocopies at that, ones that are smudged and that you've got to peer at for a long time before realizing that you're staring at splodges of ink.

There's a saying—more of a semantic tic—that I used to hear all over Lancashire when I was growing up: "It'll be reet" (right), said almost as one word. It was only after I left home and went to university and met middle-class people that I realized that there is a whole

NEXT

My heart is lost; the beasts have eaten it.
—Charles Baudelaire, "Conversation," *Les Fleurs du mal*

Jack and Kath have become KathandJack, a unit of them-ness.
I no longer distinguish between them, they are a solid bloc of
incomprehension, like the Soviet Union. There was a time when
me and Dad had an unspoken date with BBC 2 reruns; *Laurel
and Hardy* on a Saturday morning, the one where they're chimney
sweeps and the bricks keep falling on Ollie and he just sits there
resigned to, welcoming of, his fate. Or the bemused expression on
Bogart's face when he goes for a haircut in *The Treasure of the Sierra
Madre*, like he's looking in the mirror and wondering how the hell
he became Humphrey Bogart. And the bit in *Shane* where Alan
Ladd knocks Jack Palance all the way across the bar with just one
punch.

Now I stand him up, refuse to acknowledge our contract. He flicks
through the *Radio Times*—the delivery of which gave shape to our
week—and tells me that they're showing *Mutiny on the Bounty*. He
does his best Charles Laughton/Captain Bligh impression, "another
fifty lashes, Mr. Christian," the one that was guaranteed to make me
laugh. Except now it doesn't make me laugh.

I need to go to confession. And confess what? That I was the cause
of impure thoughts? That my dick got hard when it was being jerked
by my priest? That I lied, because when his viscous tongue slurped
horribly around my unresponsive lips I should have puked my fucking guts right up into his intrusive gaping mouth and drowned him
in vomited disgust, and that not doing that was not being true to

myself and so is a lie of omission? And to whom do I confess? The other priests, his fellow teachers, the ones for whom he is also head-master?

Everything is covered in cling film plastic, is being recorded through a fish-eye lens.

NEXT

When he smiled he used to uncover his big discolored teeth
and let his tongue lie upon his lower lip—a habit which
had made me feel uneasy in the beginning of our acquain-
tance. . . .

—James Joyce, "The Sisters"

If everyone carries on their lives as normal, then life is normal. If no
one says anything, then there's nothing to be said. In the weeks that
followed the first night of sexual abuse I began to wonder if what I
knew had happened had happened. Which means that not only do I
feel invaded, but I begin to doubt the sense of invasion, to wonder if
it is real.

I don't remember much about the immediate aftermath. I still go
to lessons, me and Johnny "Conrad" Mullen continue our Joyce and
Beckett as Abbot and Costello routine ("We'll call ourselves 'the et-
ceteras' and just stand there having a staring contest with the audience"). I still go to Mass.

I'm sure he's avoiding me. It's difficult to tell because I'm also
avoiding him.

Jump cut: a bit later.

Things are okayish, they're returning to their grooming-like nor-
mality. I can't remember how this came about, what happened, who
said what to whom. But I'm sitting in his office, it is nighttime, and
we are drinking red wine.

Does that sound an odd sentence? It is an odd sentence.

Having been molested by this man, I am now sat across from him
drinking wine—the kind of activity, in fact, that led me to being molested only a few weeks earlier. He tells me that he loves me. Now that

really is an odd sentence. If he loves me, then why the fuck did he fuck me? Unless the fucking was the loving.

He promises to take me to the theater. We are going to see *Who's Afraid of Virginia Woolf?*. The tickets are booked. It will be my birthday treat. Sweet sixteen.

In *Sleepless Nights*, Elizabeth Hardwick's assemblage of memories and reflections, she recalls herself and her friends meeting "a very nice-looking old man . . . a gentleman in a black suit and white shirt, wearing a kind and courtly smile. . . . He waited for us on Saturday afternoons, paid our way into the movie, bought us the whitened, hardened chocolate of summer. In the dark, with a little girl on each side, sitting straight as caryatids, he ran his hand up our thighs, under our dresses. The predator's first gift, mixed with the bright narrative on the screen and with the chocolate, was to reveal early to us the tangled nature of bribery. This at least was a lasting lesson. Bribery and more bribery—it grows within you like your molars." The shock of recognition when I read this passage was physical. I flinched, like someone had stubbed me with a cigarette. Thirty-plus years after the event, this passage explained me to myself. It explains the way in which corruption can not just coexist with tenderness, but can become part of its fiber: the tangled nature of bribery.

Kathleen had seen the movie of *Who's Afraid*, adored it, Burton and Taylor tearing each other's souls out over the course of one night. She tells me that Richard and Liz were married at the time and that the film could have been as much about them as about their characters, George and Martha. She hadn't known it had been a play, but of course I could go. It was a wonderful opportunity. To my mum's ears, the theater with my headmaster was a stop short of full canonization. The drunken PTA night ("the performance" as it became known) had proved that boys my own age really were the bad influence she had heard so much about. A school trip on the other hand would be just the ticket, couldn't go wrong. It would put her mind at rest.

The Dukes in Lancaster are putting Albee's play on in the round. I'd never come across this before. It meant that the audience surrounded the actors, an intimate otherness between our bodies and theirs. They are so close I could reach out and touch the hem of Martha's slinky slutty nightdress. I've seen this actress somewhere before. She has the poutiest mouth I've ever seen, as though she's making up her mind whether to start crying or tell you a dirty joke. I suddenly realize that the last time I saw her she was getting scalding coffee thrown in her face by a psychopathic Lee Marvin in *The Big Heat*. Tonight it is she who's dishing it out, snarling and teasing, flaunting and taunting her "poor put-upon Georgie" as she shakes her no-longer-glamorous stuff at an unsuspecting Nick. For three and a half hours I sit transfixed by this play, entranced by the woman at its ruinous center.

That night Gloria Grahame speaks to me across the decades, directly to my seat in the second row from the front. It is something about disappointment and how we torment each other to compensate for our own grandiose expectations. She tells me that I'm in love, though she doesn't say if it's with Gloria or Martha or even Edward Albee. What I do know from my night in the theater is that I want to go to university, like the one where George is, where I too will meet an imperious and destructive blonde. Except that she won't destroy me. I will rescue her, and in so doing rescue myself.

I'm full of it. In the car on the way home, I'm full of the fervor of the newly converted. I tell him that I want to write a letter to Gloria Grahame. I bet that lots of people write to her and tell her that she was wonderful in old films, but I bet not many people tell her how wonderful she was in that play. Wasn't it wonderful? The way in which it dawns on you at the same time that it dawns on the guests that George and Martha don't really have a son. And they really love each other, despite the horror they inflict on each other. And that moment when Martha shouts at him that beating him has tired her arm, the beatings for which he married her. And then the devastating sadness, the emptiness, beneath it all. It was so tender. Didn't you think so, Father? Are there other plays like this? On I go, drunk on the wonder that is Gloria Grahame. He tells me I'd like Tennessee Williams, that he does a similar thing: secrets, families, fictions. He tells me that I should read a book by Eric Berne called *Games People Play*, or try John

Updike's novels. He says that I should definitely write a letter to Gloria Grahame but didn't I think, ha-ha, that she was a bit old for me? She must, he says, be pushing seventy. No spring chicken. But, yes, I should definitely write to her. There's a silence in the car, an uncomfortable silence like when I'm at home and there's something on the telly that mum and dad hadn't expected but couldn't get up and turn off, because to do so would just draw attention to it. I don't want to write to Gloria Grahame anymore. I think, Yes she is old, an old actress. I bet in real life she's even older.

I break the silence, try to redeem myself. But this Tennessee Williams? Which of his should I read? He says that there's a play called *Streetcar* all about another (fake US accent) boozy broad and that if I fancied Martha, then I would almost certainly fancy Blanche.

It had been a mistake to mention Gloria, a lapse in judgment, like I'd made a mistake in class. More silence, the car gliding by town after town of nothing more than orange-lit clusters.

Do I know, sense, what's coming? It now seems to me so inevitable that he was going to pull into a country lane that I don't know if it seemed as inevitable at the time. What is the opposite of inevitable? Contingent? Unlucky? Evitable? I don't like the sound of any of these. At least "inevitability" offers me a certain dignity, allows me to think of myself as a version of Aristotelian tragic hero (minus the high birth). Otherwise it is merely grubby and banal. Otherwise I am grubby and banal.

And so the tongue stuff . . . What is it about the fucking tongue stuff?

His mouth is bigger than my mouth. And my mouth is a part of my face. I need to get over my mouth. Put it right out of my head.

Years later I am still obsessed with mouths, others as much as my own. I will write papers for conferences on critical theory discussing "The Scandalous Mouth of Shane MacGowan." I will write about Beckett and Francis Bacon and how the Irish mouth is a site of resistance, how it "enacts dramas of countermodernity." I will couch my neuroses in smarty-pants talk, talk of negotiating subjectivity, and liminal identities. I didn't think that then—the then that I still think of as now. Now is molestation-mouth-fuck-now, and it has carried on for more than thirty-five years and it is making me feel ill.

They're right though, those Freudian theorists. The mouth is the site where we negotiate our core identity, the orifice through which we learn the differences between inside and out, self and other, body and society. It's every infant's question: Is this edible? It is through taste that we test the world, come to understand the various flavors and textures on offer.

And just so you know, Herr Father, my memory of that night is still contaminated with the sense of your sickening gorging tongue, "like some thirsty animal lapping greedily at a spring of long-sought fresh water." Know who wrote those last few words? Kafka. The man you identified as our fellow prime number.

And the hand on my cock, the rubbing through the jeans to claim a hard-on that rightfully belonged to Gloria Grahame? How does that work? Is my hard-on your achievement or my defiance? It certainly dirties the waters though, don't it? For the record, I would like to remind you and whatever self-justificatory logistics you pulled for the twenty-odd intervening years, that my climax continued to elude you. Not that the absence of any orgasm deterred you. Was it, in fact, a challenge? Something you became determined to elicit the more re-luctant I seemed to give it up?

He sits, once again, and tells them—my parents, his allies—about our evening. About some of our evening. He tells them about the play and about how young Graham has got himself a girlfriend, a Hollywood girlfriend, his near namesake. Kathleen blushes. Not just because the thought of her son having a girlfriend is blushmaking, but because a priest has alluded to, joked about, girlfriendery, and thus about sex.

Then again, they're like that now. This new breed of priest: mod-ern, open-minded. Not like when she was a girl and you lived in terror of them. Of them finding out you'd skipped school, or missed Mass, or—God forbid—been seen out with a boy. Those days were gone, thank God. She never knew why they called them the good old days. There was nothing good about them. But here, now, this felt like something that was good. Here he sits, a man who is also a priest, a priest who is also a teacher, a teacher who is also a friend.

He doesn't mention pulling over onto a lay-by. Which is fine by me. I decide there and then that the sex stuff is my stuff and that the closer I keep this stuff, the better it will be for everyone. I decide that it's not that big a deal, that it's a small price to pay for nights at the theater, for keeping my parents happy. Besides, I know now that there's a switch. It's somewhere at the back of my eyeballs and it's connected, with pieces of twine, down through my chest, straight through the abdomen, and down into my scrotum. It's like the strings on a puppet, except that the strings are on the inside.

NEXT

The problem is insoluble. The body is harnessed to a brain.
—Virginia Woolf, *Jacob's Room*

Strategy Manual for the Molested-Puppet-Child in Minimizing Molestation.
Keep arms at side throughout. Ideally try for own hands behind own back. If this proves impossible, aim for the arms to dangle as unresponsively as possible. Aim for a bored nonchalance, a body that is somehow frigid yet indifferent. The thinking behind this pose is that although the Molested-Puppet-Child (MPC) is helpless to prevent molestation, it can, however, send out the message of countereroticism to both itself and molester. This may help the MPC later in the day/evening/morning when it comes to address its own sexual desires which, at the age of fifteen, are many and complex.

This strategy does, however, run the risk of apparent compliance, the indifference being mistaken for a silent affirmation. In order to minimize this risk, it is imperative that the MPC at no point reaches orgasm. Further complications may arise when MPC realizes that this apparent recalcitrance may also be an aphrodisiac for the molester, a spur to his ambition.

Ensure that alcoholic drink has been taken and/or is at hand. Wine is preferable due to ease of access, although beer or spirits will work just as well. The purpose of this exercise is obviously to anesthetize the MPC but, just as important, provide it with an excuse (not untrue) for when it vomits into a toilet/sink/Father's wastepaper basket later in the process. Vomit-mouth can also prove useful as a way of avoiding a second sitting of a single performance. But not always.

Take any non-being-molested opportunity to remind Father that it is heterosexual. Hope that such reminders will awaken him to the startling revelation that the MPC is not a willing participant in their exchanges (and they are therefore not really exchanges). Recurrent (though unsuccessful) examples of this strategy include: how much you fancy Debbie Harry; the made-up wet dream about friend's mum; the equally made-up though wished-it-were-true story about snogging a female at the school disco. Although this approach has proved less than successful, it does have the benefit of annoying Father Molester in its implied affront to his own desirability.

Close eyes. Repeat to self: This doesn't matter. It's not important. I'm not even here.

NEXT

Where the you of who you are is.

—Gordon Lish, *Peru*

And so the template is set, although it's not my template. I have no say in its composition. He gets to decide when he's the teacher, when the priest. It's up to him if I'm friend or pupil, altar boy or "lover."

I become adept at reading the signs, anticipating his moods and what their repercussions will be. Some days Faith is the issue. He tells me how priestly celibacy is supposed to work. It is not the absence of sexuality but the embracing of it, the recognition that sex is between all of us and so can't be limited to marriage or monogamy. He is married to Our Lady, which means that he takes her levels of loving self-sacrifice as the guide for how to live his life. But Catholics are also pragmatists. We know—don't we?—that we are destined to fall short of our own standards, and that if being good was a simple matter, then we would not need the example of Christ. And celibacy historically was about not having children, about protecting Church property from claims of inheritance. So what we are doing . . . this thing that happens sometimes . . . is not . . . is . . . well . . . it's complicated. On these occasions—our seminary talks as I think of them—I want to comfort him. I see him then as someone out of Graham Greene, a damaged antihero, torn between his desires and his duty. I think, almost tenderly, this—he—will stop. It has to. His vocation is stronger than whatever the thing is that I have (and I still don't know what that is).

Then there is the bribe, the Culture-for-Cock payoff that is now part of our Saturday night ritual. We go and see *Doctor Faustus* in Manchester, *The Canterbury Tales* in Liverpool. I sit in the audience knowing that the journey back will involve a lay-by, or a visit to his office, or a nightcap back at the priests' house. I have accepted the deal, except that my acceptance is now tinged with manipulation. If I'm going to be a whore, I want my payment up front. I am no longer the wide-eyed naïf, gobsmacked and grateful for his nights at the theater. One night we go and see a play called *The Prisoner of Zenda*. It's a crappy swashbuckly romp and I pout and sulk about how much I hate it. He makes up for it by showing me *The History Man* on a new machine that he's got at school that can record programs from the TV. He tells me that culture is how we make sense of the world. I'm getting all the culture one cultured man can throw at me. And none of it is making any sense.

NEXT

Four thousand holes in Blackburn, Lancashire . . .
—The Beatles, "A Day in the Life"

Scenes fade and merge, some stand alone, others assembled alongside snapshots of history. Kath wakes me one morning to tell me that John Lennon has been murdered, gunned down outside his apartment in New York. She seems devastated by the news. The Beatles had been her band, or rather the early Beatles had been her band, the love-me-do moptops rather than the acid-ringmasters of *Sgt. Pepper*. She had a theory, did my mum, about this decline of the Beatles, one she shared with me more than once, as though I should take this as a warning. The theory was that these four lads were just ordinary working-class lads, Catholic lads in Paul and John's case. And that they couldn't handle it, all that fame, it had taken them away from who they really were. Somehow Yoko Ono was both cause and symptom of all this, for reasons that were clearly related to her ethnicity but never stated as such. "Just think, he could have had any woman he wanted, yet he ended up with her." Quite who he should have ended up with was never made clear. Maybe it should have been Kathleen Smethurst. More likely that he should never have left Cynthia. Either way, it was an article of faith for her that he could have done better than some Japanese woman. She'd taken it badly and now he lay dead on the pavement outside the Dakota with so much to live for: a bloody waste.

I write a poem about his death because I feel that's the sort of thing that real poets do. It's a mawkish tribute of which I can remember nothing except nicking a line from Adrian Mitchell about sucking the sun like a gobstopper. I go and sit in the school chapel and try to feel sad, but it doesn't work. I don't feel sad, I don't feel anything.

It's odd, this absence of feeling, because it is itself a feeling. Feelings are like rules. People expect you to have feelings, to follow rules. But the people who are setting the rules don't seem to know what they are either, even though they're adamant that you stick to them. It is their number one rule.

I have to second-guess my parents, preempt their incomprehension. I assume that they assume that I'm doing lots of weird things—things to do with girls, maybe parties, John Lennon–type things. I need to keep this assumption alive. This assumption will protect them from the knowledge of the even weirder things, not-girls, not John Lennony things, that are also happening. One set of rampaging adolescent turbulence is a cover story for another.

NEXT

You should build an inner refuge. This too should be thick-
lined with dense materials to resist the radiation, and should
be built away from the outside walls.
    —Home Office, *Protect and Survive: This booklet tells you
          how to make your home and your family as safe
                as possible under nuclear attack*, May 1980

Johnny Goes to Cambridge—not another of our never-to-be-formed
bands (Accrington's precursor to Frankie Goes to Hollywood)—but
a statement of fact. King's College, Cambridge, to be exact, there to
read modern languages. He did Oxbridge; not the version where you
stay on and do nothing else but Oxbridge, but the one which runs
alongside your A levels. He knew it was his way out and was wonderfully unapologetic about taking it. I got the feeling through that last
year of our school friendship that he was making sure that I would be
all right after he'd gone, that certain things were in place that would
help keep me afloat.

The first of these was CND (Campaign for Nuclear Disarmament).
He'd told me about a film that was going to be shown at the library, a
film about what a nuclear war would be like. We couldn't not go. My
teenage position on the nuclear issue was like Jessica Mitford's position
on death: I was against it. All of it. Nuclear weapons and nuclear power.
I hadn't yet heard of the nuclear family, but when I did I was against
that as well. The key word was "nuclear": nothing good could come of
it. Just how much nothing good was brought home by Peter Watkins'
film. From what I remember, *The War Game* imagines the effect of a
nuclear bomb dropped on London. There's stark black-and-white shots
of devastation, children instantly blinded, mass hysteria, sirens. It was

filmed as a documentary, which meant that all this what-if horror was offset against one of those clipped formal voices that BBC announcers had after the war (was that Watkins' voice?). It was terrifying and captivating. It was case closed. The only reason people weren't against nuclear weapons was that they hadn't seen *The War Game*.

I remember something else from that film, a phrase that stuck with me and Johnny, the grotesque imagery of which we quickly made our own: "The melting of the upturned eyeball." For the next few weeks it becomes impossible for us to say anything else. We try to outdo each other in discovering things deemed to be "upturned-eyeball melting." It quickly describes all and any situations, good or bad, the less appropriate the better. PE lessons, weird people we see on the street, news headlines, girls we fancy, girls we don't fancy, ice-cold Slush Puppies that leave stains around our mouths; all are measured by their ability to melt the upturned eyeball.

We decide to perform *Krapp's Last Tape*, Beckett's monologue about an old man listening to the tape recordings he made in his youth whilst he tries to start a new recording. John would perform the monologue and I would direct: it would be a Mullen–Caveney Production. I would love Johnny's choice to be a poignant comment about loss and his leaving. But it wasn't. It was a chance to mess about with a reel-to-reel tape recorder and put on a play that we knew—hoped—none of the school would understand. It was his, and therefore our, chance to make dick jokes and get away with them. To suck on a banana and pretend that he was unaware of any potential obscenity. It was the gig we finally got to play, the one we had spent hours imagining for Cat Food Crucifixion or the Dada Trapeze Benefactors or any of the other thousand and one bands that had stoked our imagination during the four years of our friendship.

Our opening night draws maybe forty assorted students and staff. Father O'Neill is in the front row, Jock Roland a few seats back. I'm in the wings, John on stage. Bananas are being sucked, but this is laugh-at-Beckett laughter, knowing, reverential. "Box three, spool five . . ." Johnny is fully immersed, a young man playing an old man listening to his younger self. He's Patrick Magee, he's Max Wall, he's

Buster Keaton. "'Shall I sing when I am her age, if I ever am?'" He stares at the machine. "'No. Did I sing as a boy?'" He looks out at the audience, the bemused stupid stare that he has taken from Ian Dury. "'No. Did I ever sing? No. . . .We've just been listening to an old year, passages at random. . . .'" He is beautiful. He is my friend and now the stupid school will know just how clever these clever boys can be.

Then the tape machine breaks down. A reel didn't reel to the other reel. It spun and hissed and whirred, before dying a most Beckettian death.

The room lets out a snigger. Johnny stays in character, plaintively looking out, demanding to know who these people are and why are they laughing at his life. Kevin O'Neill stands up. He says that he's seen lots of Beckett, interpreted in many different ways. But he's proud and delighted that tonight he's seen a Beckett that was more Beckett than Beckett himself (the laughter is gentle now, indulgent); a Krapp, as it were, of which Sam would have approved (our audience loves him and because he loves us, they love us too). He thinks that it's a real testament to these boys that they have had the ba . . . , I mean, nerve to take on one of the most difficult writers of the twentieth century and bring him to life tonight in a way that he guarantees none of us will forget. He thinks we deserve a warm round of applause. They applaud. Curtain.

One of the reasons I never told my story as a novel—or when I tried it never worked—was that the scenes in which Kevin molested me always seemed out of character. I would write a scene drawn from an event like the one above, one in which he was the charismatic Rev. Kev. Then I would write about the abuse and the prose would start to write someone else—a villain from some nineteenth-century novel. Sexual abuse is a crisis in genre. My abuser wasn't a gothic monster. He was deeply charismatic. If he hadn't been charismatic, he wouldn't have had the chance to become my abuser.

He molested me the night of the play, having rescued Krapp from our ignominious fuckup. By this time his attitude had become more assured. Was it that he no longer feared me exposing him? Who would I expose him to? Who would unexpose me?

Had he convinced himself that I was enjoying it, that this was some consensual deal? If so, I would like to point to the stump that is my cock, the cock that refused to give up its treasures no matter how hard you pumped. And, by the way, if I was consenting, would I not also be initiating occasionally? Would I not be suggesting that you molest me in new positions, or try out a couple of new fantasies (let's play Confession)? Maybe you thought that I was thinking, I can't wait to get him home tonight where I can give him some hot molestee action. Or did you expect me to suggest we go shopping, a day trip to Manchester where we could buy sex toys, giggle our way through a selection of naughty underwear? When you saw me look at women, what did you see? Did you think, That Debbie Harry ain't got nothing on me? When I told you—with my quiet manipulative malice—about women and girls and ass versus arse, and Siouxsie Sioux in her fishnets, or Rickie Lee Jones in her red beret, what did you hear? I'm guessing that you heard a boy talk of sex, and, regardless of its insistent heterosexual content, you decided that this talk of sex was a clumsy come-on. What was it you said when the bishop finally confronted you, confronted you after I'd reported you? "It takes two to tango." That was what you said. It's there in my—our—notes. Not exactly Beckett, is it? Two to tango? As if all that cock-cum-mouth stuff was like you and me strutting along the Rio de la Plata in the 1890s, a rose between my teeth. Was it the two of us tangoing when you threatened to expel me? But now you've got me getting ahead of myself. You've got me going.

NEXT

Everything that is not literature bores me and I hate it. . . .
I have no family feeling and visitors make me almost feel as
though I were maliciously being attacked.

—Franz Kafka, *Diaries*

He takes me to meet his mother. I think there's probably a world in
which that sentence is the punch line to a joke, some sick variation on
a mother-in-law gag: "If you think being molested is bad, wait until
you meet his mother. . . ." This must surely be the time from when I
can date his transition, the point at which he made the switch. I no
longer had the sense that he was yielding to temptation. There was no
guilt, none of those mumbled apologies or averting of eyes. He had
rationalized our relationship, and "relationship" is what it had become.
I was now his girlfriend. Because he had taken my innocence I was no
longer an innocent. Because sex had been had, so sex could be had. Molest a boy once, twice, three times, and it may have the power to instill
self-recrimination. Molest him a dozen times and it stops being molestation. It becomes what you do, both of you. It becomes the norm.
Why wouldn't you take him to meet your mother? It's what couples do.

About the weekend I remember:

A night in a hotel on the way there. (Where was it? Somewhere
around the Lakes?)

A moment of relief when we enter the hotel room and I see two
single beds. (How did he book the room? I'd like to reserve a room
for myself—Father Kevin O'Neill—and the sixteen-year-old boy who
will be escorting me.)

A couple next door who are fucking. (She is making getting-fucked
noises.)

I don't make any noises. I'm silent. And bored. I make myself float up to the ceiling, where I look at a man I don't recognize fuck a boy I don't know.

His mother's name is Winnie, a wisp of a woman who appears in my mind now as a ghostly flicker, an apron and permed hair. I worry about not knowing what to say to her, to Winnie.

It is somewhere in the northeast. (Middlesbrough, Sunderland?)

We drive to the coast.

And that is it, the sum total of my memory of visiting Father Molester's very own Bates Motel. You'd think I could do better than that, right? You'd think that someone who can remember where he was when he first heard the Clash's "Bankrobber" (an outdoor record store in Accrington Market, since you ask) would be able to recall more details about a trip to his abuser's mother than some vague drive to the fucking coast. But I can't.

The inability of survivors of sexual abuse to remember the details of their abuse is one of the most frustrating aspects of their survival. Some aspects—the early scenarios—feel like they are imprinted on the back of my retinas (retinae?). Others, like the trip to Mother country, feel like they happened offstage. Jock Roland once told us that the reason Duncan's murder happens offstage is that otherwise we would lose sympathy for Macbeth. He wouldn't be a tragic hero: he would just be a murderer. Is this the reason I can't get to the memories, that I want to preserve a version of him or me or him and me as tragic, rather than merely grubby? Does it make it less abusive if I don't remember the details of the abuse, or more?

NEXT

There is reason that all things are as they are.

—Bram Stoker, *Dracula*

"Acedia" is the name given to it by Catholic theologians, a kind of spiritual ennui, what Aquinas called "the sorrow of the world" (rather than the sorrow of God). Kathleen Caveney doesn't call it that. She calls it "moping." And she won't have it. Not in her house. She won't have the "I'm not hungry," not when she's gone to the trouble of cooking a meal. But I'm not hungry. I'm not hungry because I feel sick. I look at my plate—a large mound of yellow mashed potatoes with a viscous brown stew of minced beef and onions poured over the top. It looks like how I imagine a Florida swamp to look. And sound. I can hear it breathing. I pour Daddies Brown Sauce over it and stir. It becomes like baby food, although, as Kathleen says, "It's not bloody baby food. It's Mince and Mash: it's your favorite." This used to be true. I used to plead with her to make Mince and Mash. The sound of the masher tapping against the pan would make me salivate. I say, I have to go to the bathroom. I go to the bathroom and puke up my guts. I brush my teeth with Colgate ("the ring of confidence"), come back downstairs, and we start all over again. Nothing. I'm not. I haven't. I am. What? I do. It isn't. Leave me alone.

For anyone who has been, is the parent of, or has ever met an adolescent boy, the problem here is obvious. The signs that an adolescent boy is being abused are those that mark him out as an adolescent boy. Truculent mood swings, an overwhelming sense of alienation, relentless self-absorption, wave after wave of disaffection and resentment: the problem of the "abused adolescent" is that it can almost seem a tautology. The comedian Dylan Moran used to do a great riff on kids ("They have all these charities like Children in Need! When did you last see a child who wasn't in need?") and something similar can be said about "difficult adolescents": it's part of the job description. When shrinks and doctors have asked what effect being abused has had on me, I want to (but never do) say that I haven't lived a non-abused life to which I can compare it. It's perfectly possible that I'd have been a self-loathing addict without the contributions made by Father Kevin's cock. There are, after all, plenty of other reasons to become one—social mobility, being a single child, being an arsehole. My guess is that I wouldn't have been, but there is no—can be no—proof. Adam Phillips wrote a wonderful book called *Missing Out: In Praise of the Unlived Life*. In it he muses on the ways in which the lives we live run in parallel to, or are accompanied by, the lives we feel we ought to or could have lived. He writes: "When we are not thinking, like the character in Randall Jarrell's poem, that 'The ways we miss our lives is life,' we are grieving or regretting or resenting our failure to be ourselves as we imagine we could be. We share our lives with the people we have failed to be."

I do this all the time. I sentimentalize the alternative adolescence which was refused me, whilst also knowing that this story is nothing more than a sentimentalized home movie. I mourn for the mum and dad who didn't have their son bring home his first date. I can hear the anticipation in their voices as they say hello to Carol/Sandra/Kate, can sense Kathleen's joy as Janet/Louise/Linda asks if she needs a hand with the washing up. I get dewy-eyed over losing the virginity I didn't have to the girl I didn't lose it to. I miss the kids I didn't have and imagine Jack and Kath missing their grandkids even more. My non-abused life is as real to me as my actual one, often more so. The years I didn't spend teaching in an inner-city comp, going those extra miles for that one kid who had a passion for poetry, are some of the proudest moments I never had. The fact that they never happened only makes them all the more precious.

I semi joke to Julie that the abuse couldn't have come at a worse time, as though my age was incidental to the attraction which I had for him. I say, If I'd have been a few years younger, I wouldn't have known what was happening. Which would have been better, made me less guilty, nothing I could have done.

And then I say: Or I wish I'd been raped. That way it's a straight-up case of wrong versus right. It was all those fucking hormones, the permanent hard-on which I had from fourteen to sixteen; it was them that caused the problems. I say, if you have to have sex with a teenage boy, at least wait until he is no longer a teenage boy. Or get him before he becomes one.

I don't mean either of those things, I can feel their dumbness the moment they come out of my mouth. Yet somehow they speak of a fracture I've never been able to comprehend, and it's something like this. Was it me or simply my youth that gave the priest the hard-on? It's a stupid question, isn't it? How can I possibly separate out who I was from the age I was? I don't believe that there is an essential Me to me, a little core of Caveney-ness with which I was born and which I've kept hermetically sealed in some hitherto undiscovered cavity of my Being. I realize that whatever sexual appeal I had for Herr Pater was derived from some not-so-subtle interplay of intellectual precocity and adolescent vulnerability. Yet still it nags, laps at my consciousness: Was it me or my youth?

My body and its drives are being both attacked and denied, my sense of self shattering like a cracked windscreen. There is the Catholic boy, the St. Mary's Grammar School bum boy. Then there is this other boy, a boy who is not friends with any of the others. And who watches things from the ceiling.

NEXT

We don't need no education . . .
　　　　　　—Pink Floyd, "Another Brick in the Wall"

My other teachers aren't happy with me either. I have, I am told, "an attitude," although precisely what kind of an attitude is never made clear. My school reports are now full of "fear that he is going off the rails," of "seems distracted" and "needs to concentrate." Not, of course, the headmaster's. The headmaster's report is glowing, barely containing his excitement at my ability to engage and comprehend, to make connections. When one kid looks over my shoulder and sees what Father O'Neill has written, he snorts, "Whaddaya do? Suck his cock?"

Mixed reports lead to the A-level discussion. A levels could mean university and university means a way out. Kathleen nearly cries when the word is mentioned. "University"; she moves forward to the edge of her seat, leaning into the full force of my future. Her boy and university! In the same sentence.

It'll cost them, but it'll be worth it. Science is out, just look at those reports. But English, history, Religious Education . . . It's like Father O'Neill always says, Those subjects are right up his street. He's made for them.

A levels mean two more years of being a student. And being a student, as my molester regularly points out, is what I am good at. A levels are at once remedy and poison, curse and cure.

My teachers don't know my secrets, but I know plenty of theirs. I pump Kevin for information, for the dirt on his fellow priests and lay teachers. They are part of my payoff, along with the theater trips and the swanky restaurants. I am his bratty nymphet (his himphet?), milking Father Father for the shiny candy that is school gossip. He tells me about Mr. A's marriage problems, Father B's drinking problem, the affair that nearly happened between Mrs. C and Father D. He tells me that Father E can be sulky and slams doors, and that Mr. F is lucky to still have a job. I am his confidant as well as his girlfriend, his student and his catamite. It's a lot for a sixteen-year-old boy to be. Being a sixteen-year-old boy is a lot for a sixteen-year-old boy to be.

NEXT

"I know the way you must feel about me," she broke out,
". . . telling you such things. . . ."
—Edith Wharton, *Summer*

In her office, me and Julie agree: memories of fifty-year-olds are not
the most reliable. Memories of fifty-year-olds who have experienced
sexual abuse are notoriously unreliable. Memories of fifty-year-olds
who have used drugs and alcohol to drown their memories of sexual
abuse require a new language of memory altogether.

I say, Because I was abused, I became an addict.

And

Because I am an addict, I don't trust my memory.

She says, You're remembering all the time. Not trusting your
memory is a kind of memory.

I say, It's scrappy, bitty.

She says, Then write scraps, write bits.

NEXT

"Do you know what she *did*, your cunting daughter?"
—Regan, in *The Exorcist*

I still go to Mass, but no longer take Communion. The idea that I can take Christ's body into my mouth appalls me. In the buildup to my first Communion, there had been a debate with Father Mac about whether we should receive the host into our hand or directly onto our tongues. It was agreed that our grubby mitts were no place to commune with the transubstantiated flesh of Our Lord Jesus Christ. We decided he should go directly into our mouths, like a Whopper. I remember trying not to bite into the Sacrament. Biting would, after all, be literally tearing into the flesh of Christ.

I remember the Host sticking to the roof of my mouth, its coating sucking up all my saliva, and being forced to dislodge it with the tip of my tongue. I remember thinking that Our Lord Jesus Christ had been spat on by the mob on his way to being crucified, and yet I couldn't get enough spit up to dissolve his sacrificial body.

This wasn't that. The reason my sixteen-year-old soul was not able to take Communion was not because I no longer believed in Christ, but because he was the only thing I believed in. Molestation had taught me many things, but of one thing I was certain: my mouth was not a holy place. To take his body when my own was so corrupt was a sacrilege so great that I could hardly think of it; so great I could think of nothing else. To not take Communion would be my penance. I would stand amongst the congregation and let him see me—let Him see me also—not take Communion.

NEXT

By persistently remaining single, a man converts himself
into a permanent public temptation. Men should be more
careful; this very celibacy leads weaker vessels astray.
            —Oscar Wilde, *The Importance of Being Earnest*

He is taking the service. His sermon is about a rumor that a film is
going to be made about the sex life of Jesus Christ. (Was this Scorsese's
Last Temptation of Christ? Really, so early? Or another, equally blasphemous Catholic?) He is quietly enraged, a state I've come to know by
the way his lips purse up, as though he is about to blow a kiss. He does
his riff about how he'd organized a trip to see Monty Python's *Life of
Brian*. I'd heard this riff before: it was one of his favorites, proof of his
liberal tendencies, his sense of humor. (He was, after all, the Rev. Kev.)

But this, the sex life of Jesus, would be blasphemous in a way that
he refused to countenance. He hoped that the divinity of Christ was
something that lived in our hearts even as it was being cheapened by
the proposed makers of this proposed film.

I am sitting in the third pew from the front whilst Kevin delivers
this sermon. I have no doubt, then or now, of his sincerity. For him,
the point of Christ would have been that he transcended sex. That is
what made him Christ. He may have suffered on the cross as a man
but he was resurrected as the Son of God. A film that showed Christ
having sex would not be a film about Christ. It would merely be a film
about a man called Jesus.

That the Catholic Church has some bizarre notions of sexuality is
hardly news (although I have yet to encounter a nonbizarre notion of
sexuality), but its insistence on the celibacy of its clergy is, perhaps,
one of the strangest.

In its defense one could say that the Church's preoccupation with celibacy acknowledges the centrality of sex. Priests are not being asked to give up nothing. But suppose you saw your sexuality as a curse? What if celibacy is not a renunciation but a relief? It may be why some priests want to become priests, a way of relinquishing something you didn't want in the first place. And the Catholic Church will reward you for it, allow you to build a career on this sacrifice which isn't a sacrifice at all. Was that the Rev. Kev's logic, the seminary a way not to access his desires but a way to frustrate them?

I'll soon be going to Crete. I go back to sleeping with the light on, as though I'm a young boy: a younger boy. I think: maybe the thing that I keep thinking is happening isn't happening at all. You hear about women who think they're married to some film star who they've never even met, or become convinced they're pregnant with a rock star's baby. Maybe I'm their altar boy equivalent. And if I was mad, and all this stuff was in my head, how would I know? My head wouldn't tell me if my head was mad: heads aren't like that. Heads are the problem.

NEXT

So many children want to please, try to do as they are told, imagine that what we are telling them we want is what we want. Wise children figure out that what we [adults] are after is the enticing naughtiness that comes from disobedience, their flight leaving open the child's spot so that we can occupy it.

—James Kincaid,
Erotic Innocence: The Culture of Child Molesting

"It was entirely possible that one song could destroy your life," says the narrator of Jonathan Lethem's *The Fortress of Solitude*: "Yes, musical doom could fall on a lone human form and crush it like a bug. The song, *that song*, was sent from somewhere else to find you, to pick the scab of your whole existence. The song was your personal shitty fate, manifest as a throb of pop floating out of radios everywhere."

For Dylan Edbus (the novel's hero) that song was "Play That Funky Music," Wild Cherry's disco taunt to aspiring soul brothers everywhere. Four years and three thousand miles apart, there is a song that is picking at the scab of my existence, and it's worse—far worse—than all that "dancing and singing and moving to the groovin'" endured by the invisible white boys of Brooklyn.

"Young teacher, the subject of schoolgirl fantasy . . ."

Now the epitome of earnest elevator jazz, it may be difficult to remember that Sting was once thought of as an edgy urban poet (I know!).

"She wants him, so badly / knows what she wants to be . . ."

I'd seen the Police when they were the pretenders to punk's reggae heart—a blistering two-hour gig at Blackburn's St. George's Hall. But now, now Sting has decided that he is a serious artist addressing serious subjects.

"Don't stand, don't stand, don't stand so close to me . . ."

It was the best-selling single in the UK in 1980 and, like Dylan and Wild Cherry, it felt like the song was "the soundtrack to your destruction."

Did I hate it then as much as I hate it now? I've just found the video on YouTube and it made my scrotum shrink. Sting can barely contain his own self-regard, it threatens to spill over like the biceps from his cap-sleeved T-shirt. Close-up on Sting in a classroom. He coyly looks over his Miss Moneypenny glasses, pretending to mark the girl's homework. In case we miss the point, he's wearing full gown and mortarboard. This is theater and authority, everyone! This is a serious fantasy! The lyrics are delivered in a way that he thinks is brooding and husky, but which make him sound like he's auditioning to be a sex-phone operator. "Book marking, she's so close now . . ." The bassline has the same stalkery feel, perving its way around the ankles of this girl who is "half his age." Just when you are getting ready to call the police (and there are too many jokes there to settle on one), the song erupts into its eponymous chorus. Sting is joined by his fellow band members and they too are all decked out in university gowns and caps. Hurrah! Then they all start dancing, a kicking-a-football dance in which the three roguish musicians get to show how wacky they are despite the fucking-a-schoolgirl thing.

The Police weren't alone in finding teacher-pupil fucking an enticing subject for pop music. The Boomtown Rats had made a record a few years earlier—"Mary of the 4th Form." On the face of it Geldof's contribution was just as offensive as Sting's ("She quickly drops her pencil / And slowly bends to get it / Teacher is a natural man / His hand moves out to touch her . . ."). Yet somehow a relistening to "Mary . . ." is nowhere as creepy as relistening to "Don't Stand . . . ." Maybe it's because I prefer Geldof's honest lechery to Sting's arty pretensions. Maybe it's because raising awareness of starvation in the developing world cuts you some retroactive slack when it comes to your back catalog. Or maybe it's because I wasn't being serially molested to the sound of the Boomtown Rats, whereas Sting's reign of pedo-kitsch coincided with it exactly.

It was a horrible cosmic joke, an "Our Tune" that was not my tune.

I'm making a cheap shot at Sting because of one of those flukes of history (and besides, a man needs a hobby), but there is a larger issue at stake than a pompous pop song. In an article for the *London Review of Books*, Andrew O'Hagan wrote about how the whole ethos of seventies and eighties light entertainment was predicated upon an unacknowledged sexualization of people too young to cope. Writing about Jimmy Savile (regular host of *Top of the Pops* and serial sexual abuser) and the BBC, he argues that in asking "How did he get away with it?," we are asking the wrong question. What we need is to examine the complicity of our culture at large.

> We're not allowed to say it. Because we love our tots. Or, should I say: WE LOVE OUR TOTS? We know we do because the *Mirror* tells us we do, but would you please get out of the way because you're blocking my view of another fourteen-year-old crying her eyes out on *The X-Factor* as a bunch of adults shatter her dreams. Savile went to work in light entertainment and thrived there: of course he did, because those places were custom-built for men who wanted to dandle dreaming kids on their knees. If you grew up during the "golden era of British television," the 1970s, when light entertainment was tapping deep into the national unconscious, particularly the more perverted parts, you got used to grown-up men like Rod Hull clowning around on stage with a girl like Lena Zavaroni. You got used to Hughie Green holding the little girl's hand and asking her if she wanted an ice cream. Far from wanting an ice cream, the little girl was starving herself to death while helpfully glazing over for the camera and throwing out her hands and singing "Mama, He's Making Eyes at Me." She was thirteen.

If the weird sleaziness of light entertainment produced the Savile freak show, what then of its less legitimate relation, popular music? Here is an industry that has no need for a veneer of "wholesome family fun." This is rock 'n' roll; lock up your daughters. With a brief to reach into the collective sexual psyche of adolescence, the popular music industry has had over sixty years to ask what it means to be a teenager in love. And what it means to be in love with a teenager. Let's leave Sting doing the hokey cokey in his video classroom, and listen to some of those golden oldies from yesteryear.

Let's kick off with Sonny Boy Williamson's "Good Morning, School Girl," a blues standard from the late thirties that has been covered by everyone from Van Morrison to ZZ Top, the Yardbirds to the Grateful Dead. It's easy to despise Gary Glitter, his preening "do you wanna touch?" stomps were halfway to the ugh bin even as they were being recorded. But Sonny Boy Williamson! On Bluebird records! That's another story, a story that complicates our ideas of acceptability and edginess (not to mention guilt and race).

As long as pedo pop is confined to the naff or produced by the guilty, then it's a simple matter of adjusting our sneers accordingly. Disliking bad music isn't difficult. Neither is ridiculing ridiculous people. It's when the offensive stuff is so embedded in the great stuff that it becomes difficult, when we selectively listen to our heroes because we—I—somehow believe that there are musicians that are so talented they are beyond our reach. "Now, you can tell yo' mother an' yo' father, um / That Sonny Boy's a little schoolboy too." Never mind the politics, just listen to that harp.

Let's pass over the simply odious—the Vandals' "Fourteen"—or the deliberately provocative—Sublime's "The Wrong Way" (and "Date Rape" as well, guys. Wow, weren't you the bad boys of junior high?). Let's cut Chuck Berry some slack and say that his "Little Queenie" was at least "a minute over seventeen" when he saw her in the aisle. Let's even side-step the whole issue of Jerry Lee Lewis' marriage to Myra Gale Brown, his thirteen-year-old cousin. (He claimed she was fifteen. As a defense.)

And it would be churlish to dwell too long on Gary Puckett & the Union Gap's creepy classic "Young Girl" with its poignant evocation of the self-restraint needed when encountering a girl who has kept her youth a secret. ("You led me to believe you're old enough / To give me love / And now it hurts to know the truth.")

The pedo aesthetic is so ingrained in popular music that it becomes almost rude to single out individuals. If rock is the libido of adolescence and pop its breathless courtship, should we be surprised when its stars want to go all the way? And is it fair to harp on about, oh I don't know, Ted "Bring 'em Young" Nugent and his "classic" album of 1981, *Intensities in 10 Cities*, with its equally classic tracks "Jailbait" and "I Am a Predator"? And it would be particularly shooting-pedos-in-a-barrelish to retell the story of him becoming the legal guardian of the seventeen-year-old Hawaiian girl who he'd been dating and was too young to marry.

And we certainly don't need to revisit Bill Wyman's relationship with a thirteen-year-old Mandy Smith (he was forty-seven) any more than we need to dwell on those "just-a-bit-of-fun pranksters" who set up a "countdown clock" website for Charlotte Church's sixteenth birthday.

All of which goes to show . . . that I'm a judgmental prick (tick); that older rock stars like younger women, which is why they keep on being rock stars (maybe), and put a few hooks around a cutesy-kitsch version of your daughter/niece/schoolgirl and the airwaves will lap it up in between broadcasting news reports of "stranger danger" (almost certainly).

It also shows that when I was looking for a refuge from regular sexual assault, rock wasn't just a haven, it was also a reminder. As if being fucked wasn't complicated enough.

NEXT

I can prove at any time that my education tried to make another person out of me than the one I became.

—Franz Kafka, *Diaries*

My mum tells me to preface—though she never says "preface"—my remarks to teachers with a "please, sir." I tell her that's a throwback to her own school days when teachers were omnipotent, although I never say "omnipotent."

We sit and watch *Billy Liar*, me and my dad. It's that terrifying moment towards the end, when Billy's dad confronts him about the missing bloody calendars and the missing petty cash and that missing bloody monkey wrench. He tells him that he should be bloody grateful, that it's a chance he never bloody well had. "And don't we bloody know it," says Billy. Wilfred Pickles' face is a master class, every one of its lines a lesson in the proximity between hope and frustration. He is desperate to reach out to his son but hasn't the bloody language to bloody do it. He wears a cardigan over his shirt and tie, his one concession to this thing called "leisure."

We watch it in silence but I can hear Jack's conflicted loyalties. They come out every time he clears his throat, every time he flicks his ash into one of our green glass ashtrays. He's on Billy's side, obviously. But. Doesn't the dad have a point? Isn't that what this parenting lark is all about, hoping your kid will have a better life than you? And trying not to hate them if they don't? Or not hate them if they do? Too bloody right it was.

NEXT

"It isn't Jesus. . . . It's just a fella."
—Charlie, in *Whistle Down the Wind*

Accrington in 1981 was not Bradford in 1962 and I am not William Terrence "Billy Liar" Fisher. I am Graham Can't-Afford-a-Middle-Name Caveney and I am going to Greece.

And I don't want to go. Don't mind that your grandma has given you five pounds from her pension which she can't afford, or that your aunty Mary has found a few quid which she hasn't really got, or that we've been staying in every weekend scrimping and bloody scraping so that you will have the chance of a lifetime. No. I am not Billy Fisher, machine-gunning his parents at the breakfast table. I'm better than that. I'm Lord Byron in search of his haunted holy ground. I'm Henry Miller dedicated to the recovery of man's divinity.

A priest who isn't abusing me drives the one who is, me, and two other boys to Manchester airport. (Two priests and three boys: What could possibly be wrong? People thought then the exact opposite of what people think now.)

Was the priest who wasn't abusing me abusing either of the others? The question has only occurred to me now, thirty-four years after the event. There's no reason to assume he was. Then again, there was no reason to assume that my abuser was abusing me. And did the one who wasn't abusing me suspect that the one who was was? Without a language to think about abuse, we don't think about abuse.

I look around Manchester airport and the world seems impossibly big. From Accrington to Manchester seemed far enough, but Paris? Tokyo? And where the hell is Stuttgart? I have a rucksack, several pairs of Marks and Spencer's underpants, BHS socks, jeans, and a collection of T-shirts (collective noun: a sweatshop of?). I have acne gel, sun cream, and a toothbrush and toothpaste, because Kathleen's not convinced that they sell tooth care products in Greece. I have novels by Henry Miller.

I don't really know the two other boys. They're a year—two?— above me, sixth formers, Dean Gilliver and Paul Hudson. Need I say that Dean was called "Gilly" and Paul "Huddy"? Of course not. These lads were from Accrington, a place whose idea of male nomenclature was first to shorten your surname and then soften this circumcision with an infantilizing *Y*. They were wary of me, interpreting my inability to speak boy speak as swottish standoffishness (surely not).

We arrive in Athens late at night and Kevin tells us to enjoy the stillness, says it won't last, that Athenian traffic is like no other traffic on earth. We find the hotel, two rooms for four people. I instantly know how this is going to work.

And then something beautiful happens. Gilly pukes up. It's the heat. Heat and excitement. And all the crap he's been eating on the plane. It's the kind of puke that begins life at the end of your toes and shoots up like a geyser, a fully blown, Regan-in-*The-Exorcist* vomit. I offer to help look after him, and me and Huddy take it in turns to do the "Do you want water?" "Are you all right mate?" version of looking after that is as close to compassion as adolescent boys are likely to come. We stay in the one room, the three of us.

My memory of that time is hazy, yet I do remember realizing that Dean being ill had given me a useful escape. If only he'd keep on puking for the next three weeks my holiday would be fine. He didn't, of course. A few days later we are on a ferry on our way to Crete. Yet it seems to me now that I'd worked out that two rooms/four people didn't always have to be split down the middle. Or if it did, there may be ways of making it flexible. There was a chance of a way out.

The other two don't seem to mind sharing with Kevin as much as I'd expected. Maybe it's because he isn't fucking them. Or maybe it is the two-year age gap, or the fact I've shown myself to be willing to help clean up Gilly's puke; but when I suggest that we should take turns sharing with the Rev. Kev, they seem happy enough to do so.

And so is he. Voyeurism? The chance that one of them might . . . ? I don't think so. I think that he enjoyed the proximity of young male flesh. He was vampiric. The sex wasn't a consummation of his desire for adolescent boys—it wasn't about pleasure, so much as diffusing that desire. He needed to keep us close, be around us, be one of us. I can easily imagine that his sharing a room with Dean, a shower with Paul, was as erotic (more?) to him as the cock-grabbing relief that he exacted from me when he could. The holiday was the real sex. The company of boys.

NEXT

So coldly sweet, so deadly fair.

—Lord Byron, *The Giaour*

My parents have kept the postcards I sent them. They became their postcards. And now I've kept the postcards they kept. How do I separate out what I was telling them from what was happening? What kind of record are they? Was I really "having a smashing time, eating well, walking miles, and missing you"? Maybe I was. What else could I have said? "Trying to avoid sexual assault, cock sore, wish you were here"? I remember a walk amongst the ruins of Heraklion, and a weepy moment about St. Paul. I remember baroque-style bread in a taverna in Knossos and a huge argument about us three boys staying out all night at a nightclub. I remember Gilly joking about how Cretan women had a better mustache than Kevin, and Huddy storming off because "not every fucking meal needs to go swimming in fucking olive oil."

I was amazed that there were tavernas in churches and going to a wine festival in Rethymno; Kevin disgusted at us for getting pissed on free hooch. And there was washing underwear in the sink, sand in the bedsheets, and every three or four days there were sexual assaults that I was now used to and the writing of postcards assuring Kath and Jack of what a brilliant time I was having.

Years later my lawyer will ask me for dates and places and the only thing I can tell him with absolute certainty is that it was the summer of 1981 and that I clearly remember walking up the Gorge of Santa Maria and hating the way he cleared his throat.

I'm in a hotel room, eloquently drunk on retsina and Coke. It's just me and him. There's a television in the corner. I'm explaining to him that Pere Ubu aren't just a band, they're a whole thing, a way of life. And I bet he didn't know that it was the name of a French writer who . . . What? He did know. Oh, well I bet he didn't know, because he doesn't know everything . . . And that Tom Verlaine is a French writer but an American as well. And . . . No. I didn't say that Verlaine was American. I said—if he'd just listen—that Tom Verlaine was American. No, I am not drunk actually. I am telling you something here about ME. About my . . . thing, about Television about Tom Verlaine. Pop music? No. It isn't pop music. It's music but it's not pop music. It's music that's better than music. It's not like all that shit that you pretend to like, Love grows up somebody's nose la-la-la-la . . . This is music that makes you want to fucking die. No, I don't want to die. But, yes, sometimes I do want to die. But that's not the point. That's not what I'm saying. What I'm saying is that there's this music—these people—and they're like . . . just . . .

He clears his throat in that way that he has, as though he's mildly distracted and has to compose himself for some tedious chore. It's indulgent and mocking and irritated. He says something about grow up and fucking pop stars and no idea what I'm talking about.

And I say quietly:

I hate you. Do you hear me? Hate. You. I can't bear it. Anymore. I can't fucking bear it. When you . . . touch me. Don't . . . okay? Just, don't . . . fucking . . . Touch me. Ever. Again. I don't. It's. Please. Listen. Fuck. Not hate, but . . . I don't. Can't. If you'd . . . Fuck it. Fuck you. I want to . . . not. Do Not. Touch me. Ever, ever. Again . . . Okay . . . ?

Ad infinitum.

NEXT

"No," said the priest, "you don't need to accept everything as true, you only have to accept it as necessary." "Depressing view," said K. "The lie made into the rule of the world."
— Franz Kafka, *The Trial*

So, go on, ask me. I won't blame you. I've asked myself often enough. If . . . ?

If you could summon up the courage to say No to him on holiday, then why the hell couldn't you do it earlier? Was it really that difficult?

(Look, Kevin, Father, I appreciate the attention you're giving me, I really do. I enjoy our talks about books and appreciate those trips to the theater. But this spunking-on-my-stomach thing . . . ? Well, it's just not doing it for me. I'm sure your cock's fine and all that, but if you could just keep it to yourself and let me keep my cock to myself, then that would be just the ticket. I knew you'd understand. Thanks. What can we go and see next . . . ?)

I guess I could say what Julie says, that being with the other lads gave me confidence, safety in numbers. That Dean and Paul somehow made me realize that I too was a boy, not a mini adult being indulged in a fantasy of equality within a dynamic that hid every shred of its structural inequality.

I was not his lover, best friend, soul mate, savior, confidant, therapist, and sex worker. I was a sixteen-year-old boy in the company of two eighteen-year-old boys and I had more in common with them than I did with him. I liked Gilly's swearing, and agreed that "un-be-fucking-lievable" was indeed a fucking unbelievable word. I loved the way he wouldn't eat any Greek ("foreign") food in Greece and so survived on a diet of "mia patatas," all the while spending his time yearning for Cornish pasties and sausage fucking rolls.

I loved Huddy's singular commitment to the well-being of his bowels, the constant monitoring and detailed reports on the effect that "the change in the water" might be having. When Kevin made a crack at how he must have had a difficult time being potty trained ("Freud would have loved you!"), he came across as being sneering and supercilious, not the wise old bird he was styling himself as. (And did you really have to keep talking about the wine-colored sea and Homer and how the Greeks didn't have a concept for blue?)

So, yes, Julie's right; in the company of boys I had a taste of what boyhood could mean. And not mean. It wasn't just bad poetry, Beckett, and dread. It was also nightclubs and doing stupid voices. It was crappy discos on the beach and failing to chat up an American girl who'd never heard of Talking Heads (really?). And somehow within this shift of emphasis I saw the possibilities for a different story, an alternative version of myself.

In being away from school Kevin had surrendered his power base. He never once said Mass. Or prayers. There was no classroom, no office with Head written on it, no row upon row of easy-to-impress students. I remember wondering—for the first time—just how old he was. He had always been cagey about revealing his age, evading the question with a show of mock vanity which was nevertheless as real as his Brylcreemed hair or regularly trimmed mustache.

I had always thought of his age as being Grown-up—some netherworldish state between thirty and sixty wherein all numbers were pretty much the same. But in Crete I saw him as the fortysomething man that he was, a man with sagging tits and a slight paunch.

Yet there's another reason why I said no when I did, and it's nothing to do with Gilly, or Huddy, or the legitimizing structures of power. It's not even to do with Henry Miller novels, much though I'd like it to be.

It's simply this: I'd had enough.

I'd had the kind of enough that drunks have when they finally get sober. The kind of enough that the victims of domestic violence have when they leave their violent partners. Or smack addicts the smack. It's an enough born out of weariness, helplessness, and a despairing kind of hope. It's an enough that says, "I don't care how bad the results of stopping this are, they simply can't be as bad as this carrying on." It's the enough that makes people kill people. Or themselves.

NEXT

. . . she had had an increasing sense of unreality, as if her existence had been broken off like the reel of a film.

—Antonia White, *Beyond the Glass*

Kathleen's relieved, if truth be told. She says, I wasn't going to say anything but all them school trips were taking it out of you. And if he thinks that you need to concentrate more on your studies, then that's what you'll have to do. And deciding not to choose religion as one of your A levels? Well, she can see the sense in that too. Religious study A level? It doesn't seem quite right somehow. It isn't as though you are going to be a priest (too good-looking, would be a waste, laugh) and, besides, there's no need to study religion: you're a Catholic. But what about Father O'Neill? That's one of his subjects, isn't it? Won't he be disappointed? No need to bite my head off.

So politics instead, and "British Government"? What, all together? Fancy! Jack, our Graham's going to be the next Denis bloody Healey.

And English, obviously; goes without saying. One day, luv, them books are going to see you right. They're never wasted, time well spent. Just think, you could be the next . . . You could be an English teacher.

And history too?

You know what Mary McCarthy says, Mum? History, up to Henry VIII, is Catholic history, and, after that, it becomes anti-Catholic history.

She gives me one of her best "don't get smart with me son" stares. She may not have read any Mary McCarthy, but she knows when her son's being a smart-arse. Yes, history.

Matthew Arnold would have loved my mum (and my mum, no

doubt, would have loved Matthew Arnold). When, in the late nine-teenth century, he was fretting about the Barbarians, the Philistines, and the Populace, he was worried that the working class fell short "in those bright powers of sympathy and ready powers of action" that were the qualities of the middle class. What they needed was Culture, and plenty of it. Literature, English obviously, would ennoble them, soothe their anarchic unrest, and help fill them with all the sweetness and light of humanist understanding.

Kath had never read a book in her life, but she was a card-carrying Arnoldian nevertheless. She had a blind faith in books, in reading as a moral enterprise. As I've said, she'd boast of my bookishness in the same way that other parents might flaunt their child's achievements in the high jump. When I needed to get her permission for a school trip to Stratford, she would positively glow. Shakespeare! The word was said like it was part of the catechism, reverentially, eyes closed.

The problem for me was that I shared her devotion to learning, but had nearly been consumed in its fires. Books hadn't saved my life. They'd nearly ended it. It was books that had led me to Father Him. If it hadn't been for books, I would never have found myself sitting in his room late at night, lost in all that feverish pretense. There'd been a joke going round the schoolyard. An old man in a raincoat says to this young lad, Do you want to see some photos of puppies? And the young lad says, Only if you give me a suck of your cock first. Kafka was Father K's puppy pictures, Beckett his bag of sweets. I'd had my sentimental education and it had made me anything but sentimental.

At the same time, reading was the only thing I'd got left. So books it would be: books it would have to be. I'd divorce Them from Him, the lesson from the teacher, the sweeties from the cock.

My parents approved of me getting all the qualifications I could, storing them up like the educational equivalent of my post office sav-ings account. But, as they both agreed, it was a gamble. I could see them doing the odds: sixteen to eighteen equals two years' wages: an office job, save up, possible deposit on a house. That would have been "doing very well for yourself," a close relation to "doing very nicely for yourself," but more honest, less of the got-lucky-on-the-pools about it. A mortgage and a white-collar job were not, as they said, to be sniffed at. They were the ingredients of "a good catch." And if there was one thing Kathleen was certain of, it was that I would someday make someone a bloody good catch.

Or there was A levels: hard slog with no guarantees. But if it paid off, you were made. Not just a cushy job but a decent job, a vocation of which you could be proud. Teacher, gasp. It was risky and, despite doing the pools (4 score draws 2, 7, 24, 26—our birthdays plus house number) and bingo, they weren't really gambling people.

Then there was the matter of board. The lads who left school at sixteen—my cousins, for example—would "tip up" to their parents, pay them a percentage of their wages for food and lodging. It was never said, but I knew that A levels were their sacrifice as much as mine.

Jack has an idea.

Walk up Lister Street to Blackburn Road and head towards Accrington. Pass the chemist and the hairdresser-who-does-your-mum's-hair. Go past that strange-smelling takeaway café with all the taxis outside and on past the grocer-who-delivers, then Ivan the barber with the feather cut (who can only do feather cuts) and on until you turn down King Street. Before you pass under the viaduct, there's a working men's club on your left. It has lots of glass and white brick and smells of hops. Jack Caveney has been a member all his working life. He knows everyone.

Go through the back door to the lounge (the front will take you into the concert room). A man sits behind a Formica table. He's there to check everyone's membership cards and sign anyone in who isn't a member. He still looks at my dad's card even though he was at school with him; even though Dad will have paid his dues every year; even though he comes here at least twice a week.

"And this is my lad."

The man nods towards the visitors' book, his cap moves back and forth. I sign in. He does not smile.

Jack buys himself a pint of mild and me a bitter shandy ("with plenty of shandy"). He disappears around the back of the bar and when he returns he brings with him a man dressed in a thick gray woolen suit over a tank top, shirt, and tie. It is the middle of August. This man is Tommy, the club steward. He looks me up and down and says, "Jack Caveney's lad? Hmmmm. You'll do."

Thus did I get my first job. It can't have really been like that (I must have said something), but that's how I remember it. The job was Glass Collector—Wednesdays, Fridays, and Saturdays; seven till closing, five pounds a night.

Although the working men's clubs were meant to be way past their heyday by the early 1980s, no one had thought to inform the patrons who kept my collecting basket brimming over three nights a week. And it wasn't just King Street. There was the Poplar, the Pioneer, the Miners, the Dyers, Sydney Street, and Willow Mount. Mrs. Thatcher may have decided to transform the working class into the property-owning family units of her own dark-hearted dreams, but these clubs testified to a class still deeply invested in notions of community and tradition.

The WMCs carried with them all the tensions of their history—a shaky paternalism, rigid hierarchies (the steward and the committee were the boss and the foremen of leisure), and an ambivalent relationship to alcohol itself (the influence of the temperance movement, perhaps). It was fine to enjoy a drink but shameful to be drunk ("to be too fond of a drink" was strictly for the pubs).

Women simply never went to the bar. Ever. It may well have been a club rule, like the one that forbade them from going in the games room (for their own good: "the language"). They drank halves of lager, or gin and orange, or port and lemon, and fun drinks like Babycham or Snowball. Their hair was astonishing. The women had hairdos like industrial sculptures, lacquered and backcombed and preserved throughout the week in hairnets and curlers.

The men had faces molded from the cement of the brickyard, broken-veined noses, and thinning slicked-back hair. They all had sideburns, all except the ex-military who wore their clean-shaven cheeks like medals.

Need I say that the club was 99 percent white? That the one "black fella" was called "black Trevor" and that there were no Asians (odd, considering that they were generally agreed to be taking over the country).

I spent most of my work time in the concert hall, a spacious canteen-type room with a raised glittery stage at one end and row after row of long tables leading up to it. Next to the stage was a pulpit, sorry, a raised box, where a member of the committee would sit with a microphone telling us when bingo tickets were available, when the pies had arrived, and to give a big King Street welcome to . . . Mike Marino, Casanova, the Enoch Powell Carol Singers. Okay I just made that last one up, but I didn't make up the other two. These artists—"turns"—were huge draws across the northwest and commanded a loyal following with a fee that reflected it. Their repertoire was tailor-made to an audience reared on the softer side of rock and pop. Slim Whitman, Johnny Mathis, Neil Diamond, the Carpenters, Frank Ifield, Roy Orbison, this was music which wore its nostalgia openly. Elvis was relegated to his Vegas years, "The Wonder of You" belted out, the audience happy to provide the bridging whoooo-hoooooo-ooooos.

The key to a successful turn was a question of balance. They had to take the music seriously but not themselves, create a kind of schmaltz-free sentimentality. They also had to know when to get off. Because no matter how Rhinestone a singer's Cowboy could be, or how high his *una paloma blanca* soared, he was always the supporting act to the club's star attraction, Lady Bingo.

NEXT

He gives you so much trouble, doesn't he? He simply will not understand, will not cooperate, will not see it your way. And your way, is it really *your* way? Can you honestly say that you have a way of life?

—Henry Miller, *Stand Still Like the Hummingbird*

"I'm not looking for philosophers, I'm looking for comics," says the soul-deadened agent to the group of would-be comedians in Trevor Griffiths' 1975 play of that name. "The people pay the bills, remember. . . . A good comic can lead an audience by the nose yes, but only in the direction they're already going. . . ."

(". . . and so Paddy says, yes, officer, it was definitely her. . . .")

The days when a club comic could pack 'em in had gone long before I started working there, but the gap was filled by the singers providing one-liners in between songs and the occasional "free and easy" (the WMC's open mic night). Yet the real comedians, as Jack was keen to remind me, were to be found at the bar, or in the lounge, or upstairs playing snooker.

(". . . and so he says, not to worry, we do 'em in black for a shilling . . .")

I wander round the club at fifteen-minute intervals, leaning over couples—a couple of couples usually, men talking to men, the women having a gossip (two terms whose irreversibility was ironclad). "This done?" "This one empty?" "You finished with this one?" I've got my rap down pat now, a kind of polite invisibility that, if the drinks put for me behind the bar are anything to go by, is serving me well. I know my awkward sods from my likes-to-have-a-laughs, the stuck-up cows from the all-coat-and-no-knickers. It's convivial in a way that I love the North for being, every joke a heartbeat away from an argument: "No, but you bloody will be." "I'll chop your bloody hands off, you little sod." "If you insist." On the stage Tom Jones has become Englebert Humperdink has become Paul Anka.

(". . . because fresh air's free . . .")

I bring the glasses back to Elaine, the dishwasher, a woman who insists that I look exactly like her nephew, as though this explains something important about both of us. I stand at the bar and drink. I'm allowed to drink any drinks the barmaids pull by accident, and there's always a fair few accidents.

This then is my new now, my real hometown. Not all that nonsense with the Rev. Kev. Because that's what it was, all it was: nonsense. Behind me. No more. Push on. A levels. This will do in the meantime. Won't it?

There's Johnny Regan, an Irishman who made a small fortune tarmacing people's driveways. He always smells of Brut aftershave. He drinks beer with whiskey chasers and I have never seen him drunk. At Lent he "stops drinking," which means he drinks lager. He's stood with Big Frankie Grant, a man who worked as a laborer on every A road and motorway going through Lancashire. There's Ian with his ducktail haircut and Old Stan who is a midget. They're playing dominoes, a game where they score points for making multiples of 5s and 3s. I'm not supposed to go to the bar for the punters ("otherwise you'll end up doing it for everyone"), but I go to the bar for this group. I watch and learn. So a double six scores 4 because it is 4 3; but if your opponent has a 6/3 domino he can match the 6 and turn the 12 into a 15. Which scores 8 because it is five 3s plus three 5s. Got it. They are keeping up a banter that is older than my sixteen years, jokes about their wives and people they used to work with.

Frankie plays a double blank—a domino with no white spots—and steals the points his opponent has just scored. He has a big bass laugh, chest hair made of steel. "Tha should a known I had the nigger if thy'd've been watchin'." No one blinks or coughs. There would have been more of a reaction if he'd have belched. His racism wasn't malicious or even acknowledged as being racist. It was naturalized, so deeply ingrained as to be invisible, inaudible. He said it in the same way he called the barmaid "love," or the corner shop the Paki shop. He said what he said because it's what he'd always said.

Somehow the racism nestled with the sentimentality: they shared, as it were, an emotional etymology. It's like the "I can't live without you" love of the wife beater who's just given his missus a good hiding. It's cloying; it is deeply moved by itself. The same casual disgust that gave birth to the Paki joke was a close relation to the mawkish collective "aaahhhh" that was let out at the mention of the word "kiddies." The club comedians both on and off the stage for whom racism was merely a "bit of a laugh" were the most adamant that they would never tell jokes about disability or children. Let alone disabled children: kiddies with cancer, kiddies in wheelchairs, kiddies without a proper home to go to. (Why not? If a joke's just a joke, then why not make jokes about anyone and everyone? Because those kiddies are our kiddies: white kiddies, TV poster kiddies.) And let's not forget to whip ourselves up into a frenzy of sanctimonious hypocrisy over swearing, as though the problem with the term "fucking Pakis" was the "fucking."

I want to write about the everyday heroism of my class, their triumph over the daily grind of crappy jobs or no job, of how they somehow made relationships work despite it all. I want to write about northern warmth and northern wit, the resilience and the defiance of people who put two fingers up with one hand even as they doffed their cap with the other. Yet I know it's not quite true. Or only half-true, and that complexity is not something that traditionally belongs to the inner life of the working class. Their lives (it is said) are simple and so (it follows) that their inner lives are equally as regimented or impoverished.

The ambiguity I was taught to tease out and cherish as a student of literature doesn't seem to apply to the people with whom I was brought up, and who brought me up (and even the "whom" of that sentence causes me to check my nose to see if I'm talking down it). We were reading Lawrence's *Sons and Lovers* for A level and I remember thinking that the dad never stood a chance. He's a brute, a drunk, a cutter of Paul's golden hair. He has a hard job, and hard jobs make for hard men. That is all you know and need to know about Mr. Morel.

I want to write about the complexities of my class, yet "complex" is not a thing they seem eager to embrace. When I naively ask friends of my dad about themselves, they say things like "There's nowt to tell" or "Whaddya wanna know for?" It was a weird question to them; intrusive, impertinent. When I got to university I was filled with envy for the ease with which middle-class people spoke about themselves. They had been taught that they were interesting, that their stories were worth listening to. They accepted my curiosity as their birthright.

The truth is that my own class embarrasses me. All those names and their un-glamour, the auld Tommys and the Big Jims, the Our Dorises and the Your Hildas. Their stereotypicality has not been forced upon them; they embrace it willingly. They do it to themselves, internalizing their oppression, emerging at birth pre-stereotyped and ready for the brickyard, the shoddy; factory fodder. They still speak broad Lancastrian, most of them, "thee-ing" and "tha knows-ing" their way through a series of anecdotes, most of which celebrate a certain kind of stupidity. A defiant, no-nonsense stupidity, a dumb insolence, one that appears to speak commonsensical truths to posh la-di-da power. And fails. It fails because they're in a double bind, what I would later find out is called a dialectic. If they aim for something "better," they fail to see what's better about it. Or rather: the very thing that makes it "better" is its exclusivity; is precisely that people like them don't go and see it, hear it, read it.

There were advertisements on the TV around this time for complete record sets of mainstream classical composers. The ad featured Johann Strauss' "Blue Danube," which the voice-over would promise was just one of many of the great waltzes that had been recorded especially for you. Kathleen would toy with the idea of buying this. Or rather of me buying this for her. Because if I bought it, I wouldn't have wasted the money ("it's the sort of thing you'd like"), whereas if she bought it, she would have. Because she will never listen to it. She likes the idea of liking all those old Strauss waltzes. They signify an elegant form of deference, one which can be fantasized as being courtly and romantic ("Just think, them balls! Them costumes! All that bowing!"). And she knows the "Blue Danube" because everyone knows it. But this familiarity is fake. It also reminds her that that's all she knows (Johann or Richard, Kathleen?) and that if she did really buy that three-box record set, she wouldn't know any of the other tunes. And they didn't come cheap.

What was she going to do? Finish working at the bingo, the factory, or on the home help where she would later work? Come home and make the tea. Do "a bit" (it was never "a lot," even though it was a lot) of housework. Maybe mend some clothes, do whatever bit of old people's washing the home help were told they didn't have to do but that all of them did, and then tell Jack to turn off the telly because she fancied listening to a couple of hours of Johann Sebastian Strauss? Too bloody right she wasn't. And besides, there's the bingo.

I am sixteen and I am picking up glasses, and for three nights a week I listen to different turns butcher the same old songs. Yet that's not all I'm listening to. John-no-longer-Conrad sends me a tape of the Fall's *Totale's Turns (It's Now or Never)* from Cambridge, with a handmade postcard of Gene Hackman in *The French Connection*, the back of which says: "Keep picking yer feet in Poughkeepsie." When I first play it, I think that it's bootleg, a bootleg from some secret gig that John is showing off about. I'm half-right. Most of it is recorded live, but not at the Corn Exchange in Cambridge or any other punk-friendly venue. It's recorded live in working men's clubs in Bradford and Doncaster, and if there is a better internal soundtrack to collect glasses to in the King Street WMC, I don't want to hear it. Each track moves further and deeper into an ecstasy of loathing. There's a three-way loop of disgust between Mark Smith, the band, and the audience; their hostility is perfectly triangulated. "We are the Fall-a, the crap that talks back . . ." Smith shrieks, "the difference between you and us-ah is that we have brains . . ." He introduces the third track, "Rowche Rumble," with a goading reminder to the punters, "Last orders half-past ten." It's his *Waste Land* moment, his own punk spin on Eliot's "Hurry up please it's time." And so King Street became a different space.

NEXT

The boy next door is me.
—The Feelies, "The Boy with the Perpetual Nervousness"

Picking up glasses gives me an In, and therefore a way out. King Street men start to recommend their local pubs, urge me to pop in, give me the thumbs-up. I learn of the good pubs, the hard-man pubs, and the tarts' pubs; of where they serve a good pint and a late pint (rarely the same thing). When I go down to the Elite snooker club, I no longer go to play snooker. I go and sit in the back room, the one which says Bona Fide Members Only and where none of the members are bona let alone fide. There I sit and watch men play jacks or better—a version of five card draw poker. I watch Big Frankie play in a school with a couple of Asian taxi drivers and Colin from the front desk and notice that Frankie's friendly straight-talking racism seems to stop talking when he's in the company of other races.

Earning fifteen quid a week makes me eligible to join this school: it's the only qualification necessary. There's no "going easy on the kid" breaks either. If you're old enough to win, you're old enough to lose. The lessons taught to me by my granddad serve me well. I know to concentrate on the other person's hand, and appear nonchalant with my own. My grand-dad's advice had been simple but effective: maximize your good hands, minimize the bad. I start to win, respect as well as money. I'm not, I'm told, as daft as I look. Which makes me wonder how daft I do look.

And so I become socialized in the ways of men, different kinds of men than the ones I'd known or thought I wanted to know. Julie tells me that I was man tasting, checking out the different flavors of masculinity available to me. The Rev. Father had had a bitter aftertaste, I needed to find something with less complex notes, a fuller body.

NEXT

It really moved me.

—The Passions, "I'm in Love with a German Film Star"

I returned from Crete to my parents like the prodigal son. Except that I hadn't been prodigal, I'd been molested, the whore with whom others have been prodigal. But now I've stopped it and it's no thanks to them. If it hadn't been for their blind Catholicism, their creeping deference, their fawning over all things better than them, then I wouldn't have been molested in the first place. Or be sitting here: watching *Seaside Special* and trying not to hate them for laughing at the comedian whose entire act seems to be saying the word "Germans" in a stupid Scouse accent. Or watching *Are You Being Served?* and trying not to wish that I was still going to Manchester's Royal Exchange, or the Bolton Octagon. Because I miss him as well as despise him. I miss the trade-offs, the cultural kickbacks, the bookish bribes.

I am triumphant at having stood up to Father the molester, but bereaved at my loss of Kevin the mentor. I want to be back, rooted in the solid dependability of my parents, although they proved to be neither as solid nor as dependable as I needed them to be. For they too were seduced.

I will, of course, make them pay. Never again will I entrust them with those secrets that children are meant to be able to take to their parents. When Kathleen tells me that I should know that I can always talk to her about anything, anything at all, and that there's nothing we won't be able to work out, and that nothing is ever as bad as we think it is, I'll grimace through gritted teeth and call her names to myself that I was told men should never ever use about women. When Jack asks me for the hundredth time that day about A levels, jobs, the possibility of university, he doesn't know that I'm going to fail my exams on purpose, and that he won't be looking so fucking pleased with me and my future and therefore himself when I: marry a foreign girl, turn myself gay, go to Cambridge to live with John Mullen in a squat, hitchhike around America, get a job that is as boring as yours to punish you for wanting me to have a life that is more interesting than yours.

Kevin has forced me to grow up too quickly and thus prevented me from growing up at all.

NEXT

It is disconcerting that the director always credits the patient with total cinematic recall, instead of showing the blurred, spotty, personalized texture of spontaneous recollection.

—Manny Farber, "The 'Psychiatry Movie,'" *Farber on Film: The Complete Film Writings of Manny Farber*

Diary:

Go back to church, get a clean slate for your soul.

And:

god's a cunt.

More than ever now I think in and through film. I need flickering images: I want to internalize them, possess them. There's an aerial camera permanently fixed outside my bedroom window. It lingers on me stretching in the morning, wondering why Paul Newman's white vests look so cool whilst mine have threads hanging down and stains on them. It tracks my newly bought Dr. Martens shoes as I stride along Blackburn Road like Lee Marvin in *Point Blank*. It cuts to a close-up of my face as I stand at the concert room bar, my inner voice narrating a voice-over à la William Holden's in *Sunset Boulevard* or Fred MacMurray in *Double Indemnity*. I don't so much speak as script my sentences, listening to the dialogue play out as other people fade and dissolve at my editorial will.

And again:

Try to feel like you feel when you're watching films when you're not watching films.

On a premolesting school trip to London I'd gone to see Polanski's *Tess.* Postmolestation, I try myself out as Nastassja Kinski, cringing at the absurdity of the comparison even as I conjure it up. Besides, Kevin ain't no Leigh Lawson. I'm not sure who he is. My inner casting director is fickle, restless, overambitious. I'm a tragic heroine from a nineteenth-century novel. I'm the angriest of angry young men. I'm a ruined Emma Bovary as played by a young Alan Bates. I want to have attacks of the vapors, swap my school uniform for Brontëan bonnets and fucked-up petticoats. If I cast it right, the film in my head might still redeem me.

And:

Feel sad for Jack and Kath. It will help you to like them.
Try to picture them crying.

Film is my way in, my way back and through to my parents. I know what Kath likes and scour our weekly *Radio Times* to find them. "Women's pictures" she calls them, a bafflingly elastic term when I first heard it, but one that I'm coming to realize has rules like any other. I'm searching for dates (1948–58) and actresses (Bette Davis, Joan Crawford) and those haiku-type reviews which I always complain about but secretly rely on. I'm looking for women who are well off but unhappily married, or happily married but about to become ill and die. I need—Kath needs—women who have been betrayed yet remain defiant, or who have sacrificed duty for desire, or whose love lives promise to be the death of them. I want staircases and smoking, sobbing and slapped faces, I'm looking for *Jezebel* or *All About Eve* or *Mildred Pierce.* Nothing doing. Then I see it, tucked away on a Tuesday night, some weird time, 5:20 or 6:35, never a straight o'clock. *All That Heaven Allows.* Got one, I say to her. And a date is made. There will be tea and shop-bought custards or apple turnovers. There will be "How old is Rock Hudson now?" and there will be "Shhhh."

I know I've made a good choice two minutes into the film when it becomes clear that Jane Wyman is a widow, and rich. And that she is disappointed with her life because it is peopled with tiresome neighbors and uninspiring men. I can feel Kath's empathy for this character, except it's not quite empathy. It's an identification with the character's inner life that is also a fantasy of something like revenge. The film is a way of letting Kath have it both ways. She loves the otherness of this world whilst being reassured that it is not that different from her own; even beautiful rich American women and their country clubs are riddled with petty jealousies and quiet despair. It's why she never liked British films, I think. There was nothing fantastical for her in seeing Rachel Roberts fetishize the boots of her dead husband in *This Sporting Life*, or watching June Ritchie slowly turn into Thora Hird in *A Kind of Loving*. She had a phrase for films she knew well, like *Now, Voyager*: "I could play that part myself." She meant she knew the dialogue off by heart. Yet she was also saying something about playing a role, about her fantasy, about how she knew she could've been Bette Davis.

I didn't think that stuff then. Then, I would enter a distracted trance and wonder about the creases in men's trousers and why they all wore hats. And I would hope that Kath was enjoying it, beaming at her when Jane and Rock hit it off, snarling with her when Jacqueline de Wit is a right old cow. My responses were Kathleen's responses; for ninety minutes we shared a common language. In having chosen the film, I was being given access to her inner life. I would watch her watching Rock Hudson and know at that moment that my mum wasn't just my mum: she existed in 3-D.

NEXT

A photograph is a secret about a secret . . .

—Diane Arbus

Kath's right. My skin does look better. And, yes, I have thinned out, lost that puppy fat. And, yes, I did need a haircut. There's Dean looking all mischief eyed, arms crossed, his red footie shirt contrasting with the ice-blue ocean behind him. And Paul, sulking at being dragged to yet another site of ruined grandeur. And me, alternating between bumblebee shirt, a white cheesecloth number, and a bare chest. There's nothing particularly arresting about any of these holiday snaps. They're holiday snaps. Me and Dean. Paul and Dean. Me and Paul. Me and Paul and Dean: mountains, sea, taverna. I can't remember whose camera was used, but it's obvious who snapped them. Because he's not in them.

There's one picture of the three of us taken as we stand around a sign with writing in Greek and English that says: Military Controlled Area and underneath Taking Pictures is Forbidden. My hand grips the pole, Gilly's also, both of us appearing to smile at the obvious joke. I remember how he was keen to take this particular image, how he kept laughing, saying that we were a threat to national security. Kath's not amused though. Forbidden is forbidden. If you weren't meant to take pictures, then you didn't take pictures. They didn't say these things for the good of their health, you know. He of all people should know that. I say, It was a joke, Mum. No harm done. I defend him against her, partly because she didn't defend me from him. It's her punishment.

I have spent too much of my life looking at—thinking about—this photograph, about its cheap and transparent staging of rebellion.

At times I've used it to remind myself that Kevin's sense of himself as maverick had no more depth than this Kodak moment. Taking a picture of a sign forbidding the taking of pictures? Well, move over, Weegee, how very rock 'n' roll. It's essentially a schoolboy prank, and looking at it reminds me of how schoolboyish he could be. I remember him sulking as we came back through customs and him buying up his duty-free allowance and asking me to take through a bunch of cigarettes and me refusing. And I remember my feeling of contempt for him, for the way he was desperate to be the Rev. Fucking Kev with his hipper-than-thou cutting-edge self-image. So this photograph keeps him small, keeps him at a manageable level of wannabe desperado.

At other times this picture torments me. When I'm feeling grand, I compare it to that portrait of Lee Miller in Hitler's bathtub. It torments me because the "joke" of the photograph is being bought at my expense. He is, after all, the photographer. It's not his sagging middle-aged spread that is draped over the forbidden sign. It's mine, and those of two other boys. Did you make copies of these, Father? Did my, your, our holiday snaps keep you company on the long winter evenings after I cut off your supply to adolescent flesh, or at least to my adolescent flesh? Did you keep them under your pillow? Did you save the "taking pictures is forbidden" one until last? You did, didn't you? I know you. I've had my whole life to think about you.

NEXT

It was extraordinary how my absolute conviction of his secret precocity—or whatever I might call the poison of an influence that I dared but half-phrase—made him, in spite of the faint breath of his inward trouble, appear as accessible as an older person, forced me to treat him as an intelligent equal.

—Henry James, *The Turn of the Screw*

Hot water, says Jack, as hot as you can stand it. It softens the bristles, opens the pores. He gives me a badger-hair shaving brush and tells me that it was designed by a badger, and I laugh even though I've decided to stop laughing. He shows me how to scrape down on the cheek and up on the jaw, working first with, then against the grain. I nick myself just under the nose and, in the words of my newest companion, Alex from *A Clockwork Orange*, red red kroovy flows real horrorshow. I'm transfixed by the sight of myself performing adulthood, that there is a me who is taking on the trappings of a man. I'm impatient to be rid of my childhood whilst feeling that it has yet to begin. I'm losing something I never had, and thus am I doubly bereaved.

I shave the skin that is no longer covered in acne, that has improved in the Cretan sun. I now wear my tie loose or not at all. I am allowed to tie my jumper around my waist and wear trousers that aren't strictly regulation so long as they're black. People stop telling me to get my hair cut.

School isn't school anymore; it's college, sixth form. There are boys from other schools who have arrived to sit their A levels, boys who don't believe in the One True, or any, God. There are boys who didn't know me from before: new and cool boys, clean-slate boys. There are girls.

It is easier than I'd thought to become invisible, to slip beneath Kevin's headmasterly radar. No longer taking RE means no more classroom contact. I bury myself in my other A levels, long hours in the library. I think of the other teachers as a buffer between me and him.

"Politics" doesn't seem to be about politics at all. In fact, it seems actively hostile to it. It's about how Westminster administrates itself, the efficacy of select committees or the drawbacks to the single transferable vote. I become quite good at it. The time I would have spent with St. Paul I now spend with R. M. Punnett. I think of it as being like Latin: irrelevant but strangely noble.

I'm fired up by history, American as well as European, a new and slightly disreputable combination at the time. I remember being impressed by how not very far west and not particularly old the Old West was. I like the way the South was the villain, and lost a righteous fight, but that everyone seems to prefer it. It's my new lost cause, and I play the Band's "The Night They Drove Old Dixie Down" with the satisfaction of my new insider knowledge.

And I dissolve into English lit: Keats and Chaucer, double Shakespeare, Lawrence, Pope, and Tourneur's *Revenger's Tragedy*, which Jock Roland assures us is much funnier than we think it is. Sometimes I sit and look at him and wonder if he too wants to fuck me. And then I try not to think that. I tell myself that just because Kevin wanted to fuck me doesn't mean that anyone else will want to fuck me. But it doesn't mean that they won't.

It means negotiating between the fucking that has already happened with and fucking that might yet occur, and knowing that there is no relationship between these two things whilst suspecting that there is every relationship between them. Also, I suspect I may want to pursue some consensual fucking of my own at some point, an activity that books and films suggest can be complicated enough in its own right. I tell myself to shut up. I go and sit in the library.

And it is also true that:

It's impossible to be invisible, to slip between the cracks of Kevin's authority. The other teachers ultimately report to him; he's their headmaster too. He pops in on lessons, a friendly face advertising his accessibility to staff and students alike. He takes general studies lessons, he takes morning assembly. I see him in the corridors, hear him on the playground. Nowhere is Rev.-Kev-free, not even the library.

I befriend a few of the new lads—Dave "Harry" Harrison, Martin "Eggy" Eggleston, Phil Curran. Our record collections morph and bind us together, commingling through the magic of TDK C90 tapes. Music allows us to tell each other who we are, or who we think we might want to be. Our compilations advertise our credentials. They are performances. Each track in conversation with every other track, suggestive, revealing.

Bowie and Iggy bootlegs were highly prized (have I dreamt this but did people even charge just to make a tape of *Live Santa Monica*?), but also Can, Beefheart, and Hendrix. Of the postpunk bands it was Joy Division who I remember most clearly as being spoken of in jaw-dropping terms, Curtis' suicide sealing the deal on their legacy. Yet even more important than our bids for obscurity was the announcement of what we were not, and what we were not was: soul boys, disco kids, or funk freaks. It wasn't that this music was "black" music (although it was and, as such, not ours); it was also that this music all seemed to be about having a good time. And if there was one thing me and my friends were certain of, one thing that united us in our collective secondhand overcoat, it was that we were not, nor would we ever be, in the business of having a good time.

Starting smoking was an extension of this unpleasure, a statement of my anhedonia and commitment to fashionable misery. Considering Jack and Kath's forty-plus a day habit, it is amazing that I remained smoke free until I was sixteen. But when I did start it felt right, as though tobacco had moved from black-and-white to Technicolor.

NEXT

For he alone knew what no other initiate knew: how easy hungering was. It was the easiest thing in the world.
—Franz Kafka, "A Hunger Artist"

He was in wonderful form that particular morning. Another of the Irish hunger strikers had died, or maybe the strike was being called off. I remember having been mesmerized by the news footage that had been coming out of the Maze, the grainy footage of men sitting in cells that they had smeared with their own shit, the unmistakable Northern Irish accents demanding to be treated as political prisoners. I particularly remember the dustbin-lid protests, hundreds if not thousands of women each night banging their bin lids on the cobbled backstreets of Belfast and Derry. I remember thinking that someone should make a record with this sound as a backing track, or that they should form themselves into a full-blown orchestra and perform cover versions of English classics (the Brotherhood of Man's "Kisses for Me" as performed by the Falls Road Ensemble, three hundred housewives wielding dustbin lids and various kitchen utensils). I write to Johnny Mullen and tell him this, joking that our next band should be called the Blanket Men and we should release our first EP ("Our Toilet Is Your Shame") in the Gents of the House of Lords. He writes back and tells me that it's already been done. It was called "God Save the Queen" by the Sex Pistols.

Father O'Neill clears his throat as a cue to start morning assembly. He says, It's nothing to do with any of us, here in Britain, what a bunch of criminals get up to in a prison in the North of Ireland. We've no need to ask why they would go to such extraordinary lengths, such desperate measures as starving themselves to death just to be recognized as people who had a rationale for doing what they did. That, he says, is nothing to do with us. He looks around the assembly and smiles. Every student there is, or is friends with someone whose parents are, Irish.

It is nothing to do with us, he continues, voice a semitone higher, if those men who are guilty of terrible crimes also wish that we acknowledge the context for their crimes, or to acknowledge that their crimes were not born just out of wickedness or spite but out of a long and complex series of events. That has nothing to do with us. Has it, Mr. O'Brien, Mr. O'Toole, Mr. Horrigan?

And so he goes on, not defending the hunger strike exactly, but certainly not condemning it either. He took Thatcher's pious intransigence and unpicked it piece by self-serving piece. If he hadn't been my sexual abuser, I would have loved him. He was brilliant, he was Mark Antony come to bury the Republicans, not to praise them. He keeps on saying how it is nothing to do with us, each time showing us precisely how it is. And his rhetoric is peppered with direct appeals to the students, the O'Rourkes, the Flanagans, the O'Byrnes. And the Caveneys.

When he says my name it is the first time he has acknowledged me since our return from Crete. Did I imagine it or was there a longer pause before he chose my name, a fraction in which there was time to register that my name was not as Irish as the others, was the odd one out in his roll call of descendancy. He knows that I hate my name, the un-nickname-ability of it. He also knows that it somehow makes me feel bogus, or he should know. I used to tell him often enough back when we were "courting," back when my every insecurity was listened to with his complete groomer's attention. He knows that I wished that the granddad whom I'd loved had either been properly Irish—a no-nonsense O'Kaveney or a lilting Cavanaugh—and not the bastardized change-it-at-Liverpool Caveney that he became.

And so I hear my name as a punch line, a faintly ludicrous tag-on to his sermon on the H-Block. Or maybe he meant to reach out, to include me in his litany of the oppressed. It may well have been a kindness. The problem being that once you've been fucked, you tend to be suspicious of kindness, especially when it comes from the one who was molesting you.

I'm called to his office.

He says, I was wondering if you're all right. You seemed to be uncomfortable this morning. In assembly.

I'm fine.

It's been a while since we had a proper conversation. I've been worried about you, you're not . . . Your attitude. Seems to have changed. This punk thing. Doesn't suit you.

I'm fine. Not a punk. Just music. Doesn't matter.

It does matter. Very much. So long as you're a pupil . . . My pupil . . . At this school . . . It matters a great deal. Teachers tell me you're doing well . . . The workload. But it's not just the work . . . That was never going to be a problem . . . It's everything else. The smoking . . . You don't seem . . . You're not the boy I used to know.

It goes on for fifteen hours. It goes on for fifteen minutes. It's the grilling of a witness who knows that the lawyer cross-examining him is the one who has done it. And that the judge is his accomplice.

I'm aware of him becoming Father O'Neill, how easily he is able to shed the Rev. Kev's skin and adopt the weightier body of the Headmaster. Every time he crosses his legs he seems to be advertising his ownership of the office. His posture is confident, hands folded calmly on his stomach, head slightly back. He sits in a chair with its back against the window. The sunlight is a spotlight, beaming from behind. His voice is rich, homiletic. I have sat in this office dozens of times, sat with him in these same chairs, drinking wine and talking about how we were both prime numbers.

It's not the same office, he's not the same man. And me? He's right, I'm not the same boy. I'm a sulky spoiled bastard who wants to smash this office up but knows that he can't. I sit perched on my lower-than-his wooden chair unable to speak. I don't mean that I can't find the right words. I mean that words—the right ones or not—don't belong to me. A couple eventually come to me, on loan. I don't know whose they are but I'm grateful for them, say them anyway, blurt them out . . .

I don't believe in God. Or anything, really . . . So . . .

I don't say fuck you, but he can hear it anyway.

He says, Think about what you're doing at this school. And, Re-consider your position. He doesn't say, Expulsion, but it hangs in the air between us, like incense.

NEXT

We are not hurt only by tragedy: the grotesque too carries weapons, undignified, ridiculous weapons.

—Graham Greene, *The End of the Affair*

There's days of not sleeping, and not eating, and sulking around my house saying I don't feel well. And pinching Jack and Kath's fags and thinking that if I was Siouxsie Sioux's slave, then I would be happy (I still think that). There's the King Street WMC and accidentally pulled waste-not-want-not pints of beer. There's the Doors and the way they sound like music that hasn't been made yet. There's writing letters to Johnny in Cambridge and talks about a visit. There's diary entries with bad poems about secretly fancying skinhead girls. There's a visit to the doctor who tells me I should take up cross-country running.

And then there's Big Frankie Grant, the domino player for whom "nigger" is just another word.

I don't remember exactly why I was round at his house on a Saturday afternoon, what my thinking was. He had been asking me round, reminding me of his address every time I saw him ("Pop in, tha knows where I mean . . . ?"). Nothing particularly strange about that. People asked each other round. It was what mates did. But "mates," a man in his midforties and a boy of sixteen? It didn't seem as odd as it does as I write this now. And, besides, I had form, I was used to being befriended by men who were older than me. Did I think he'd shed light on my situation at school? Was there a sense in which he was the antidote to everything that Kevin was not? The rarefied air of books and schools had proved to be not so uplifting after all; perhaps I thought that a no-nonsense man-mate may offer me some clarity, cut through the fog.

He is next to me on the settee. There is porn. It's the first proper porn I have seen. I'd stumbled on some in the park near our house, torn-out pages of a grubby *Penthouse* that had grown grubbier as they'd become entangled amongst twigs and dead leaves. But this wasn't that. This was clinical stuff, nothing pouty or cheeky here. There are close-up pictures of what I know must be vaginas; and horses' cocks and women with faces covered in semen. There is his hand around the back of my neck, the other hand clutching his erection. There is a whispered question that is also a threat: "Dost tha want to suck it?" He's in the zone, muttering variations on this sentence like it's a chant. "Tha wants it, don't you? Say it. Say tha wants to suck it." This man drills holes in roads for a living. The phrases "hands like shovels" and "viselike fingers" are more than metaphoric. This man is hard. We used to say the word all the time at school, "hard." It was much coveted, spoken with awe. We meant "able to fight," capable of doing some serious damage, but also not frightened of doing so. Someone who wasn't afraid of the consequences. This man, the man I'm calling Big Frankie Grant, is hard.

I don't know, I can't think, I don't remember. It's flickering and it's like the ride on the Big Dipper at Blackpool just before it reaches the top. It isn't like anything. It isn't Kevin being lost inside his own abjection, it's this man and his absolute presence, and his absolute presence as a man. It's in the chest and it's running away and it's something animal in me.

A door handle, something about how sticky the door handle was, how it made opening and twisting more difficult. His mum? Fuck, yes. His mum around somewhere, the kitchen, just back from town? He didn't. I'm not. I'm on Burnley Road. I think of going to the Accy Vic Hospital and then think how stupid because there's nothing I can tell them and nothing they can do anyway. I can't go home. Why, why can I not go home? Because things are supposed to be normal there, and I'm far from feeling normal.

There is a phone box. I pull the trick I've pulled scores of times, ringing the operator and telling her that the phone swallowed my money and what should I do and she says what number were you trying to ring caller and I tell her it because I know it off by heart and when someone answers I say the same words I've said scores of time too. I say, "Can I speak to Father O'Neill, please?"

I sit in the chair I have sat in back when he loved me and I loved him and I don't say anything. I don't remember the bus journey, or the walk up the hill. But here I am, back in the priests' house, a brandy to steady my nerves. I cannot tell him that I'd been sexually assaulted, that a man who I knew, who my parents had trusted, had tried to force me to suck his cock. To tell him that would have meant talking about his cock, or my own cock. And I knew that our cocks were strictly out of bounds, were no-go-zone cocks.

It would have meant saying something like: Father, you know the way I really loathe the way you used to touch me and shove your cock around on my stomach and come all over me? Well, another man wanted to do something similar to me. Bastard eh? No, not you!

Accusing one would have been to accuse the other, and I wasn't up to an accusation just then. I go to him in the hope of comfort. And I get it. I find comfort from one attempted abuser in the company of an actual abuser. He doesn't bother me for details of why I'm there. He doesn't try to fuck me, a non-fucking for which I feel pathetically grateful.

I took the secrets from one man who tried to force them upon me and hid them with a man who had made me carry secrets of his own. It's the logic of abuse. Secrets start to migrate to each other, they divide and multiply. Like cells, or bacteria.

I never did tell Kevin—or anyone else until now—about the assault. I must have fallen asleep, as I woke up on his sofa with sheets around me and an unused bucket by my side. He took me home, straightened out the parents.

I decide that nothing happened. And that nothing matters. And that somehow this nothingness is the same as freedom.

I flinch when people touch me. I miss myself.

I tell Julie that I feel almost grateful to Frankie Grant for allowing me to hate him with such unambiguous passion. There were no book-ish kickbacks with him, and therefore no ambivalence.

Compared to Kevin I hardly think of Frankie at all, but when I do I hope that he died alone. I hope that he died in his dead mother's house, surrounded by empty beer cans, pie crusts, and hard-core pornography, and that his body wasn't found for a week.

Julie thinks that I channel the complexities of my emotions for my first abuser into this seething loathing of my would-be second. She's right.

There is, I think, an emotional economy to sexual abuse that is similar to the law of diminishing returns. It is a logic that says the more sexual abuse there is, the less abusive it becomes, as though the abusive experience is somehow diluted through its repetition. If the abused get used to their abuse, as they must in order to survive, then it somehow ceases to register as abuse. Indeed the more abuse an abused child reports, the greater the suspicion that any "real abuse" has occurred at all.

The status of victim becomes problematized by the number of perpetrators. It's like a version of Oscar Wilde's joke about bereavement. To have had one abuser is unfortunate; to have two starts to look like carelessness. The presence of a second abuser lessens the impact of the first: it may even undermine it altogether. People begin to detect patterns. They start to wonder.

The matter is further complicated by the fact that the once abused become easier prey for their abuser in waiting. The abused are vulnerable, availably damaged, in need of all sorts of validation. If ever there was a group that was open to sexual exploitation, it is the already sexually exploited.

My old cognitive behavioral therapist called it a boundary issue. Which is one way of putting it.

NEXT

Inside out
And round and round

—Diana Ross, "Upside Down"

In my single bed, with its tightly tucked-in poly-cotton sheets, I lie
and think about how words divide up between odd and even numbers.
Ideally I'd like all words to be evenly numbered palindromes. I like
"palindrome." Not just a neat ten, but each of the two fives sounding
complete in themselves, complete enough to be words to which a solitary *s* need only be added to make both of them even. ABBA was of
course palindromic, as was their hit single "S.O.S."—a state of affairs
that I looked on as a personal triumph at the time. "Madam" is a palindrome, as are "level" and "refer." They are all five-letter words. I need
to find a non-five-letter palindrome or something terrible will happen.
"Civic," "radar" . . . five again. I put my hands on the sides of my head
and massage my temples, as though I could squeeze words out of my
brain like the juice from a lemon. There's got to be others, others with
more than five letters. My bedside clock is ticking. There has to be . . .
"Race car!" Thank Christ for that.

It's going to be light soon.

NEXT

Believe, and you shall be right, for you shall save yourself.
Doubt, and you shall again be right, for you will perish.
The only difference is that to believe is greatly to your advantage.

—William James, "Rationality, Activity and Faith"

Johnny is back from Cambridge. He arrives replete with hair and the overcaffeinated energy of the underfed. When I ask him about university he says, "There is nothing more stupid than a right-wing academic," a statement I instantly believe to be true even though I have no idea how. He tells me that the Labour Party is over, that he is going to get Barclays Bank to disinvest from South Africa, that the way to grow a beard is to shave twice a day (and then stop; obviously), that he is teaching himself Japanese, and that he has met Adrian Mitchell. He tells me that he has decided to like the Monkees more than the Beatles ("It annoys people") and he tells me we are going to the Hyndburn peace group.

I expect the Hyndburn peace group to be perfumed with joss sticks, populated with hairy men in Afghan coats and doe-eyed women who look like Melanie Safka. These people, I think, will be my people. They will share my utopian vision and hear the poetry in my soul. There will, I think, be a girl there who might snog me.

We are in the back room of the Labour Party office, a gable-ended terraced house opposite Accrington railway station. There is indeed an Afghan coat, belonging to an aging dropout called Sid, who it turns out isn't really called Sid but, "seeing as that's what everyone calls me, I may as well be." I recognize several faces from the *War Game* screening. There are a smattering of trade unionists (collective noun:

a discontent? a belligerence of?) who are sitting, with a row of empty chairs between them, next to a handful of people who clearly have god (small *g* as I now think of him) on their mind. There are the usual Labour-supporter suspects, their faces sallow from years in committee rooms, their postures already defeated. Opposite these, resplendent in combat trousers tucked into Dr. Martens boots, army jackets over slogan T-shirts, are the Accrington branch of the Socialist Workers Party.

There are three of them. One, male, late teens, has dyed red spiky hair and a ponytail that is dyed blond. He looks totally emaciated, as though he has just been kicked out of a hostel and can't remember where he lives. The second, a couple of years older, is what used to be referred to as "a big woman." Casual misogyny notwithstanding, it was also a term that was spoken with a certain reverence, an appreciative nod and respectful outbreath. This woman is a big woman, and she carries it with pride. Her hair is black and curly on top, shaved sharp at the back and sides. She has one of those disdainful mouths, its lips poised somewhere between a sneer and a dirty laugh.

Between them is a tall man with John Lennon specs and a woolen hat. He wears a mustache with which he has yet to feel comfortable and sits cross-legged, looking around him as though he is both deeply curious and bored at the same time.

I know that they are the SWP because they have copies of *Socialist Worker* tucked under their chairs and red-fist badges proclaiming their allegiance pinned to the lapels of their jackets.

I don't know what a socialist worker is exactly. I suspect I may already be one.

I sit with Johnny toward the back, near the table selling copies of other left-wing papers and pamphlets and books from publishers I have never heard of. The meeting was about the Tomahawk and about how the Americans were planning to launch their missiles from UK bases and how this was part of a wider move to mutually assured destruction. I remember being amazed that there were so many disagreements amongst a group who I thought were all in agreement. I had never really sat and thought about multi- or uni- or gradual disarmament, or the military-industrial complex. And what the hell was "a people's bomb"? I thought the purpose of the meeting would be how best to tell people that nuclear weapons were bad and that peace would be better. I thought the problem was that people simply didn't know. The issue, it seemed, was more complex than that.

Just how complex is revealed when the man with the Lennon specs stands up to speak. He is slightly hesitant; he has a diffidence that seems to be at odds with his height and that endears him to me straightaway. He says something like, "I firstly want to say that our society is organized violently or has violence at its core. All of our transactions and interactions are conducted from a place of inequality, which means that there is someone who has got the power and someone who hasn't."

He slowly settles into his argument, allowing his words and thoughts to find their rhythm. He says that the peace movement isn't necessarily the same thing as the CND movement, and the campaign to rid the world of nuclear weapons might be anything but peaceful. The people with lowercase god are beginning to shuffle. He says that we have to be careful not to fall back on a lazy anti-Americanism, of how there is a big difference between opposing a government's policies and opposing the people who have to live under that government, many of whom are as opposed to it as we are. (He must like Springsteen, then. I can be like him and still keep my record collection.) He says that the antinuclear movement needs to have what he calls a "class analysis," that we will continue to have these weapons only so long as people are prepared to keep on building them and that what he wants is a more fundamental rethinking of what it is that people should build.

I think, That's what I want to think.

NEXT

Why did girls never play air guitar? Did we sing along because singing along was what girls did or was it that girls only sang because they didn't play air guitar? These are not questions I asked myself at the time. I was pushing away such complications.

—Lavinia Greenlaw, *The Importance of Music to Girls*

In the Railway Hotel I sit and am introduced to another Accrington, an alternative Accrington that runs in parallel to the one I know but challenges all of its assumptions. I'm like Alice in Wonderland or Captain Kirk, boldly going down a rabbit hole where people are talking in coded acronyms and hallucinatory possibilities. I go there every night I'm not on King Street, and occasionally when I should be. I go there every Saturday lunchtime when I know they will have finished with their paper sales, petitions, and seemingly endless campaign collections. There's talk of TOM, who I never meet, but I'm assured wants the troops out of Ireland. There's the WRP and the RCT; the CP, the IMF, and the IMG. There's people who want to smash the PTA, which I think is a slight overreaction to the Parent-Teachers' Association until I find out they mean the Prevention of Terrorism Act. There's the Right to Work organizers who tell me that they are marching for the Right Not to Work. There's the ANL (Anti-Nazi League) and RAR (Rock Against Racism); there's entryists, separatists, and revolutionary defeatists. There's the Third International and Militant Tendency, the permanent arms economy and permanent revolution. And then there's Gary and Sara.

Gary was the guy who had spoken, the one who had convinced me of what I already suspected I thought. A journalist on the local paper, he took his profession seriously. He knew lots of people and had a rare gift for a newsman (let alone a Marxist) in that he liked people. Genuinely liked them, was fond of their eccentricities. He was a talented mimic and had a repertoire of voices that would wend their way in and out of his monologues. He loved to argue and he loved to drink, and in the Railway we did lots of both. It was rhetoric as much as revolution that excited Gary, the making of phrases, verbal jousting. He called me a "callow youth," a phrase whose assonance he clearly savored. He teased me for being "ideologically promiscuous" or "decidedly suspect" and of falling prey to "bourgeois distractions." Sara was the woman who sat with him, the ill-looking punk their friend Neil. Sara had dropped out of Salford University and was back living with her parents.

Within weeks I'd been "contacted," quickly befriended, eagerly adopted. Sara was my first woman friend and I adored her with every inch of love in my twisted postpriest sixteen-year-old soul. She was sharp and imperious: detector of bullshit, shredder of male ego. I would offer up my literary pretensions to her knowing that, hoping that, she'd shoot them down, her judgment prompting me on to greater folly and further frustration.

I told her that after the revolution everyone would be a poet, to which she said that she sincerely hoped not. When I told her that my favorite poet was e. e. cummings and he'd said that "a pretty girl who naked is / is worth a million statues," she sighed with the magisterial scorn of a headmistress nearing retirement:

What?

Er . . . a pretty girl who naked is / is worth a million statues.

What kind of statues?

Um . . . it's poetry.

Why does she have to be naked, and what do you mean by "pretty"? And why is that a compliment? Who made those statues and why does he need a million of them? What are you talking about?

As I said, I loved her.

Her heroines were Colette, Simone de Beauvoir, and Rosa Luxemburg and I devoured their stuff with all the passion of the newly converted. She introduced me not just to new music but to new ways of thinking about old music. She handed me a copy of Dylan's *Desire* with the barbed recommendation, "You'll probably like this. You can have it." She said she used to quite like him, but that after she heard a song he'd done called "Just Like a Woman," she couldn't take anything he said seriously ever again. Dylan! The man to whom me and Eggy and Harry and every other Picador-packing sixth former had been paying dutiful and attentive homage, summed up and dismissed. She didn't care that he had changed the lyrics to a song when he performed it live at the Budokan. She didn't even care that he had played the Budokan and "left his soul there." She just wanted him to stop singing about women who broke like little girls. I didn't know you were allowed to do that. Or certainly allowed to do that and still be cool. And Sara was cool. She'd been to Jim Morrison's grave in Paris and written "They've got the guns but we've got the numbers" on it. She bought her clothes in charity shops and assembled outfits that juxtaposed girly frocks with men's jackets, monkey boots and leggings. One night she was walking me home and a sleazy old man shouted something at her and she spun around and said, almost smiling, "If you talk to me like that again I'll cut off your dick and dangle it from a lamppost."

It was Sara who taught me about the Slits and Gang of Four, and it was Sara who took me to Salford University to see the Au Pairs. Until then my punk had been mostly American punk—New Wave—a term that seems less emphatic and more willing to find out what it wanted. Tom Verlaine's Television was recording songs that lasted more than ten minutes, longer than most UK punks' entire sets. The New Wave were allowed to do cover versions or record with Phil Spector or make records that flirted with other genres. In Sara's front room in her parents' house on Willows Lane, I discovered postpunk, a new world being built out of punk's initial declaration of year zero.

When she first played me the Au Pairs' *Playing with a Different Sex*, we danced. And not the jumping up and down dance that seemed to be the only dance available at the time, but a new one, a mock-militaristic-type strut with arms punching and head chicken-necking like Wilko Johnson's had not too many years before. It was strident, its anger in the hips as well as the stomach, abrupt and erect.

"I don't mind if you want to sleep on your oooooown," sings Lesley Woods. "I don't mind if you want to bring somebody hooooome, for the na na na na night." On maybe the fourth or ninth or eleventh listen, later the same night, it dawns on me that she is singing not just about relationships but about how relationships seem to be all about possession and ownership, about power and the proprietorial claims that people in so-called love appear to make on each other. "You must admit when you think about it that you're mine," goes the chorus, a mantra that becomes more sinister each time it is repeated. I was listening to a band that was deconstructing the love song even though I didn't know the word "deconstructing." I knew that love songs were always about people staking claims, surrendering, or belonging, that heartbreak was when you no longer "had" the person you thought you had, and that ecstasy was "getting" the person you wanted. I knew that because love songs told me so. Except that the Au Pairs didn't seem to think so. They seemed to think that it was a business transaction that sold both parties short, a dream soon rinsed out in the washing machine.

Gary was showing me how politics shaped the world, Sara how politics shaped me. I learnt that there was a totality to political life, that it went all the way through a person, down into their fibers and molecules. She told me why the word "cunt" is the worst swear word there is, about how language inscribes all of society's worst preconceptions about women and sex and sexuality. Politics, it seemed, was as much about bedrooms as barricades, as much concerned with private intimacies as it was about public demonstrations. It was the first glimmering I had that there might be a way for me to articulate what had happened to me.

I let Sara cut my hair: she spikes it up, but not too much. Kathleen is delighted. She asks me if Sara is my girlfriend.

They take me for a curry. I must pass at least five curry houses on my way to work, another five on the way to school. Yet it has never once occurred to me to go into one of them, any more than I would have popped into the local mosque or Methodist church. I silently shared my parents' suspicion that they smelled funny. I didn't believe the stories that were doing the rounds in the pubs and the school-yard, the ones about pets going missing or about how "they" didn't wash their hands properly after they'd been to the toilet. (I didn't, did I?) We all order lager and start to talk about how society deforms us, lies to us, makes it impossible for us to live authentically. (So why have I never gone for a curry before? Why did I get so angry with Jack and Kath when I saw the look on their faces when I told them where we were going?) Lager arrives and we talk about how the Front, as we now all refer to the National Front, is planning to march in Accrington, deliberately planning to march through Asian areas. (It certainly wasn't due to racism. Take a look at my record col-lection; all those thin white boys with their angry guitars. Just how much more anti-racist do you want?) Biriyani? (There was one Asian, or half-Asian, lad at school. Everyone called him Zebra, or Johnny Zeb, on account of the half-Asian half-white thing. It was, as we said, just a laugh.) Yellow food, with raisins? And everything mixed in to-gether, so you can't tell what's what? Crisps for starters that weren't really crisps, gravy that was nothing like proper gravy. I watch Gary and Sara tear chunks of naan bread, the ease with which they dip and scoop and seem blissfully unperturbed by all that glistening ghee. I listen to them talk about the coaches coming over from Salford and Manchester, comrades who will be helping to smash the Front. They're kind and confident and generous and I think of how much I wish I could be like them. And I think, I'm not very good at this.

I wasn't very good at being a vanguard Revolutionary Marxist gen-erally. I never actually joined the party, for a start. Which didn't help. I helped defend their paper sales in Blackburn during a time when some Nazi thug used to go and stand in front of them and stare for what seemed like hours. I went on some of the demos, especially the ones with bands. I loved sitting and talking with them, their passion and humor infectious, their commitment unquestionable.

And yet . . .

And yet I never quite believed any of it.

I didn't believe that the working class (or Jack and Kathleen Caveney as I called them) would suddenly find their consciousnesses permanently changed through the heroic experience of class struggle. I didn't believe that a revolution was going to happen, but if it was going to happen, and happen with all the historical inevitability that I was told it would, then why the hell did it need me to usher it along? I didn't care whether Russia was a deformed or a degenerate workers' state, or whether it was state capitalist or whether or not history would have been different if Trotsky hadn't got an ice ax or Lenin lived longer.

I knew my own religion well enough to know that class unity was not going to miraculously heal the wounds of the North of Ireland and that knowing all the words to Peter Gabriel's "Biko" was not the same as being an expert on apartheid.

It was partly a question of temperament. I either am, or was made, a skeptic. Father O'Neill saw to that. He turned me into a skeptic who is skeptical of his own skepticism, a skeptic par excellence. The Catholic Church had been my one totalizing system of belief, and I was damned if I was going to throw myself into another. Especially one which seemed to be as equally enthralled by the World to Come as my recently lapsed faith. The comrades would talk for hours about what life would be like after the revolution, a vision of utopia which had more than a passing resemblance to the Sermon on the Mount. I'd had one version of messianic redemption and it would be fair to say that it hadn't worked out too well. Both the Church and the party wanted to save mankind, only the party had a better soundtrack. And they didn't want to fuck me.

I go to a meeting, a big one, addressed by Tony Cliff, leading theorist of the SWP. He is marvelous, a Jewish Palestinian stand-up who moves from anecdote to analysis with liberal sprinklings of misplaced "bloodys." After the gig (and it had all the qualities of one), I talk to him for about fifteen minutes. I ask him about his own doubts, about how he manages to overcome his ambiguities. Arrgg, he says half amused, half disgusted, Hamlet! There was a man who was never a bloody revolutionary.

He was right. He wasn't. And neither was I.

The SWP didn't fix me. They couldn't. It wasn't their job. They were class warriors, whereas I was the victim of a different kind of war, one that was equally political but not one whose dialectics could be so easily synthesized. No picket lines were going to be formed demanding the emancipation of my twisted sexual oppression, no calls for industrial action. What would their banners have read, their chants have been? What do we want? Graham to be un-fucked! When do we want it? Er . . . ?

The comrades didn't really do the inner world, certainly not the politically unsound netherworld of the libido. It was all a symptom of a sick society, the outcry of an oppressed preacher, pornographer, psychiatrist. I remember Gary saying that there was nothing wrong with adults and children having a sexual relationship in itself, but that the dynamics of capitalism were such that a relationship like that would have to wait until after the revolution, until the inequities of power would (presumably) wither away (along with the state). I'm not sure he believed it then, and I'm sure he wouldn't believe it now, but at the time child fucking was being reclaimed by the left as sexual liberation. I went to find solace amongst the champions of the oppressed only to find that my oppressor himself was just another oppressed minority.

Their arguments were insistently right, and, therefore only half-right. It is no use just describing what people are, so the position went. We need to ask why they are the way that they are. What are the socioeconomic conditions that have constructed this thing we call the human being, what ideological forces have gone into producing their desires and hopes and dreams? Once they had achieved this task (and why wouldn't they?) and identified the machinations of capital as being the driving force of human history (which they unquestionably were, weren't they?), it seemed but a short step to building a revolutionary vanguard party (which would be them). The party would then galvanize the energy of the proletariat who, as they were the ones whose labor created capital in the first place, were the only ones with the power to overthrow it. Marx would almost certainly be quoted here: philosophers have always interpreted the world, the point, however, is to change it. Amen.

We go to see *Scum*, just me and Sara. There's a lean Ray Winstone, proving that he's the new fucking daddy by battering the old fucking daddy with pool balls wrapped in a sock. There's a cocky Mick Ford polishing his feet with boot polish, reciting his name and number to a jaded and bitter Bill Dean, a screw more battered by his job than any of the kids in his so-called care. And then, of course, there's a fragile Julian Firth, gang-raped in a greenhouse whilst the screws are on a cigarette break.

We walk out in stunned silence, tacitly agreeing not to speak until we get to the Railway. Once there Sara buys me a drink and we start to talk. She loves the way the film showed how the institution used race to divide the boys, like in the gym when they were deliberately set against each other. But it also showed that race wasn't an issue in the riot scene. They'd found some solidarity; and even though it unleashed the full brutality of the prison, it showed that the inmates could be a real threat when they found their common cause. She thought that the rape scene was entirely justified. It wasn't there gratuitously or to titillate. It was absolutely about how power is used sexually and sexuality is used violently. Brilliant film. She's right. Of course she's right. And I love her for it.

And I have something to tell her.

NEXT

It might indeed be possible to cover my face; but of what use was that, when I was unable to conceal the alteration in my stature?

—R. L. Stevenson,
The Strange Case of Dr. Jekyll and Mr. Hyde

I'm back in his office. Strange how this office has transformed itself whilst remaining exactly the same. It wasn't that long ago that I was here to sort out his books, my first job, although I didn't consider it a job at the time. He's let them slip again, his theology spilling over into his lit. crit., his desk groaning with collected Shakespeare. There's no wine on offer today, no chance of a sherry. I haven't brought him bad poetry, neatly written with my Parker pen. Neither do I want to talk about Beckett or Kafka or any other of our prime-numbered literary heroes.

He's not threatening to expel me either. There's no need, for one thing. I'll soon be gone of my own accord, and he can chalk me up as one of his success stories. He wants to talk about universities, about my choices. I can't remember now if I've already made the decision or if it's already been made. Either way, it's a subject he's keen to talk about. It is, after all, his school. But before that he says . . .

. . . that he heard me talk in the common room, the school debate about the Falklands War. Unsurprisingly enough I was against it. I'd cobbled together an argument that was half SWP and half common sense: no one knew where the Falklands even were, let alone that they belonged to the UK; British troops were being killed by weapons we had sold to the Argentinians; er, something about imperialism and, er, a cynical distraction from the real issues of the day. Like . . . unemployment, and stuff.

He said that he'd heard me and that I hadn't said a single thing that he hadn't known beforehand that I was going to say. He could have predicted it to the letter. I had talked in "isms" as though they were truths and seemed happy to wrap myself up in jargon, jargon (throat-clear) "of the most vacuous kind." And on he went, dismantling my performance limb from cliché-riddled limb.

I'm not the golden boy anymore. This isn't "How I know God" and a world of "aren't-you-clever" grooming. He's no longer entranced by my curiosity or eager to lend me books. There's no suggestion of a trip to the theater. This is: remember whose school this is, whose boy you are.

Maybe it's because I no longer know God, or maybe it's because I don't want him masturbating onto my stomach, but he's decided that I need taking down a peg or two. And he's right. Show me a seventeen-year-old boy who doesn't need their pegs taken down. It's what makes them boys, this placing of pegs.

I recall this conversation with more bitterness and shame than I do all the grooming and sexual assault and grubby furtive invasions combined. It seems to me a cruelty on which he really spent a lot of time and effort. Had he sat and rehearsed it, calculated the most efficient way to remind me of my insufficiency? Or was it more inspired than that, a semi-improvised riff that he warmed to as he watched my arrogant face try not to crumble?

In its own way, it was a masterpiece. It took power and pedagogy and politics and enacted them in such a way that all three became one. Like the Holy Trinity. It was a speech designed purposefully to undermine my status and reinforce his, to inscribe each other in the structures of the classroom. It said, I have created your rapacious adolescent ego and now I will expose it.

Thirty-three years later I still replay that conversation, just as images of him groping and grabbing and fucking me replay themselves: unexpectedly, intrusively, all-consumingly. I should have said, Lucky that Catholicism (and sneered when I pronounced the last three letters) is so refreshingly free of "isms," that it has no catech . . . ism or trinitarian . . . ism or that it's impossible to predict to the letter exactly what the Church's position is going to be on, oh, I don't know, abortion or contraception. And then I would say, Was that jargon free enough for you, you failed vampiric celibate?

But of course I don't say that. I don't say anything. I stand there and perform the trick I'd learned before, the one he'd taught me in his bedroom. I close my eyes without closing my eyes.

Julie says, It was payback; you had seen him naked and he had nowhere left to go. She says, He must have been frightened. He didn't know who you might tell, or what you might tell them. He thought you had power, and he needed to show you that he had more than you. And he knew that ideas were what you prized the most and so what made you most vulnerable. It was his job to know those things. He'd had years of practice.

So I close my eyes whilst keeping them open, and let his words become sounds, like the voices in an out-of-sync film. He is nothing more than traffic noise now, mild feedback. But he wants more.

Hull is relatively close, should you choose it as your university. He chews this over, as if being close is a factor, as if he is going to be popping over on the weekends. A few of our boys have gone there. Larkin's the librarian.

I didn't know that. I imagine Philip Larkin stood behind the desk, stamping piles of books and collecting overdue fines, sssshhh-ing people. It never occurred to me that Larkin would have another job. I wonder how much poets get paid. I know that I won't be going where any of my contemporaries have been, or are planning to go. My plan is to become a virgin.

He says that I don't really appreciate how far away Kent is (I do because I've looked it up and thought, Kent's a long way away), that it's one of those places that sounds great (it sounds great) until you realize how difficult and expensive it is to get home (I won't have to come home) and how that can be very isolating (isolating? I know!) and that reading English can be isolating enough as it is.

The film is back in focus, back in sync. He's talking to me and it's my turn to speak. I say, Not English, English and American literature. I don't say this as well as I say it in my head. I say it in the shallow-breathed way I seem to have developed, where words don't come out at first, but then once they do come out I have difficulty in turning them off. I think, but don't say, You did English. American literature is my way of reclaiming English literature. I'll make it mine again. I'll read books you haven't read.

He barks a cough, catches it in his fist.

He doesn't know much about Warwick except, wasn't it the stomping ground of "that bitch" Germaine Greer? (I forget, you hate women. Not just Greer, but I've noticed: the girls in the sixth form, the female teachers. You don't know what to do with them. Or to them.) And E. P. Thompson? He's building up to an aphorism, some bon mots that he'll quote himself on later. He clears his throat. Here it comes: a redbrick university that builds revolting students.

It sounds wonderful. It sounds like heaven.

NEXT

. . . his armor-hard back.
—Franz Kafka, "The Metamorphosis"

The head down, the eyes darting up in a way that is both accusatory and furtive. Cigarette held between thumb and middle finger, the reverse of the extended two fingers favored by girls. Smoke released with a cocky indifference. Cuticles of fingers chewed, the autumnal stains of nicotine to be sandpapered away later with the side of a matchbox.

Spit to be spat every ten or fifteen minutes; options of hawking or flobbing or squirted from between the teeth.

Hands—where else?—in pockets.

Subject of discussion: Fit Girls, The Fitness of Girls, Of Girls and Their Fitness.

Gradations thereof: 100 Percent Fit, Totally Fit, Fairly Fit, Really Fit, Absolutely Fit: occasionally a single and emphatic "Fit!"

Taxonomies of Fit: arse on that, tits on her, lips and their cocksucking potential.

Gestures: the side of the left hand brought karate-style into the inner cleft of the right arm causing elbow to raise the forearm in a mock erection with closed fist taking the role of "bell end." Thumb and forefinger placed in an O for okay and then penetrated by the finger or fingers of other hand. Tongue extended and flickered.

Noises: slurping, howling, barking, groaning, bleating.

I'm getting better at this, this pantomime of sexual bravado. I run my hand through my hair (stop that!) and make sure the gel's still doing its job, keeping the spikes in place on what is a not-quite punk mullet haircut. I say, I'm saying nothing . . .

It gets me an appreciative laugh. I say it in a way that suggests just how much I would have to say if I were to say something, but that I'm too grown-up to say it. Which is true, but not in the way that they think it's true.

My schoolmates talk about sex all the time, which means that I don't have to. I use my silence about the sex I'm not having as a cover story for the silence about the sex that was done to me.

They play games of "would you rather?," a competitive form of gross-out in which "I wouldn't" is not an option. Eat shit or suck dick? Suck snot through a sock or go down on your granny? I think, One of them is going to say, Fuck the Rev. or . . . ? If they say it, then I'll choose it, because saying it might just exclude me from the suspicion of having done it. Saying it could even be my alibi. But then again it might stick, might become a defining joke. It's a high-risk strategy: there's sour bile in the back of my throat. But of course no one says it. Why would they? It's not that kind of game.

I wonder if I'm the only virgin amongst them, a virgin who also knows more about what sex really is than all of them combined.

One of them has an actual girlfriend. They have, he's told me, full-blown condom-wearing sex. She is called Kay and wears pencil skirts and low-cut jumpers. I decide that I'm in love with her.

My grown-up leftie mates don't seem to approve of sex, which is fine by me. It's one of the reasons they're my mates. They think it's overrated, an empty system-propping pleasure, like shopping or going to a disco. Sex replicates the power relationships of capitalism, coerces us into compliance, divides us into monogamous units. Sometimes that also sounds fine by me, though I don't say that bit.

Kay has decided I'm her safe not-going-to-try-anything new male friend. Her favorite records are Pink Floyd's *Relics*, Deep Purple's *Machine Head*, and *Kings of the Wild Frontier* by Adam and the Ants.

I somehow know that the best way to guard secrets is to get other secrets, ones that are easily discovered. Wear this secret well. Be a triple agent. Your secret will be that you are someone who has secrets. Advertise the fact that you have secrets and you'll be allowed to keep the secretive secrets secret.

I bring Kay to the Railway where she meets the comrades who

she doesn't think of as comrades. They think she's my girlfriend even though they don't say the word "girlfriend." I enjoy the perception of having her as my girlfriend and know that it's much much better than her actually being my girlfriend. An actual girlfriend would want to touch me, and even though that's what I want, I worry that it will make me sick. And I don't want her to think that she makes me sick.

NEXT

One can begin so many things with a new person!—even
begin to be a better man!

—George Eliot, *Middlemarch*

Yet somewhere and somehow I find Dave Hesmondhalgh. Or he finds
me. Ask Dave how we met and he'll tell a couple of stories about
having met me as a young lad, twelve or thirteen, playing Ping-Pong
down at the local sports center. He'll tell you about a lad with long
hair who was notably and intensely competitive, ungraciously celebrating his every fluke. I don't remember this, but I do remember
seeing Dave at the peace group, a lad my age with a nose for the issues, keen to make a difference. I remember an afternoon drink in the
Railway and a conversation about the Mighty Wah's "The Story of the
Blues." I remember an invitation to Oxford, where he was studying,
and being slightly affronted that I wasn't the only clever kid on the
block. I remember him reading things with a pen in his hand and
the way he gripped the pen like a chopstick. But what I remember
most vividly about Dave "Hesy" is thinking that here is someone with
whom I want to be friends.

He was an Accrington boy but not a Catholic, although his mother
had been. He was an athlete without the sportiness, a lad without the
laddishness, an activist without the dogma. It was Dave who reminded
me of what a life outside Accrington could look like, yet also what
there was in this strange little mill town worth keeping hold of. Dave
was the first person I met who made being kind look charismatic.

He invites me to Oxford for the summer after my exams.

Exams are all I can think of.

NEXT

Now I am quietly waiting for
the catastrophe of my personality
to seem beautiful again.

—Frank O'Hara, "Mayakovsky"

Escape. I need to get out of Accrington, away from Jack and Kath. I need Rev. Kev to stop looking at me in the corridor, in the library, in the smokers' corner when I'm smoking with Kay. I need to get to university. Which means doing well at A levels. Which means studying. Which means spending time at Jack and Kath's, in the library, and smoking with Kay.

I'm looking now at the diaries I kept then. There is page after page of homework schedules, revision timetables, the day broken down into the free periods in which I can cram notes from books into the inside of my head. Jock Roland recommends that I go over every essay, every notebook, and underline the most relevant paragraphs. I do this. I then copy out those paragraphs and go through them again, underlining the most relevant sentences in them. I then copy them out, and so on. And on. I record my entire history notebooks onto a portable cassette player. I go to sleep to the sound of my own voice talking about the Declaration of Independence and Causes of the First World War. I work each night from six until nine, when I then go down to the Railway, notebooks in hand. I take *Sons and Lovers* down with me to King Street and memorize quotes about Miriam being frigid. In between collecting glasses I underline couplets from *An Epistle to Dr. Arbuthnot*, and when anyone asks me what I'm doing I say "nothing."

I still miss god who, as John Lydon's Public Image Limited now reminds me regularly, spelt backwards is "dooooog." I miss Dave Hes., even though I've only just met him. And I miss my mum and dad, even though I hate them. Me and Jack just don't fit together anymore. The last time we did was when we went to see *The Long Good Friday* together, John Mackenzie's brooding vision of an old-style gangster watching his London, his "manor," slip away from him. I can feel Jack's discomfort at the swearing, but also his sheer pleasure at watching Bob Hoskins swagger around the docklands, a man torn between impotent rage and crumbling self-belief.

We walk home and he says how they don't make them like that anymore, and I say they obviously do because they just made that. He says Hoskins was like Cagney and Helen Mirren like Bette Davis, especially in that hat with the veil. I say that they were also like John Cleese and Connie Booth in *Fawlty Towers*: he keeps messing things up and she keeps straightening them out. He says no they weren't, they were like Bogart and Bacall. I say no they weren't, they were like Kermit and Miss Piggy. He says you're like Kermit. And Miss Piggy. And the scruffy one that plays the drums, and I love him like I used to love him before.

But we don't go to the flicks anymore. Or skim through the *Radio* and *TV Times* together, hungry for the week's films. Neither do we go for walks, or play snooker; and we definitely no longer joke about me being one of the Muppets. Take away the movies and he can't find a way in. I overhear him and Kath, his complaint that he "can't do right for doing wrong." It's a phrase that used to send me into paroxysms of rage, the closed-circuitry of it, the way in which its tautology seemed inescapable. Kath too is at the end of her tether. She knows it can be difficult, what with the work and the exams. Much though she likes Gary and Sara, she's not sure that it's good for me, to always be around people that much older than me.

She suggests that I get in touch with Father O'Neill. He, of course, is not a person who is older than me. He is not a person. He is a priest, and as such wise and ageless. If anyone will be able to sort out her son it's surely his headmaster-mentor-teacher.

I punish them with my reticence. I tell myself that nothing of mine will ever be theirs again, that their blindness to the abuse-that-I-still-don't-call-abuse disqualifies them from all my future intimacies, confidences, troubles. Fuck them and their petty-minded deference. Fuck the rosary beads that are draped over the luminous statue of the Sacred Heart that still stands on the chest of drawers in my bedroom. Fuck the old pope and the new pope and every groveling pope lover who descended on Manchester when he came to visit the other month. Fuck Lourdes and the stupid fucking holy water that we keep on the sideboard next to the missionary box. Fuck also everyone who goes to Lourdes: if they're stupid enough to believe that jumping in a river will cure them, then I hope they fucking drown. Fuck Mass and confession and the stupid fucking dog collars that Father Fuck once told me would look good on me. Fuck the Holy Ghost, the baby Jesus and particularly fuck the Virgin fucking Mary.

What was it about the Marists, about the Society of Mary, that appealed to you, Herr Reverend? Why not the Jesuits, the famed Society of Jesus, a bunch of intellectual heavyweights if ever there was one. Not up to it? Or too long? Their gig lasts seven years, doesn't it, a long time to be kept away from young boys and all that young energy. But no, it wasn't that. Or just that. It was a mum thing, a woman thing, a mum who is a woman but doesn't have sex thing. I could see it when you took me home to meet Winnie (and fuck her too, while we're at it). I could see the way you were solicitous of her, needed her to bless the unholy fucking pedo-rimony that was taking place under her roof. You needed her to like me, and me to like her. (I didn't, by the way. That night's sexual assault kinda distracted me from appreciating her finer points.)

NEXT

The house next door is never the sanctuary it at first appears
to be.

—William Maxwell, *Time Will Darken It*

Which raises the following question. If I am as enraged as I seem to be
by the Holy Roman Church, then what am I doing defending it to a
pair of revolutionary socialists in the bar of the Railway Hotel?

I can't remember how the subject came up, although if you are
drinking in a pub with Gary and Sara the topic of politics and state
control is never far from the surface. It wasn't Catholicism in particular, it was Christianity in general. Which meant God and goodness,
the truth of material conditions versus the idealistic fantasies of the
well-intentioned. It meant "opiate of the people" and religion as a
form of ideological anesthesia. It meant "no need to bother about this
world, be happy in the next." Gary and Sara are adamant that religion
equals political passivity, a way of getting the docile masses to embrace the status quo.

Although . . . ?

Although what . . . ?

Well, it's also true that the reason I'm sat here with you two tonight
is because of my religion. I mean the reason I hate all this capitalist
stuff is because it's wrong. What it does to people. The way it pits
them against each other. It's un-Christian as much as anything else.

So what you're saying is . . . ?

That maybe religion can inspire people as much as oppress them. I
mean isn't the "opiate of the people" thing a good thing too? Opiates
can help you dream. There's this poet I'm into called Baudelaire and
he was into opium and he . . .

Opiates drug you, keep you where you are. In bed or in the gutter. Listen, comrade (a sure sign that the stakes were being raised). Spending your life on your knees before some imaginary being is just being on your knees. It doesn't matter if it's God or . . . No one ever changed society with an opium pipe or sticking a needle in their arm. God's just a drug for people who don't do drugs.

Drinks are drunk, cigarettes rolled and lit. I agreed with him. So why was I disagreeing with him? Why could I hear my blood flushing through my head like water through a cistern? Why were my hands shaking? I can't talk properly when I can't breathe. So: breathe.

But why is it either-or? It doesn't have to be pray or strike. Obviously you could do both. Look at Solidarity. I bet they're mostly Catholics.

I didn't say it was. (Bristling) You're mixing me up with one of your poets. (Ouch) I'm saying that the ideas people have in their heads come from the actual world around them. They're not beamed in telepathically by some extraterrestrial or some pope who's never wrong. Infallible fucking pope? How's that for control? "I am the mouthpiece of God and therefore I cannot be wrong."

Papal infallibility doesn't mean that. It means . . . never mind. The point is that your version of socialism is going to be pretty bloody soulless if there's no room for poetry or the spirit.

Poetry that ordinary working people never read or understand, you mean . . .

And the joke about it is . . .

Joke?

And the joke about it is that you have your own version of papal infallibility, it's called the party line . . .

I disagree with the party all the time . . .

About tactics and the odd film review maybe. But you're not prepared to question the fundamental premise of the party, which is that you're right, and you know better and that you're the fucking messiahs who are going to lead us poor bastards to the promised land of socialism . . .

I thought you of all people would know that religion is the very

worst pretext for every form of oppression imaginable . . . (And looking becomes staring. Glasses pushed back.)

(What does he mean? Me "of all people"? He means I'm a Catholic.
That's what he means. That's all he means.)

And every kind of liberation imaginable . . . Look at the priests
fighting in Nicaragua and El Salvador. They've got more revolutionary
fucking spirit in their little finger than you've . . . (Fiery)

Scratch any history of oppression and you'll find some religious jus-
tification for it, someone with God on their side telling other people
what's good for them . . . (Pugnacious, head up)

And the hunger strikers and the IRA and the bit in the Bible where
Jesus trashes the moneylenders and rich men and the eye of a needle
and you are so fucking smug and you don't even know what you're
talking about and . . . (Trembling, the catch in the voice)

Or worse. People using their so-called belief as a smoke screen for
doing whatever they want . . . for all sorts of . . . for controlling and
brainwashing and . . . keeping them in . . . and . . . Priests. And sex.

And altar boys.

I know then that he knows. That Sara has told him what I told
her after we saw *Scum* and that I asked her not to tell anyone. Looking
back it seems ridiculous for me to have thought that she wouldn't tell
her partner, that a young (twenty-four? twenty-five? year-old) woman
could have carried round the burden of my secret without feeling the
need to share it with someone, someone with whom she shared not
just a bed but a whole political worldview. It was something that she
could not have not told him.

That isn't what I thought then. What I felt then was that there
is nowhere left for me to go. Not my family (nor the WMC job that
was its extension). Not the school and its panoptical library, not my
laddish mates with their "would you rathers." And not, it would seem,
my newly found friends. It wasn't just the telling. It was that my secrets had proved to be less important than winning an argument, my
suffering secondary to scoring a political point.

This wasn't the first of our fallouts, and it certainly wasn't the last.
My would-be comrades were not my therapists. They had no obli-

gation to carry my wounds, let alone heal them. They were guilty of not understanding something I didn't understand myself, of failing to provide a cure for a condition that had not yet been diagnosed. Which didn't stop me from hating them.

I would behave abominably to Gary and Sara: not then, but later. Marinate resentment in two years of alcohol, bring it slowly to a boil in a cocktail of psychiatric diagnoses and prescription pills. Add the deflated political commitment of two people who had relocated to Sheffield in support of a strike only to witness the demolition of those people and the community they were fighting to defend. Add arguments about AA and failed bids for sobriety. Let those rekindle the flames of arguments about Higher Powers and God and what we think we owe to each other. Throw in the Leadmill nightclub and wraps of white powder, simmer over petty grievances, and serve in the early, truth-telling hours.

Yet there is a wider issue here, one that justifies neither my disproportionate rage nor the comrades' emotional myopia. It's to do with the left's inability to deal with the complexities of the inner world (not just mine). The party would insist on how capitalism was riddled with contradictions. They would insist again and again that it was capitalism that produced the human subject. So why then were they unable to acknowledge the fact that the human subject was therefore riddled with all sorts of contradictions? It seemed that the oppositions inherent in being a person produced by the capitalist system could be resolved by the simple act of joining the SWP, an act in which the person would emerge enlightened, Buddha-like, with an understanding of the world so politically acute that those pesky dialectics of history would dissolve in the time it took to sell a copy of *Socialist Worker*.

There was a machismo and muscularity to the left in the early eighties. They were suspicious of all those other outsiders who dwelt at the margins—queers, artists, pacifists, nonaligned lefties, veggies, cautious progressives. There was a puritanical contempt for anything they considered frivolous—sport, fashion, a whole world of popular culture that was seen as little more than "bourgeois deviation."

And they simply did not know what to do with or about sex, let alone sexual abuse. It was, at best, a conversation to be postponed until after the revolution. Meanwhile, sex could not help but reproduce the social relations of capital, and as such was deeply suspect. "Out of order" was the phrase I remember most clearly, as though other people's thoughts, emotions, and opinions were like the toilets on a train.

NEXT

"... the peace of a whole family,—the feelings of a father,—
the honor of a mother,—the interests of religion,—the eternal salvation of an individual, all suspended in one scale.
What do you think could outweigh them?"
    "Nothing," I replied ardently."
                    —Charles Robert Maturin, *Melmoth the Wanderer*

How do you disclose your secrets to someone when your secrets are so
shameful they remain a secret to yourself? How are we to reveal our
selves when we have no language with which to shape or define or recognize ourselves, when we have no frame of reference?

One answer is that we fall back on approximations. We make do.
If there isn't a conceptual framework available in which we can articulate ourselves, then we use the ones that are available—euphemisms,
insinuations, disavowal.

If the secrets that are thus shared are shameful, their guilt turned
inward, then the inadequate nature of language becomes part of the
problem. We feel we have lost some intimate part of ourselves and
if we want to communicate this loss, we are forced to do so by this
secondhand, jumble-sale, ragbag thing called language. No wonder
disclosure feels like a betrayal. The abuse is itself a betrayal and now
we need to talk about this betrayal through a medium that is bound
to betray us.

In disclosing my experiences of sexual abuse I am bound to sell myself short. The available language is inadequate and so I have to cut
my experiential cloth accordingly. I tidy it up, or minimize it. I may
ironize, or dramatize, or contextualize, and yet after each statement
what I want to shout is: But it's not that. Not really. It's something else.

This is, I think, one of the many reasons people are reluctant to come forward. There is not only the shame, the fear, the guilt, but there is also the sense that what they have to say is so deeply embedded (and embodied) that talking about it would be failing to do it justice. Each statement or revelation would in a sense be just one more injustice, another thing stolen from you, just another way the inner world and the outer world fail to connect.

This is true now. It was certainly true in 1983. I used to hear my parents talk in theatrical whispers about rumors they may have heard about a friend of a friend, or someone at work, or at the bingo. Eyes would dart and widen, lips would purse. I would feel the whole atmosphere of the room grow solemn. "I'm not saying . . ." The conversation would always begin with a plausible deniability. I soon learnt that "it" was the worst thing someone could be accused of, that you had to be "very, very careful" (two "verys," serious stuff) of what got said, of malicious gossip ("you know what folks are like").

The most explicit phrase that was used was "interfered with," the last syllable to be said in a way that trailed off, as though fully enunciating the words might bring them to life. Before I'd actually been interfered with, the phrase "interfered with" would always make me think of a science fiction film in which some newfangled discovery backfired on its inventors.

"Interference"; is that what had happened? It didn't seem right somehow; nowhere near.

When I told Sara that I had something to tell her, I told her that something "like that" had happened to me, the "that" being the rape scene from *Scum*. This wasn't accurate, but it was all I had. It hadn't been rape as I understood it. Nothing violent, nothing stuck up the arse in a Borstal greenhouse. I was lying to her even as I revealed myself. I'd said "something like that happened to me" because I wanted to tell her that *something* had happened to me. I wanted her to know I'd been interfered with without using the words "interfered with." The closest I had was an Alan Clarke film.

Dealing with abuse means talking about something you don't want to talk about, telling people things you'd rather they didn't know. It can feel like a violation, or coercion. It can feel like abuse.

If this was a novel, then the scene in which I tell my "something" to Johnny Mullen would start: "And so I tell him. I tell him everything." It would be a breathless recap on the whole sorry saga; the grooming, the drunken seductions, the molestations. But it isn't and I don't.

We're in the Railway, where else? He's back from time abroad, Spain or France? Part of his course. I mumble something about being in a relationship that I hadn't wanted to be in. Or had wanted to be in, but only at the beginning. Or not really a relationship, but sort of. But then it went wrong. I went wrong. It got all fucked up. It was my fault. I'd led this person on, been flattered, used him for all sorts of things. He knew, knows the person. I tell him who the person is. It's complicated.

I'm not racked by uncontrollable sobbing. I don't wrap my arms around my shoulders and sit, head down, rocking to and fro as my shoulders heave and snot accompanies my barely audible confession. There's no catharsis or clarity, and no close-up.

I'm looking at my friend, who must be what—twenty?—but who is impossibly wise by virtue of going to university, to Cambridge University. And by virtue of being wise. He still cuts his own hair; there's bits of red in it and a plait that he's made at one side that he tugs at all the time we're talking. His secondhand jacket is covered in badges, including a badge that says Wearing Badges Is Not Enough. There's a pause that lasts for about a minute but feels like ten. And then he says, "Fuck."

"Fuck" felt right: it still does. It captures the mixture of outrage and futility, an excuse for the jaw to drop and the mouth to remain frozen. It was a "fuck" that registered disbelief even as it registered the truth of what I was saying, a "fuck" that acknowledged the impossibility of saying anything else.

I've had my share of therapists over the years (collective noun: a sincerity of? a self-harm of?) and not enough of them have said "fuck." A few have said "bastard," which sidesteps the ambiguity and makes me

NEXT

I want no secrets or soul-states, nothing ineffable; I am neither virgin nor priest, to play at having an inner life.

—Jean-Paul Sartre, *Nausea*

I was made guardian of secrets, made to protect myself from the adult world whilst protecting adults from each other. And themselves. I swallow the injustice whole. It makes me seethe. It makes me generate internal dialogues, dialogues in which I emerge vindicated and victorious. I say to myself that when he says . . . I will say . . . He might say This, and I will say That. It will be beautiful, my saying of the That. It will be a That that everyone will understand, and, once I've said it, all the other This-es will fall into place. But I also know that I'll never get the chance to say anything, which makes my rehearsals all the more frantic.

And, looking now at my Dear Diaries from then, I see that:

My handwriting has become fucked up. I used to have "a lovely hand," or so I was told; the kind of hand on which you could build a career (clerk, cushy job. Look at his hands). My parents and teachers were committed graphologists; both believed that legible handwriting was the sign of a trustworthy character. And so my *J*s and my *G*s announced themselves with a flourish, imperiously self-contained in upper case, swinging and flirtatious in lower. I was taught to turn a page upside down once it was written, to appreciate the harmony between the vertical and the horizontal, the bold slants and promiscuous vowels.

Now (i.e., then), postfucked and moody, I'm told that I have "doctor's writing," a phrase I'm pleased with until I find out what it means. Now (i.e., now) I see exactly what it means. My handwriting has become a thing trying to hide from itself, something that is reluctant to express what it is there to express. My *M*s and *N*s are indistinct, as are my *I*s and *L*s. My once proudly descending *Y*s now seem apologetic, embarrassed, whilst the upstrokes of my *E*s and *C*s guiltily merge into the next letter as though they are ashamed to show their face. My handwriting is the bearer of bad news: it resents itself and wants me to know that it is there under protest.

None of which would really matter if I didn't have to sit A levels in six, five, four, and counting weeks.

My interview at Warwick University has gone well. A giant of a man, with jam-jar glasses, crazy hair, and a booming voice told me that Warwick University is nowhere near Warwick, but that I should be thankful as Warwick is a ghastly place. That it is closer to Coventry, which is also pretty ghastly but redeemed by the fact that no one from the university lives there. That those who are at the university live either in Leamington (students mainly: fairly ghastly), Kenilworth (admin staff and the occasional poet: completely ghastly), or London (lecturers: ghastly, obviously, but in ways that often mitigated against its ghastliness).

It was love at first sight.

The giant's name is Tom Winnifrith. He gave me a poem by William Carlos Williams which began: "I will teach you my towns-people / how to perform a funeral." I had ten minutes to think of "something, anything, interesting to say about it." The only thing I knew about Carlos Williams was that he was mentioned in the sleeve notes to Dylan's *Desire* ("Dr. Poet WC Williams dying nearby said, 'A new world is only a new mind.'"). This, I suspected, would not be sufficient to appease the other doctor, not dying, waiting even nearer by.

I went into his office and said, "Alienation! From death! And everything! Once people died and everyone was, er, sad, grieving. And now people die and we don't know how to, um, be sad, or, like, grieve, not like they used to. . . . It's like Bob Dylan said . . ."

Tom Winnifrith sighed. It was a sigh that belonged to a benevolent Greek deity looking down at the tenth mortal this week who had come to ask for a favor that would be his undoing. He may not have actually said, despairingly, "Oh God," which doesn't stop me from remembering him saying it. But grant me the favor he did: he made me an offer. I'd be accepted if I got two As and a B at my A Level.

NEXT

"I should like to bury something precious in every place where I've been happy and then, when I was old and ugly and miserable, I could come back and dig it up and remember."

—Evelyn Waugh, *Brideshead Revisited*

I go to Oxford to stay with Dave Hesmondhalgh; he's working at a cinema (Penultimate Picture Palace?) and takes me to see *Chinatown*. When Nicholson tells the "fuck like a Chinaman" joke, unaware that Faye Dunaway is behind him, Dave shuffles in his seat, and, for a second, I think he might be bored. Then I sense that he can barely contain his delight. At that moment he's my favorite person. We go to *Pat Garrett and Billy the Kid*, *Eraserhead* the night after. He carries a Faber copy of Robert Lowell in his jacket pocket and he cooks me spaghetti. We take drugs and talk about how difficult it is to talk about fancying women without sounding like a wanker, and he tells me a story about his ex-girlfriend and then says he's just realized that that makes him sound like a wanker, and I tell him it doesn't and he says thanks for saying that, Graham, and I think how not that many people use my name. I tell him about Warwick and Tom Winnifrith and he tells me about meeting the poet James Fenton and we agree that our lives are going to be interesting.

NEXT

I hope to God you're not as dumb as you make out . . .
                                        —Orange Juice, "Rip It Up"

Even though they call the results "your" results, they don't send the results to you. You are still property of the school, your accomplishments are theirs (although you know that your failures will be your own). And the school is still the property of the Church, even though it is now a sixth form and there are no more blazered boys skidding down the corridors. What there is is a group of unblazered boys (collective noun: a slouch?) and pencil-skirted girls (a pout of?) loitering nervously outside the headmaster's office. They are telling each other that they don't care, that they already know they've done crap, messed up, fucked up, screwed up, didn't do any work, can always do re-sits, got a job anyway so it don't really matter. Except it does matter. To me it matters more than anything has ever mattered. It means:

no more office and the being called to and the sitting there in a lower chair with the sun in my eyes and being told what I've done wrong and remembering the That that I can't acknowledge even though I don't want it acknowledged even though it's everywhere in the office in the space between the chairs

The boys emerge from his office one by one.

no more WMC and the look at what he's wearing and he's probably one of them punk rockers and get us half a bitter and two fat ladies and Frankie Grant looking at me like a butcher eyeing up a carcass and a big King Street welcome for whoever's love is in the air and you'll have this glass when I've bloody well drunk it

There's shrugs, stoic smiles, tears angrily brushed aside.

no more clinging to the Railway like a life raft hoping that the revolution arrives whilst I've still got the time to enjoy it and doesn't "merciless criticism of all things existing" mean appraisal and not just finding fault with everything all the time?

It's a sixth-former's waltz, each person egging on the other to go before them: After you, no, after you, no really, after you. After me? Surely after you? It's like a Marx Brothers routine.

Just. Fucking. Go. In.

I go in. He's perched on the edge of his desk, wearing a black priest suit and white dog collar. I know this film, I've seen it dozens of times. Like Kathleen says, I can play this bloody part myself. I click the camera on behind my eyes. It's connected to the switch in my chest, which is the reason I find it hard to breathe sometimes. The projector is running smoothly, its whirrrrring like a lullaby. He's Leonard Rossiter as Mr. Shadrack in *Billy Liar*, carpeting Billy about the petty cash. He's Donald Wolfit as Mr. Brown giving Joe Lampton the third degree in *Room at the Top*. He's Captain Bligh and Miss Mackay, Colonel Kurtz and Baby Jane. There's a slow-mo shot of him handing me an envelope, cut to a close-up of his face, inscrutable. I'm Steve McQueen in *The Cincinatti Kid*, Paul Newman in *The Hustler*. I'm a bratty Ann Blyth and De Niro's Johnny Boy and a silky Cary Grant.

I open up the already opened-up envelope.

Inside the envelope is the best book I'd ever read: it said, You can be rid of the person standing before you and meet people who know nothing about you. It said, All knowledge comes with a price but some books will pay you back. It said, You can turn your back on this man's needy greedy soul and his joyless seedy cock. It said A, A, B.

NEXT

It is after all a little difficult to catch the reflexion in your own armor.

—Patrick White, *The Living and the Dead*

Jack and Kath didn't tell the entire earth's population that their son was going to, had been accepted at, been offered a place with. They spread the news even more widely. They descended on relatives I never knew I had, cousins by marriage, a woman who lived in Bacup who had been "like an aunty to my dad when he was younger" (what?), the bloke in the cake shop whose daughter had once babysat and who "still asked about me." My aunt Mary was the one with the phone, which meant increased visits and "while you're there, ask her if you can give Gladys Arkwright/Mrs. Pickles/Pat from work/Vera from bingo/Ida from church/Elsie from the hairdressers a quick ring and tell 'em your news."

So I rang and told them my news. Apparently I didn't tell enough of 'em, as Kath was forced to go to the *Lancashire Evening Telegraph* and the *Accrington Observer*, holding in her hand a piece of paper, like Chamberlain just back from Munich.

I wasn't sure if Sartre's mum had rung up a local Parisian newspaper to tell them that "our Jean-Paul has just been accepted to the L'École normale supérieure (and make sure you spell his name right)," but I was pretty certain that his dad hadn't told the steward of his local working men's club, and that the steward hadn't then told whichever garçon called out the bingo numbers, and that there was therefore no announcement for Jean-Paul (in between the announcements for the arrival of pies, rolls, and, presumably, croissants) that we'd like to give a big Le Roi Rue congratulations to a young man, you all know him, who has served this club faithfully for the past couple of years and who will be leaving us to go to university and that there was no big "oooooo" sound, a sound that would echo in J-P's head every time he sat down to write *Being and fucking Nothingness*.

It is on King Street that I spend my last night in Accrington. I'm told I can go early. (It's a long way to Coventry. Should have been sent there a long time ago. Etc.) Tommy slips me an envelope with a card addressed to the Professor. It contains ten pounds plus my wages and is signed by all the bar staff. I sit in the lounge with Jack and Kath. I can feel a conversation brewing. If there's one thing I don't want, one thing I can't have, on the night before I leave home, then that's a conversation about leaving home.

Jack says, This time tomorrow you'll've left home . . .

Kath says, But you can always come back home, if you don't like it down there. We won't pressure you. This will always be your home.

And then she cries.

Whilst my mum is crying, do I really think: You should have protected me but couldn't protect me and so I won't miss you even though I will miss you because you loved me and are decent and that the pride you have in me is misplaced but, no, I won't be coming back, ever? Probably not.

By my reckoning, Kath and Jack were born, worked, and died within a four-mile radius. The distance from the house in which my dad grew up to the house in which my mum grew up is about one hundred and fifty yards. Because they were both Catholics, they both attended the Sacred Heart school, the school that took its name from the local church in which they (along with both my aunties) were married. I would also attend this school, be baptized and confirmed in this church, and serve on its altar.

With the notable exceptions of . . .

One trip to London in the early sixties in which they saw *Oliver!* on a West End stage.

And

One pre-me holiday in Spain which they hated due to hotness of weather and lateness of food. (Ten o'clock! For your tea!)

And

Annual trips to either Blackpool, Fleetwood, or Morecambe (trips, as I've said, that were really extensions of home).

. . . they had never left Accrington.

Which means what? It means that they were, in the parlance of the social psychologists, "outside in." It means that their sense of identity, their core beliefs, the ways in which they validated themselves, had been produced, reflected, and reinforced by the world in which they grew up. At its best it meant that a community had nourished and nurtured them, had (in soc. psych. speak) allowed them to develop meaningful connections amongst their peers, form supportive networks and lifelong-lasting friendships. It meant pragmatism and resilience and a sense of communal well-being. It meant that Accrington had seen them right.

Yet it also meant fear: fear of the world outside that community, or of people from the outside coming into it. Fear that you weren't somehow good enough or clever enough or that people would think you'd been born yesterday. It meant letting pride shade into bitter exclusivity, pragmatism into a lack of imagination. It meant letting humor become a cover story for prejudice, and straight talking becoming a shortcut to cruelty. It meant letting "the community" become "looking after our own" (and sod the rest) and looking out for each other a smoke screen for parochialism and backbiting and gossip.

Would that those oppositions could be neatly divided, but they collapsed themselves daily, sometimes within the same sentence. My heroic working class was also the petty proles, their common decency a tabloid headline away from moralistic outrage.

And so I sit with Jack and Kath in the lounge of the King Street WMC and I sip my drink and I watch my mum cry and I try to summon up a sadness at leaving a place with attachments I no longer feel attached to.

Tomorrow I would be at university where I would find out that I was a recognizable type, that my story was part of a bigger story. I would learn about social mobility and the precarious advantages bestowed upon the working class by Butler's Education Act of 1944. I would hear about education being a form of enlightened false consciousness and how boys from my background had to straddle two worlds and yet would belong to neither: the worlds of the confident and self-assured middle class and the deep-seated uncertainties of the exam-passing working class. I would read books like Richard Hoggart's *The Uses of Literacy*, which would describe my intellectual trajectory to its boldly crossed T and I would blush in recognition at the description of: "He [who] has moved away from his 'lower' origins, and may move farther. If so, he is likely to be nagged underneath by a sense of how far he has come, by the fear and shame of a possible falling-back."

But I would also know that this was not it, this was not it at all. The story of precarious working-class "self-improvement" was one that I held on to in the absence of anything else, all the while raging at its inadequacy. My parents were outside in, but I was inside out. I was inside out in ways that went further, cut deeper, than knowing about wine or meeting people who went skiing. The outside that had nurtured my parents had ruptured me. The world would no longer be allowed in, or would only be allowed in through the frozen watchfulness of a trauma that didn't recognize itself as such.

"Brains are the currency by which he has bought his way, and increasingly brains seem to be the currency that tells," writes Hoggart: "For he tends to make his schoolmasters over-important, since they are the cashiers in the new world of brain-currency. In his home-world his father is still his father; in the other world of school his father can have little place: he tends to make a father-figure of his form-master." His characterization of the nervously uprooted scholarship boy had little to say about the impact that fucking him may have on his sense of dislocation. Safe to say, it doesn't help. And when the "father-figure" is also a reverend Father, what then?

I sit beneath the strobe lights in the lounge of a working men's club and I drink another pint of a beer that I still don't really like with parents who I love but will be glad to leave and I try to separate: parents from teachers; teachers from headmasters; headmasters and teachers from priests; priests from Catholics; Catholics from parents; parents from the working men's club in which we're sat on a Friday night in September 1983.

It's not working. It's like trying to separate H_2 from O to make more sense of water.

So I will leave it all behind instead. I will go to a new place, and meet new people, and do new things.

NEXT

"What you say is true," the professor said, staring through his study window at the sky, "but not so very interesting."
—Renata Adler, *Speedboat*

This much I knew:

I knew that there were politics and that there were Politics, and that the lowercase kind were the stuff of people's lives, and their ideas about their lives. I knew that strikes and racism and nuclear weapons and CND were the only politics that mattered, or at least the only politics that I could relate to. I also knew that Politics could be the enemy of politics, a way to stop nonpolitical people from being politicized.

I knew that there was literature and that, like my hero Kafka: "I am made of literature. I cannot be anything else."

And I knew that there were literary figures who were political, and that literature was capable of playing a role in the kind of politics about which I cared. I had read Paul Foot's book on Shelley, seen a production of Brecht (thank you, Father K), and listened to my best mate recite Neruda's "Come and see the blood in the streets" whilst drinking cans of cider in the local park (thank you, Dave Hes.).

I assumed therefore that politics would mean, that its end point would be, the emancipation of the working class in order that they may better read Literature. It couldn't mean anything else.

The literature that I had been lucky enough to read (abusive priests or not) was the only literature that mattered. I believed in Penguin. I trusted in Pelican. I used to amuse myself by imagining that socialism would mean me and Jack and Kath arguing over translations of Kafka.

The first lesson I learn at Warwick is that my assumptions about Literature are themselves political, that there is a Literature and a literature, and that the pleasure I found in my reading had as much to do with a thing called "ideology" as it does with me being just a naturally sensitive little sod.

Perhaps it wasn't a question of giving the working class access to Great Books, or High Culture, or Literary Taste. It wasn't about connoisseurship but of understanding that the very definition of Culture itself is a matter of class (amongst other things). Maybe, maybe even in my teenage socialist utopia, Jack and Kath wouldn't want to read Kafka; or if they did, they may do so with a mind-set that is not searching for the eternal truths that I'd gone looking for.

I'd heard of F. R. Leavis, but had certainly never read him. This, I soon discovered, hadn't stopped me from being one of his most devout disciples. It turned out that I was committed to "a particular version" of literary criticism, one that was all the more "problematic" for refusing to acknowledge itself as such. (I liked the idea that I was problematic.)

It's a version that is predicated on "humanism" (lift an eyebrow), "universalism" (tilt the head), and "transhistoricism" (breathe in sharply). It assumes that the job of the literary critic is to unpick the various ways in which the literary canon (make quote marks with the index finger of each hand) reveals eternal truths (ditto) about the human condition (shrug shoulders and moan).

Furthermore, I think of these great works as part of a Tradition, one that I have inherited, ready-made and validated through time. And yet I fail to see that this story is itself part of an ideological construct, one that privileges certain authors (and I should think about the word "authority") over other, more marginalized voices (women, colonized subjects, immigrants, gay and lesbian writers).

It's true: I do do that. I thought that that is what we were supposed to do. And I was good at it. I thought that reading English and American literature at Warwick would be like doing A-level English but with a few more—a lot more—books. And without getting fucked.

I thought that I would plow through wonderful books written by wonderful men (and a few wonderful women) and discuss the ways in which they were wonderful. I had my three Practical Criticism ques-

tions written down in my sixth-form Prac. Crit. notebook, and I expected that for the next three years I would be applying these same
three questions to the entire history of Western Literature.

They were:

a: What is the author's intention?
b: How does he [*sic*] go about expressing this intention?

and

c: Is he successful in doing so?

There. I could do that.

The intention of this Larkin poem was to express his ambiguous response towards a wedding/tomb/church/his parents. He did this by internal rhythm (cite relevant example), assonance, enjambment, litotes/
bathos (I was never sure of the difference), metaphor, alliteration, and
onomatopoeia. He was successful because I now also feel ambiguous
about these things. And what is more (and this is the really clever bit),
Larkin wasn't alone in thinking that weddings, tombs, churches, and
parents were ambiguous. Other writers had thought that too (name
one before for influence on Larkin, and one after for Larkin's influence).
Can I have an A?

I suspected that getting a first class honors degree might be a bit
trickier than that, but not much. I knew that there would be a lot
more reading (it was the reason I was there), but it had never occurred
to me that I would have to question the whole notion of reading itself,
to question what I soon learned to call my "subject position." Or that
the books would be called "texts" and treated with a certain disdain;
as though they were secondary to the real "critical project," which was
to upset binary oppositions, or locate them within "the materiality of
history," or "embarrass the mechanics of their own production."

Within weeks I went from being a simile-spotting Leavisite to a
textually suspicious materialist, from someone who could identify a
half rhyme at five hundred paces to someone "deeply suspicious of the

whole notion of canonical value." I had a handful of phrases that saw me through, phrases which, if said without blinking, could imply a position arrived at via months (rather than minutes) of critical reflection.

Whereas I once thought that Beckett wrote about the tragicomic void of our common humanity, I soon found myself saying things like "his work is gendered in really interesting ways." If I had once warmed to myself as a literary critic, I now swaggered along the fifth floor of the Arts Department as something much sexier, even scary. I was a literary theorist. Barthes' "literature is what gets taught" could get me out of any scrape, so long as no one asked me where it was from (where *is* it from?).

Yet the fifth floor of the Arts Department was not a place to inflect your reading with any ideology, Marxist or otherwise. Theory had arrived at Warwick, but it had arrived via the philosophers and the sociologists, rogue historians and refugee linguists. It came seeping in from the Birmingham Centre for Culture Studies just up the road. It was in the bars (all five of them) and it was in the athletics union, which weirdly had a drinks license for opening in the afternoon. It was in the music press, which was running articles that wove together music reviews with the far outposts of poststructuralist theory. It was the currency of the postgrads, who all seemed to be researching things like desire, excess, and abjection. Where it wasn't was on the fifth floor of the Arts Department.

Take a stroll along the English corridor and chances are you would hear Dr. Bill Whitehead warmly reminiscing about his time at Oxford and how Chaucer is as relevant to us today as he's always been. When, in my second or third week, I went to see my tutor for European Epic and told him that I was struggling to get to grips with the *Iliad*, he seemed slightly baffled and said: "It's like when you go to the opera. Listen for the arias." I would try to remember that. The next time I went to the opera.

"Culture is ordinary." With these three words did the critic Raymond Williams open up my world. For if culture is ordinary, then the ordinary is cultural. Something more than my sensitive sensibility would be needed here.

NEXT

Don't call me Scarface.

—The Specials, "Gangsters"

I often thought of Tom Winnifrith's opening interview joke, about how Warwick had nothing to do with Warwick, or anywhere else really. There was something nowhere-ish about the university campus, something barren. The students used to joke that it was modeled on a Latvian prison or an out-of-season holiday camp. There was a bar called the Airport Lounge and the whole place shared that sense of anxious in-betweenness.

We were no more than three miles from Coventry, and the place was effectively run by people who lived in Coventry—cleaners, bar staff, shop and canteen workers, security. And yet no one seemed to mention the fact, let alone celebrate it. People talked about Stratford as though it was on the doorstep which, at twenty miles and with a regular supply of cheap theater tickets, made it a much sought-after neighbor. Coventry, on the other hand, was the rowdy lot the next street over. Don't tell them we're having a bash, they might want to come.

The Students' Union was closed to nonstudents, which meant that our free Saturday night gigs (Divine, the Men They Couldn't Hang, Pete Shelley, Jonathan Richman) weren't open to the locals. It was invisible class apartheid: we had subsidized beer, grant-funded educations that were going to get us better jobs, an Arts Centre that catered to our every creative whim. In Coventry unemployment ran at 20 percent.

The Union's housing officer regularly warned members about the dangers of student-bashing, yet seemed to make no connection with these dangers and a policy that excluded nonstudents. The Specials had recorded "Ghost Town" a year or two before ("Bands won't play no more / Too much fighting on the dance floor"), a song that was a regular fixture for the Alt Music Soc.

When a recently elected Thatcher arrived to open a new Business Park (what else?), she was met not only by the usual mob of jeering Trotskyites but by a group of Young Conservatives clutching placards demanding More Cuts. I'd never met a Tory. I don't mean someone who voted Conservative because their tabloid had told them to, but a real card-carrying, flesh-and-blood Tory. I'd always imagined them as claret-swilling jowly idiots, replete with three-piece suits and pocket watches, slightly bewildered by their discovery that they seem to run the country.

These Tories weren't that. These were Young Conservatives, a new breed of class warrior for whom the free market was as much an ideological commitment as state ownership had been for the left. They joined the Students' Union in an attempt to disband it. They had a vision of a Privatized Utopia, unfettered commercial freedoms whose only responsibility would be to the laws of supply and demand and a thing called individual choice. They would call each other "comrade" and taunt the left by referring to Mandela as a terrorist. A few of them wore T-shirts calling for him to be hanged.

They had chosen their target well, for if you wanted to upset the left on the mid-1980s, you had only to mention that you were unsure of where you stood on apartheid. Any student found not wearing an ANC badge in the lapel of their secondhand jacket was shot and their corpse propped up as a picket outside the campus branch of Barclays. It was compulsory to name every bar after imprisoned South African activists (as though what would really comfort the Mandelas in their time of struggle would be the thought of students drinking cheap lager and throwing up in each other's underwear).

NEXT

And class happens when some men, as a result of common experiences (inherited or shared), feel and articulate the identity of their interests as between themselves, and as against other men whose interests are different from (and usually opposed to) theirs.

—E. P. Thompson,
The Making of the English Working Class

Inadvertently, incidentally, inevitably, Warwick University teaches me the ways in which I'm working class.

Jack and Kath didn't teach me the meaning of my class. They'd taught me ways to compensate for it, to rise above it, to feel its shame and convert it into something that could pass for pride. In the language of Marx, they taught me "class in itself."

The SWP hadn't taught me about class either. They may have been in search of class consciousness, for Marx's "class for itself," but that was a goal, an ideal, not a description of its soul.

It was the middle class who taught me fully the meaning of what it was to be working class, who gave me my class self-consciousness.

At Warwick I came to understand that I had "a background," and that this was something different from "an upbringing." There was something robust, wholesome, about an upbringing: it suggested an ongoing, cyclical consensus, like cultivating a garden or Morris dancing. A background, on the other hand, was something out of which one stepped, something murky and disreputable that would be best left to fade away.

I hadn't realized the importance of the first-person pronoun, that there was something unseemly and overly possessive about prefacing "dad" or "mum" with "my"; or that saying "my holidays" was provincial ("holiday" was quite sufficient).

I hadn't realized that you passed the potatoes before helping yourself, or that being on time was bourgeois, or that supper was tea and dinner lunch, or that it was boring to worry about money. I hadn't realized that having a bath and not a shower was unhygienic or that we could always get a taxi. I didn't know that parents were in a line of work rather than having a job, and I certainly didn't know that you could call them by their first names. I didn't know that "lovely" wasn't necessarily lovely or that "charming" probably wasn't charming or that dull was the worst thing you could be. I didn't know, couldn't even have guessed, that everything was okay, amazing actually. And would just carry on being amazing; because why wouldn't it? And what I definitely didn't know, but would be reminded of daily, was that I had a funny/charming/strange/strong/distinctive/sweet/delightful way of talking. People felt free, compelled even, to do imitations of my accent within the first thirty seconds of meeting me. Bad imitations. Imitations that moved across the Pennines and up the coast and swerved back round via Newcastle and Carlisle. The imitation would invariably involve "whippets" and saying the words "mother," "ey up," and "by gum" in various combinations. Failure to greet being mocked to your face with anything less than full-blown hilarity would result in the charge of chips on shoulder and the need to get over them.

What strikes me now is just how annoyed people were by my being working class, as though I was doing it on purpose, just to provoke them. There was a need to challenge me, prove me wrong, catch me out. I remember one housemate saying that I didn't need to keep "reminding us how working class you are" (as though his own behavior and values were classless); or another saying that now that I was at university I was middle class too (although in the holidays I was going home to work at Asda dairies; she was going to Venice).

And so you learn to shut up. You learn to hide your class "tells" beneath an apologetic smile and constant self-screening. You soften your vowels and become your own Professor Higgins, correcting and cajoling your inner Eliza Doolittle.

NEXT

Love'll get you like a case of anthrax.

—Gang of Four, "Anthrax"

She kisses me. And I kiss her.

I'd seen too many episodes of the TV series *The Young Ones* to think of myself as a feminist (they thought it meant getting to do Felicity Kendal's laundry). Yet I'd been around too many lefties to think of myself as anything else.

Lips, neck.

It seems common sense—shitty wages, shitty men, too much childcare. She tells me that "common sense" was a way for oppression to disguise itself, of making itself seem natural. So maybe it wasn't.

And so on.

There are two books doing the rounds, compulsory reading: *Our Bodies, Ourselves*, and Nancy Friday's *My Secret Garden*. I spend a lot of time with both of them. Especially the Nancy Friday. And especially a girl called Bobbie in the Nancy Friday.

I say, It's okay. I don't mind. I like it.

I think that the having-been-fucked thing should mean that I'm their ally, one of them even, an honorary woman. I'm annoyed that it doesn't.

It may be the wrong time to be thinking of William Carlos Williams, but it is William Carlos Williams that goes through my head: "They taste good to her / They taste good / to her. They taste / good to her."

Her name is Lisa and she is perfect. I know that thinking she is perfect has all sorts of problems, not least the problem of her imperfections.

My nose? Chin also?

I don't recognize any of the male privileges that I'm supposed to benefit from, but then again I wouldn't, would I? Their invisibility is part of the privilege.

It's not really a moan; not quite a gasp. Somewhere in between.

She has scarily impeccable credentials: Greenham Common visits, university women's group, spiky black and blond hair with the tips dyed a red that reminds me of snooker balls. She wears monkey boots with multicolored laces.

Soles of her feet. On my back. Like soft sandpaper.

She pulls me up. She has the dirty smile, where she bites her bottom lip as if she's still undecided where she wants this to go. I know where I want this to go. I want this to go where she wants this to go. I think something like, This is who I am, even though my sense of who I am seems to lie somewhere else, with her maybe, or in the space between us, which has a definite shape and texture. She pushes me onto my back and climbs on top of me, her knees on either side of my hips. The record has come to the end of its side, some reggae that I didn't know I liked but plan to start liking. I've sat in this room every night for the last ten nights. I've drunk cold coffee until two, three, four in the morning and walked the three miles back to campus. We've agreed—or rather she's said—that the boyfriend-girlfriend deal is bollocks, patriarchal nonsense, and I've agreed. I've agreed because I want the boyfriend-girlfriend deal, and it seems the best way to get it is to pretend that I don't want it. She's told me to stop putting her on a pedestal, that she sweats and burps just like anybody else, and I've said yes I know, that's why I've put you on a pedestal, and she laughed and told me that I'm a pervert.

We've agreed that men are wrapped up in power and power is wrapped up in patriarchy and that patriarchy is like capitalism, it's everywhere. She's agreed when I've said that it's more complicated than that, that men get screwed over too and, anyway, what about class? She says, I'll trade you, you can have class and I get gender: Deal? Deal. She lends me books published by Virago. I give her a copy of Kafka short stories and worry that she might not like them.

We'd been on a date that we didn't call a date to see a film called *The Big Chill.* She hated it. She hated the smug bunch of wankers all fretting about their cozy fucking lives and being so pleased with their liberal fucking credentials and preening about their successful fucking marriages and their successful fucking jobs. Like I said: she's perfect.

And so I'm here on top of her bed in a terraced house in Earlsdon, Coventry. She puts one hand over my face, feeling the contours, as though she is blind. The other roams over my body, my nipples and stomach. Farther down.

Why has she just tasered my cock? There, she's done it again. Tasered it, and now I'm somewhere on the ceiling watching not her but an abstract composite of Lisa-shaped flesh. And watching a boy who looks like me. I'm absolutely calm, clinically calm. I'm like Diane Keaton in *Annie Hall*, leaving her body in the middle of making love to Woody, picking up her drawing pad: "Now that's what I call detached." And again. Taser, flinch. Flinch without moving; flinch in the stomach. The cock that isn't my cock but which seems to be attached to my pelvis is erect. It's a phantom limb. I watch it do its thing. Whoever is projecting the film has used the wrong filter, or overexposed it. I know I'm in Lisa's room, but it's a hologram of Lisa's room, or one of those flimsy cardboard film sets that they use in cheap productions that wobble when the actors slam a door. And cut.

The story is inescapable. It may have minor amendments, footnotes, or variations. It is played out in a million movies, it's the gag (sometimes the only gag) in thousands of stand-up routines and scores of sitcoms. It's the stuff of folklore and ancient myth, genetic speculation and cultural theory. It's a story in which we find motivation, tragedy, and hubris. It's a story whose pitfalls we already know, but which we embrace anyway, embrace its pitfalls as essential to its abiding truth.

The story is this: men need sex.

They need it like they need to empty their bowels. They need it beyond, despite of, or instead of emotion. They pester women for it, they marry women for it, they pay women for it. They may not particularly like it, are probably not very good at it (whatever that might mean), but they need it. Like air, like food. It is, we are told, hardwired into our DNA. Our need for sex, so the story goes, is who we are, what we are.

Unsurprisingly, women have had a lot to say about this (as have some men). They have rightly challenged its status as "the dominant discourse," its crudely reductive biological determinism, its potential for excusing a whole range of behaviors from infidelity to rape. They have opposed the way the story is used (sometimes literally) as a get-out-of-jail-free card, as an all too convenient abdication of agency and responsibility. And yet . . .

And yet, it's a story that we were born into; it's our inheritance. It is reinforced daily; we are surrounded and produced by it. It lives inside our pores: men need sex.

I hate the story. I hate it now, and I hated it when I used to tell myself it from the other side of the room in a bedroom in Blackburn whilst my body was being used by a man who needed sex but whose religious vocation prevented him from having it. I hate it politically, and the way in which it swaggers its way out of the mouths of groups of men who, when gathered together, are so frightened of boredom that they fall back on the story to keep their other desires at bay. I hate it aesthetically, and the infantilizing representations of Men Behaving Badly or New Men behaving disingenuously or Papa bloody Hemingway's Men Without Women.

But I hated it the most when I felt its presence between me and Lisa in a bedroom on the outskirts of Coventry.

I don't tell her about Kevin. I don't tell her about Kevin because I haven't told myself about Kevin. Or rather, I've come to Warwick to stop telling myself about Kevin. I want to be ex-Kevin; non-Kevined. And so I tell her bullshit. I tell her that I have problems with the whole blah-blah of penetrative sex, that the blah of phallocentric blah is to perpetuate a whole notion of blah. And I thought as a feminist she'd be pleased? (And had she read those Kafka short stories I gave her?)

It's a long walk home that night, longer than it has been the previous ten nights. I wander round the green bit in Earlsdon that's more waste ground than park and one of the townies who I never call town-ies shouts at me, "Whaddya spend yer grant on?" And I tell him to fuck off and he seems surprised that I haven't got a posh accent, and we face off and then both walk away because we're both men and it seems that we need to save face as much as we need sex, and maybe needing sex is a way of saving face and I think it'd be easier if I was gay even though I know it wouldn't be and I feel guilty for thinking it. And I start to laugh, laugh a lot, because I think how in a way this is exactly like one of those films where the boy walks round a waste ground late at night because of his problems with a girl, even though it's exactly not like that, because my problems with a girl are the opposite of the problems that boys usually have with girls, whatever they are.

I wander back to my rabbit hutch on campus and go past the Arts Building where my tutor keeps saying how we are all unwitting vic-tims of the Romantics and how their emphasis on spontaneity has made us enslaved to a spurious idea of authenticity, and how "authen-ticity" is no more authentic than any other conceit and how we need to appreciate that "artifice" doesn't mean artificial.

And I can't remember if I wondered then as I wonder now about what twentieth-century English lit would be like if, instead of all that phallic rain pounding and pounding into the thirsty loins of an await-ing mother earth, David Herbert Lawrence had been repeatedly nonced by his headmaster? Or if the complaint that Portnoy was so famous for was that every time a woman touched his dick, he flinched as though someone had tasered his groin? And if Henry Miller's celebration of his thrusting Self would in any way be diminished if his couplings with Anaïs Nin had been shot through with the memories of a priest's mustachioed mouth bearing down on him from a single-bedded room in Blackburn?

NEXT

Every day is like survival.

—Culture Club, "Karma Chameleon"

I return to Accrington for Christmas. It feels like one of those spooky stories, an episode of *The Twilight Zone*, where a place has been transformed into an exact replica of itself, the inhabitants all replaced by look-alikes. It wasn't just me; something really had happened, something so deeply unimaginable that hats were still being eaten as I stepped off the coach.

It had happened on the ninth of June 1983 to be exact, a time during which I was lost to a regime of A-level revision. More exactly it had happened during the early hours of the tenth, when, after six recounts, and by a majority of twenty-one votes, the returning officer announced that the new Member of Parliament to represent the Hyndburn and District Constituency was one Joseph Kenneth Hargreaves (Conservative).

A Tory. In Accrington: a place that was such a Labour stronghold that, so the joke went, the party could (and often had) put a goat up for election and still be assured of victory.

And not just any Tory. Ken Hargreaves was a Conservative who was loud and proud of his Catholic values.

And not just any Catholic. A Catholic whose Catholicism had been forged in the loving embrace of St. Mary's College, Blackburn, my alma mater, home to my very own alma abusive pater.

I know without asking that Jack and Kath have voted for him. I know it the same way I know they will be going to midnight Mass, or that we'll be having fish on Friday; or that my mum will cross herself whenever she passes the church or make sure her head scarf is on when she goes inside. In their mind, Jack and Kath hadn't voted Tory, they had voted Catholic.

And as if a Tory MP in Accrington wasn't enough, I come home to find that a phone has been installed. For the last ten weeks I have had to phone Aunty Mary (remember, Graham: no need to say "my") on a Saturday, 12:30. Kath will be there for her dinner. The problem was that Mary never really got the pips-money-talking equation. She'd answer the phone as though she had only just discovered it, baffled and suspicious, as though there was no connection between the fact of its ringing and her having picked it up and holding it in her hand. She'd be amazed to hear my voice, even though she knew that I'd be ringing, and would then launch into a series of non sequiturs about her dermatitis and the weather forecast and "her up the road" and did I still watch *Star Trek*? By the time Mary's monologue was finished I would have thirty seconds left to fib to Kath that I was eating well and to discover that no one had died.

So a phone-owning household we became, though not much of a phone-using household.

I think that my parents found something disreputable about spending time on the phone. It wasn't a medium for pleasure or friendship, it was an unpleasant necessity, like the first aid box. It was kept on a shelf in the hallway as you came in, away from the living space, private, but a privacy that was always on the verge of being interrupted. Any call that lasted more than two minutes would bring Jack's head round the living room door and he'd pointedly look at his watch. I tried explaining to him that it wasn't costing him anything if people rang me, but he either didn't believe me, or this wasn't the point. The point was, I think, that he didn't like the blurring of categories; talking that wasn't circumscribed, the intrusion into his home of other voices.

Yet their modernity was not confined to the buying of a telephone. Keep walking down the hallway and go into the living room, look at the rug which used to serve as my stage when I put on my air-guitar concerts, look at the three-piece sofa that my parents had bought on the never-never (the shame of a payment installation plan). Look at the color telly that we got in the late seventies because Jack "liked them nature documentaries." Look underneath the telly and you'll see a silver rectangular box. On its front is a black panel with small gray buttons which control the numbers that are displayed above it. There is a small slide door that reveals tiny sockets and tinier diagrams on its inside that say things like "tracking." Push a button on the panel and a metallic mouth shoots up out of the box, announcing itself with a no-nonsense ta-da. It is a Panasonic (I think) VCR top loader, rented from the local electrical store (because buying was too big a risk). It is a time machine.

Here was proof that there would be a cure for cancer, that all them moon landings weren't so daft after all, that the working class had indeed become cosseted by the technological indulgences of the modern age. Kath's argument was both pragmatic and saintly. She wasn't that bothered about the telly herself: so long as she watched her soap operas *Corrie* and *Emmerdale* and maybe *Crossroads*. But you and your dad were always squabbling, always falling out about what films to watch. Now it was simple. Take it in turns, watch one, record the other. And so it came to pass, Jack would watch Cagney assault women with grapefruits, and I would watch Isabelle Huppert smoke and stare out of windows.

What the bloody hell's going on here . . . ?

It's called a jump cut. It's a way of disrupting temporal linearity and . . .

Well, it's giving me a bloody headache. Record it and let's watch *White Heat*.

White Heat is on tape. We can't record this and watch *White Heat* at the same time. Stick with this, there's only another two hours and twenty minutes to go . . .

The corner shop now has a video section; the man on the market who used to sell me my James Herbert books now sells secondhand videos: "Classic Movies," "Action," "War," "Westerns," and a category for anything arty and/or mildly pornographic: "Foreign." I go foraging for Kath, return home armed with dramas featuring Bette Davis and her broken heart, or Lana Turner breaking hearts, or Barbara Stanwyk pretending not to have a heart at all.

NEXT

Only two English words rhyme with culture, and these, as
it happens, are sepulture and vulture.
　　　　　　　—Raymond Williams, *Culture Is Ordinary*

I thought I'd chosen my moment well: the day after Boxing Day, the
third Christmas dinner in a row, Jimmy Stewart waiting for us to stop
him from killing himself. It's something I'd been building up to saying since I got home, something that was obvious I should have said
after the first three weeks at Warwick. It would have been fairly easy
not to say anything, to simply do it and tell them afterwards. But, as
they always reminded me, they'd raised me right, and being raised
right meant that if I was going to do it, I needed to tell them first.

I take a deep breath and say what I always say when I say something that I know will make them worry. I say, I don't want you to
worry. But I've been thinking . . . I want to change my course to Film
Studies. I'm not sure if . . .

Someone has just told Kath that God does not exist. Worse, he does
exist but has decided that her last eight years of sacrifice have been
worthless, that all the ambitions she had for her son—a teacher!—are
being thrown away because he wants to be an actor, or a director, or
some such bloody nonsense. And it's her fault, all them hours spent
watching Joan Crawford. She bloody knew it.

Jack is more circumspect. He tells me that it's my decision, obviously, but that I should know that there's lots of people all trying to
"make it" in film; he has a cousin (really? Who?) who trained to be an
actor down in London (years, it took him) but it didn't work out and
now he's doing (horror) odd jobs, living from hand to mouth.

If there's one thing guaranteed to enliven any family Christmas, it's a lecture on cultural relativism from your nineteen-year-old son, the son who's just told you he wants to walk away from the chance to be an English teacher (and all them holidays). I tell them it's not about wanting to work in the film industry, it's about looking at (did I really say "reading"?) films in much the same way I'd been looking at books (did I really say "texts"?), and that anyway the distinction between popular and literary (please tell me I didn't say "a hierarchy of") cultures was not one that I found useful.

Apparently it was a distinction that Jack and Kath had found useful. They knew that there were things that you liked on the one hand and things that were good for you on the other. Film may have given them untold pleasures over the years, fed their rites of courtship, offered them a medium through which they could map their inner lives. But there was one thing it hadn't done, and that was to get either of them a decent job. Just the opposite, hadn't going to the movies been a way of escaping, getting up to all sorts, doing something you shouldn't? Weren't they about sex and smoking and this thing called glamour, glamour being a thing, like playing the trombone, that was fine to look at but not something you'd want in your home.

Literature—English literature—on the other hand was noble, truthful, and wise. They believed this without having read any. Because they hadn't read any. It seemed that Leavis was going to be more difficult to shake off after all. Literature was life, and books were wonderful. Whether you liked them or not.

NEXT

> . . . it's not at all unusual for a manual worker to study so hard in his spare time, and make such good progress, that he's excused from practicing his trade, and promoted to the intelligentsia.
>
> —Thomas More, *Utopia*

I'm reading Dante that Christmas, continuing my state-funded whistle-stop tour through the European Epic. I view my fellow Accringtonians through his descriptions of the damned, joyously casting them into whatever circles of Hell I see fit. I wander around the market with a bag of broken biscuits and bemoan "these wretches, who had never truly lived." I eye up passersby for telltale Hargreaves-voting tendencies and sentence them to be stung by hornets for eternity, maggots collecting in the pus.

Not uncoincidentally, I'm working in a factory that Christmas; a two-week, six-days-a-week, twelve-hours-a-day gig at Asda dairies.

At one end of the production line stands a burly man unpacking boxes of cartons of milk and juice onto a conveyor belt. Along the length of the belt stand half a dozen women sorting out the juice from the milk, getting rid of any damaged cartons, and putting them back into the right boxes. I stand at the other end and seal up each box with brown gaffer tape and stack them onto a nearby pallet.

Sorry, were those last three sentences boring? Did they sound flat and monotonous as though they were trying to just get the job done and move on to something more interesting? Do you want to read them over and over and over again from seven in the morning to seven at night with a half-hour break for lunch and a company-bought fish and chips tea that you got in lieu of proper overtime?

Brecht once said that putting a factory onstage will tell you nothing about the nature of capitalism. He's right. Factories are the last place you want to be if you want to understand capitalism. They're noisy for a start, so you can't really think. And you can't have conversations with people; they're too busy and, besides, they hate you. They hate you because you're taking a holiday in their misery. And when you've finished working, you don't want to talk about working. You want to go to the pub. And talk about other stuff, exciting stuff, like shagging, drinking, and fighting.

My diary entries about Asda make me cringe more than those about sex. They say things like:

"These people have to do this job all the time" (with "all the time" underlined so emphatically that the pen has scratched through the paper)

And:

"Why does everyone there not go mad?" (with six question marks underscoring my outrage)

I'm reading critics like Terry Eagleton and learning about how capitalism alienates us from ourselves, reduces its workers to an abstraction. I think my foreman had been reading him too because he kept saying I "was a good, safe pair of hands," as though he was employing my hands, and they were nothing to do with me. Which he was. And they weren't.

After work I go to the Railway, sit there in my overalls, performing my version of the working man in his scruff. I see Gary and Sara, who tease me that they're going to start a paper sale at my factory, a special edition of *Socialist Worker* calling for a general strike to get Asda's fish-and-chips-for-tea policy to include portions of mushy peas. I tell them about Dante's *Inferno* and how there's a section in which middle-class lefties are forced to explain dialectical materialism to haggard old men sat on toilets reading copies of *The Sun* who explain that said lefties have never done a bloody day's work in their life.

We're all three of us trying to be okay with each other, which is probably a sign that we're not. No mention of religion or abusive priests or drunken rows that we regret. They're no-go areas and I can hear their silence straining the laughter, making our jokes sound more barbed than they're meant to be. Gary's a student himself now, a place at Ruskin, a trade-union college down in Oxford. Sara's off to Sheffield, going to train to be a mental-health nurse, a job she will be great at. In a few months the miners will go on strike, an event that will bring us back together in lots of ways, and wrench us apart in others.

I leave the pub and call Lisa from a phone box on Blackburn Road; get her to call me back. We don't talk about me freezing every time her hand touches my genitals, about how I have no more control over it than I do my knee jerking when a nurse used to tap my knee with a toffee hammer. We don't talk about how me going down on her has become a way of us not fucking and how we both collude in the idea that this has something to do with feminism. We don't talk about the fact that women need sex as well as men, but maybe need it for different reasons and/or in a different way. Or that the way in which heterosexual women need sex is bound to be folded into ideas about how heterosexual men need sex. And I definitely don't say, I'm sorry but I'm too damaged to have a girlfriend, even a nongirlfriend girlfriend. Or I need a girlfriend because I'm damaged. And that's probably the worst reason to have one.

NEXT

Pictures came and broke your heart
        —The Buggles, "Video Killed the Radio Star"

Hayley Mills has seen Horst Buchholz shoot his wife. He's just back from sea and he suspects—no, knows—that she's been having it away with another man. They've been arguing. In Polish; having a right row. We can't speak Polish but we know it's not good. Hayley is watching through the letter box, horrified, fascinated.

"Bitch, bitch, bitch!" His missus (Yvonne Mitchell, moving between hysteria and contempt) is not having any of it. "Yes, and your bitch has had enough of it. Crrrraaaaawling every time you come back to her. No more. Sailors shouldn't have real women to play with . . ."

Then, bang, bang, bang. Dead. Hayley is looking. She has some gun caps in her hand, been given them to play with by her auntie. She drops them: bang. She needs to hide; there, a cubbyhole. Where Bruno has hidden his gun.

Jack presses the pause button whilst Kath goes to make some tea. And tea means biscuits, and biscuits mean fags. Do you like it? (I do like it.) *Tiger Bay.* We saw it when it first came out, 1958. No it wasn't, 1959.

Restart. Best thing we ever got. Amazing what they can do now.

Hayley is going to late for Mass. She's an altar boy; even though she's a girl. She puts the gun in her cassock, shows it to the snot-nosed boy standing next to her in the choir. He's impressed, starts singing stupid words to the hymn: "chocolate spread" instead of "righteousness."

Hayley is dynamite. Dynamite wrapped in cotton wool. She is pitched perfectly between angelic innocence and calculated devilry.

She's an angel with a murder weapon, but she does it so nonchalantly that you wonder why all angels don't carry round loaded revolvers in their cassocks.

Kath is beaming. Her boy is home for Christmas. Jack has even done his bit, whipped the cream (strong wrists), washed up. We're settled down.

Kath says, "Remember when you were on the altar?" She's been doing this ever since I got home, flights of nostalgia prompted by whatever we're watching. It's a version of a thing she used to do when I was a kid, which was to address strangers by talking loudly to me. If we were in a supermarket and someone pushed in, she'd say, "Some people have no bloody manners, do they, luv?" And if the person said anything in return, she would haughtily tell them that she hadn't been talking to them, she'd been talking to me.

I decide that using films to talk to me is like using me to talk to strangers. It's a way of avoiding having to talk directly, of taking responsibility for what you're saying. I know this because I do it all the time.

I say something about not wanting to take a stroll down memory lane, and she says not to bite her bloody head off, and Jack says something about not talking to your mum like that. I say something sarcastic and Kath says there's no need to be sarcastic. Jack says to leave it, the both of you, and Kath tells him to leave it, because I'm his son too and it's his religion and, whilst we're on the subject, it wouldn't have killed me to put in an appearance at Mass on Christmas Eve. I ask them if their mate Ken Hargreaves was there and they say no he wasn't, but what if he was and, anyway, what's that got to do with anything.

I say and they say and we all three of us say that we'd better not say anything we'd later regret.

I walk around Accrington and try to figure out how I would know if I was going to regret saying something until I'd actually said it. And if I could regret not saying something. And if I could regret saying some things only because I regretted not saying others, and how would I know the difference until I'd said them and saw what there was to regret.

I remember it was snowing and when the streetlamps came on, I felt like I was inside one of those glass globes that you can shake.

I think, I'm enraged by the smallest things because they feed into big things. And because I know what the big thing is, I know that the small things aren't small. I somehow think that other people must know this too, must be able to see it.

I was wearing my regulation Oxfam overcoat, a long scarf, and a peaked blue cap that I think makes me look like a folk singer and Jack says makes me look like a cartoon pirate.

I think, I must have brain damage.

I arrive at Dave Hes.' house and his parents give me home brew and ask me if I have had a good Christmas. I say what I always say, "Fine thanks, you?" I feel guilty for thinking that Dave's parents are nicer than my parents. I still haven't got the hang of calling them by their first names, John and Maureen. I wish my parents had central heating. And a car.

Me and Dave walk over Dill Hall Lane to Clayton, past where my grandparents used to live, and I tell him about playing cards during the power cuts and how I feel bad for not seeing my grandma much after Granddad died. He tells me a story about his granddad that makes me want to put my arm around his shoulders, but I don't. He knows a pub where we'll get a lock-in, a pub where they'll sell us drinks even when they've "stopped" selling drinks.

I say something like, How do you stand it?

I'm half expecting him to say something about families, or Oxford, or a book he's been reading, or (his favorite) the wide range of stories available to posh people and how we should be suspicious of the "got out and made good" story that we seem to have been lumbered with.

He doesn't say any of that. What he says, with a face as flat as a pancake, is this: "What I think is that love is like oxygen and if you get too much you get too high, not enough and you're gonna die. Love gets you high . . ."

And on he goes, delivering Sweet's "Love is Like Oxygen" as though the words have just occurred to him and they carry the gravitas of all ten commandments. He's stroking his chin, nodding at his own wisdom: "'I can't shake off my city blues, everywhere I turn I lose.'" He's playing it straight, in the style of Oliver playing Richard III." "'Some things are better left unsaid. I'm gonna spend my days in bed.'"

I can't stop laughing, snorting. I pull myself together. . . .

"Really, David? Interesting that you should say that, because I often think that love is the drug, particularly when I troll downtown to the red-light place and lumber up and limbo dooooown."

Dave stays in character, not missing a beat, nonchalant but officious: "A fine thought, Mr. Caveney. But have you ever considered that people may have had enough of silly love songs?"

"I have indeed, Mr. Hesmondhalgh, but I look around me and see it isn't so . . ."

We do this all the way to Clayton.

We sit in the pub, and drink, and talk. The landlady has put out a table groaning beneath plates of pork pies sliced into quarters, the insides glistening with gelatine. There are sausage rolls that don't seem to have any sausage in them, and bowls of nuts and crisps that are suspiciously damp. There are sandwiches, thick white bread just starting to curl; basins with pickled onions; and mince pies heavily dusted in icing sugar.

People are wearing paper hats with glitter on their faces. The next table over a man is blowing a party horn and singing the wrong words to Paul Young's "Love of the Common People." I say to Dave that it's like that scene in *Educating Rita*, the one where Julie Walters is berating Michael Caine for raising her expectations of life, and how it cuts back to her sitting with her family having a sing-along in the local, except that she can't sing along because she knows there's better songs than this.

Dave had been irritated by it, thought that it sentimentalized both sides of the equation. I didn't know quite what I thought of it. I had sat watching it, thinking, So it is possible to be schooled without being seduced, to be mentored without getting fucked. Yet there had been something sexual between them; no doubt about that. The bit where he comes back from holiday and has brought her some cigarettes and she says that she's stopped smoking. It's a minibetrayal, the kind of incidental hurt that a lover might inflict.

But he hadn't fucked her, or tried to. He'd held whatever it was between them within himself. He'd been reckless with his drinking and his career, but he hadn't been reckless with Rita. It was intimate and flirtatious without being sexual. I'd been mesmerized by it.

I don't say any of this to Dave. It would take another two years and my first nervous breakdown before I'd tell him what it was I needed to tell him. Meanwhile, we drink bitter with a proper head on it and hit the whiskey towards the end of the night. And when the inevitable moment comes and someone plays Slade's "Merry Xmas Everybody" on the jukebox, we put our arms around each other's shoulders and sing "everybody's having fun." And we were.

NEXT

Forget everything. Open the windows. Clear the room. The wind blows through it. You see only its emptiness, you search in every corner and don't find yourself.

—Franz Kafka, *Diaries*

The new year is still on its first legs the day I go back to Warwick. I'm going early. I'm going to look for a house in Coventry, get the hell off campus. Kath has packed me some sandwiches, corned beef and brown sauce, wrapped in tin foil; an apple to counteract Christmas, a KitKat to counteract the apple. It's sunny, the kind of crisp winter sunshine that should make me want to take myself off up the Coppice, or Pendle Hill.

But I'm not going to either of these. I'm going back to Coventry. I'm going to find a house near Lisa, even though I've said that being near Lisa isn't a factor in me finding a house. I'm taking the coach. It takes longer than the train, but it's cheaper, and (Jack's convinced) more reliable. No threat of the strikes that they keep having, even though they haven't had one for about ten years.

I put my suitcase in the luggage compartment, down in the bowels of the coach which are built into its side. Like I say, it's sunny, warmer than it should be for January.

The coach will stop for a break in Manchester, but before that it goes to pick up passengers all around the small towns round about: Colne, Bacup, Rishton, Rawtenstall. It's a long journey, best part of a day Kath says; three, four hours maybe. We set off.

I sit next to the window and look out and think just how green it is around Accrington. I always forget this. I think of Accy and I think of pie shops and women in hairnets and pubs and factories and school playgrounds. But it's a valley: it's why it was so useful for the cotton trade, the factories powered by the water that ran down into its center. So, yes, it's green and rolling and beautiful; the kind of landscape that produces the kind of poety types that I see myself as being.

It's really hot now, I'm sweating.

Along with the food, I have a flask and a book, all packed in a little leather holdall. I take out the book: Elmore Leonard, my new discovery. He writes crime novels with titles that sound like they could be noirish movies from the 1950s, titles like *Cat Chaser*, *Unknown Man No. 89*, and *52 Pickup*. They're funny also, cracking dialogue. I start to read.

I'm reading but also looking out the window, which means that I'm not really reading. The words are a bit fuzzy. The window is made of glass.

The coach is quite busy, but then again it's a Friday, and not everyone will be going to Coventry.

The window's made of glass, but it's as though the world outside the window is made of, no, not made of glass, but has glass all around it, like a fishbowl.

First stop . . . Clayton-le-Moors, is it? I'm not really paying attention; I'm thinking about the sweat trickling down my back. It doesn't look like anywhere. It looks like everywhere. It looks like a new thing, a thing that's nothing to do with me, a thing called Outside. People are getting off.

People are getting on. I put my hands on my forehead just to make sure that my head's still in one piece (nervous laugh), and they come away damp, and I'm not sure if they're damp because of the sweat on my forehead or the sweat on my hands. And there's tingling in my fingers. And static in my head.

The woman in the aisle opposite me is looking at me and I don't know what she's thinking.

There's tingling in the tips of my fingers, but when I rub them against each other they also feel numb. Tingling and numb. And my chest.

She's probably thinking, What's that bloke doing, what's wrong with him? Does she think I'm a bloke, what's a bloke? When did I become a bloke?

And my chest is like someone is pushing down, or kneeling on top, or stretching. No, it's coming from the inside. My lungs. There's dry ice in my lungs.

She's staring now, and nudging her husband, and they're talking about how weird I must look. Except I can't hear what they're saying because they're so far away, even though they're right next to me and they're inside the fishbowl too, which is outside, outside of me.

Where are we again? Where am I?

There's dry ice in my lungs. Which is why I can't breathe and why I need to start breathing; breathing, breathing quickly, breathing hard.

Great Harwood? People getting off. Get off. I can't get off. There's nowhere to go to if I get off. My stuff's way down in the innards of the coach. And why do you need to get off? There's nothing the matter. Everything's fine; stop being so stupid.

People get on.

I look out of the window, try again with my novel, put the novel away, look again out the window.

It's happening again, except this time I know that it's going to be worse. I know it's going to be worse because my bowels are churning, turning to water.

Scramble inside the bag. There's sandwiches, and an apple, and a KitKat biscuit.

My bowels are turning to water. Which means I'm going to mess myself. On a coach. In front of the people on a coach. There'll be shit, there'll be the stench. Of my shit, and the people on a coach, and the inside that's neither inside nor outside.

Breathe. The problem is that you can't breathe. I tell myself this with the one voice that I've still got left in my head that I still hear as my own, a voice that I'm trying to hang on to, a voice that's fighting with the other voices. Who are saying . . .

You are going mad. You have gone mad. You are going to die. You are going to go mad and then die. You will shit your own death. You are disappearing.

Rishton? People get off, people get on. Getting off is not an option now because my legs won't move. My legs won't move because they're tingling and numb. And if I try to move them, my intestines will explode.

Breathe, gulp, and fight for breath. I'm not me anymore: I'm you, and you are going to die unless you . . . you are lungs that need air, and a throat that can't swallow, and a mouth with no saliva. You are a stomach that's trying to stay on the inside. You are shit trying to hold itself in. You are one thought, and it's not even a thought, it's more primal than that: it's visceral, and desperate, and clamoring to be heard. It is:

I have to get out of here. I have to get out of here. I have to get out of here.

NEXT

... so much to answer for.
— The Smiths, "Suffer Little Children"

I'm in Manchester Coach Station. I'm still shaking, but I'm able to walk. I was right, people were looking at me strangely. They still are. They're looking at me as I get off the coach, and as I ask the driver how long he's stopping for, and is it all right if I get off and come back on.

It's the early days of 1984 and I have just had my first panic attack.

There's a bar in the station and I have to wait for forever until the barman serves me, and I get a pint of bitter and go and sit in the corner and wait for my hands to stop trembling so that I can put the glass to my mouth.

In 1984 people didn't have "panic attacks." They were mad, or crazy, or a bit doolally. Not right upstairs.

I have no idea what has just happened to me. I feel like crying but am too overwhelmed to cry. I feel like I have had a premonition of something dreadful about to happen and, at the same time, that it has already happened.

They were destined for the funny farm, the nut house, the loony bin.

It is 1984, and I've just reread Orwell's *Nineteen Eighty-Four*. I wanted to compare what he thought it would be like with what it was like. I think, This is my room 101. I think, It's like that bit with the rats. When they find out that Winston Smith's biggest fear is a fear of rats, and they put that cage over his face. He's screaming, begging, saying that he'll do anything they say; just tell him what they want him to do and he'll do it. And they say, "You'll know what it is we want you to do: when the fear is great enough, you will know."

And he says, "Do it to Julia! Do it to Julia!" Because he knows then that his fear is bigger than his love, that fear is absolute. And the man—O'Brien—who has known this all along says something chillingly simple. He says, "The thing that is in Room 101 is the worst thing in the world."

This then was my Room 101. Whatever happened on that coach must never happen again. Do it to Julia, but don't let me experience anything like that ever again.

The diagnosis was to tap the finger to the temple, or roll the eyes, or make a whistling sound which was similar to the one that was reserved for an unmarried male relative. Kinder voices might insist that you were mental, or that it wasn't your fault, and you would be listened to with an indulgent sympathy usually reserved for the recently bereaved.

But in twenty minutes I have to get back on the coach. And sit there all the way to Coventry. Sit there knowing that those feelings are still bubbling away, that they could descend at any minute, that they are inside me as well as outside me, and that they don't seem to notice the difference.

That—whatever that was—cannot happen again. I will not, cannot, survive it. It is the worst thing in the world.

I say to the man behind the bar, "Can I get some cans to take out, please?"

NEXT

. . . and the poisonous world flows into my mouth like water into that of a drowning man.

—Franz Kafka, *Diaries*

They're happening regularly now. And when they're not happening, I worry about them happening. Which can make them happen. I still don't call them panic or anxiety attacks; those words are not yet available to me, not part of any common vocabulary.

Mental health had not been discovered, or invented, in 1984, let alone become an industry. If anything, "mental health" was an oxymoron. If you were "healthy" you were "normal," and if you were normal you certainly weren't "mental." Despite evidence to the contrary, people didn't seem to have "issues" or "conditions," didn't openly share about their neuroses. All I knew about psychoanalysis was that Woody Allen had had it. And it hadn't worked. (And, as he said, if you killed yourself, they made you pay for the sessions that you missed.)

Or maybe there was such a thing as mental health, and this was yet another of those things that my class background (or was it "upbringing"?) had made me deaf to? I remember my family talking about so-and-so having had a "bad do with her nerves." Aunt Mary, we knew, "suffered terribly with her nerves." Nerves weren't good, you wouldn't wish them on anyone. They got on your nerves.

Yet there was never any acknowledgment that nerves were connected to the nervous system, and that the nervous system might be a response to emotional history. Instead there was a sense that there was something deeply shameful about them, and that their treatment should remain furtive, unseemly, like contraception or hemorrhoids.

A "bad do with your nerves" could also be shorthand for being "work shy," slacking off, nothing that a hard day's graft wouldn't cure. Nerves were soft and namby-pamby, the result of too much mollycoddling. The best thing for nerves was a bath, or a good night's sleep, or a bowl of hot soup.

You didn't want to start with your nerves. Once you'd started with your nerves, you'd not know when to stop.

So when, in Coventry, I eventually go to my doctor, I don't go armed with acronyms, or with a self-diagnosis gleaned from conversations with friends. I go and I say, I think I'm going mad.

And this being 1984 he doesn't refer me to a wellness clinic, or counseling, or recommend that I practice mindfulness. He doesn't tell me about breathing into a paper bag to short-circuit hyperventilation. He doesn't explain about the hippocampus and the amygdala, and how the primal part of our brains responds to perceived threats by sending warning signals to the more evolved parts of our brain to set in motion the sympathetic nervous system, and that that produces a flight-or-fight response which is trying to protect us from threats even though there may not actually be a threat present, and so that even though these panic attacks may feel like they're sent to destroy us, they are really just the body's misguided way of keeping us alive. He doesn't talk about exposure or desensitization, relaxation techniques or counseling.

What he does is say, "Of course you're not going mad."

And he reaches for his prescription pad. And he writes me a prescription.

NEXT

As though everything I possessed had escaped me, and as
though it would hardly satisfy me if it all returned.
                                    —Franz Kafka, *Diaries*

I'm sitting in the Warwick Arts Centre waiting for the bar to open.
One of the cleaners comes up to me and asks me if I'm all right, I don't
look well.

They're still happening, these attacks, these whatever-the-fuck-
they-ares. They are in me but not of me, which means that they get to
decide when they come and visit me. They seem to like it when I'm
outside, particularly on public transport. They also like cars, cars on
motorways, dual carriageways. In cars they like that I'm both confined
and exposed, closed in next to someone but surrounded by no one, and
nothing, nothing "safe" anyway. Like houses. I go to a Buñuel double
bill in Birmingham, get a lift with a friend. I hyperventilate all the
way back, squirming and sweating in my seat, trying not to go mad.
I'm embarrassed and he is kind, says that he thinks it is claustro-
phobia. Or agoraphobia: some mixture of the two. I think he's right,
though I'm not sure what it means. Something to do with the Greek:
"agora" meaning "market" or "place of assembly." Except we're not in
a marketplace. It's an outside-ness thing, a spatial vulnerability thing.

I sit in the Arts Centre and think about all the situations in which
they might happen, and how utterly devastating it would be if they
happen in those situations, and how there's nothing I can do to stop
them from happening.

And so the cleaner says, "You don't look well." She's right. I don't
look well. In movies, when the actor is messed up, looks bad, they
always seem to look good-bad. They may be sweating and shaking,

but they still look like movie actors sweating and shaking. They still look cool.

I don't look cool. I've been throwing up into a toilet, thrown back up the cottage pie that they sell in the Arts Centre café that I didn't want but thought might make me feel better because I'd not eaten for the last couple of days, but which didn't. I cover my mouth with my hand because I'm ashamed of my breath and tell the woman that I'm fine and that I just need a moment.

I don't just need a moment. I also need the pills that the doctor has given me to kick in. But I think I must have spewed out the pills that the doctor gave me when I threw up the cottage pie that I ate. I look at the white label on the bottle of pills. It says: Ativan: 30 tablets, 5 mg: May cause drowsiness: If affected do not operate machinery. Do not drive. Avoid alcoholic drink.

Which means that I need an alcoholic drink. I know that pills that tell you to avoid alcoholic drink only do so because they make the pills (and the drink) a little bit stronger. And what I need are stronger pills.

The bar staff is getting ready to open, lifting up the shutters. Earlier I had left a lecture halfway through, had felt the dread in my stomach and the sweating palms that I think of as my warning system. I can now add "lecture hall" to the list of places to avoid, yet another place that can't be trusted, or that I can't trust myself to be in.

It's getting long, this list. It already has on it: supermarkets, banks (if there's a queue), buses during rush hour, public transport if tranquilizer has not had time to work, public transport to unknown destinations, the all-night garage, Leamington Spa and now lecture theaters. It doesn't include bars, or places that have a bar like the Arts Centre. It doesn't include those because they sell alcohol, and I know that the one thing, the only thing, guaranteed to tranquilize me if my tranquilizers don't work, or if I've spewed them back up, is alcohol. Only I've taken to spewing that back up lately as well.

It's getting complicated. The things I do to make myself feel better are making me feel worse.

I see my friend Heather. She saw me leave and wants to know if I'm okay, has noticed that I've not been around much this term. Heather's a rare thing in 1984. She's a mature student and a single parent, not to mention a white South African with a distrust for the more pious end of student politics. I love and trust Heather, can talk to her about anything. Anything except the dread in my bowels and the fear in my stomach. I can't talk to her about those things because I know that talking about them will make them real, will bring them forth like some deranged self-fulfilling prophecy.

She has hold of my hand. I squeeze her hand back and say that I'm fine, really, that I'm just drinking a bit too much, hitting it a bit too hard, she knows how it is.

She does know how it is. She has a friend, Simon, who was an alcoholic, says that alcoholics are born and not made. She's mentioned me to him. She buys me a drink—a bottle of strong lager, one that my uncle Jack used to "have" to drink because he was diabetic. We talk for a long time, about our course and how studying literature wasn't what we expected, whatever that was. She tells me about stuff that happened to her back in South Africa and I feel slightly ashamed at not knowing what to say, and about not knowing anything about anything really, despite the fact that I'm always mouthing off. I tell her some of the stuff but not the cock-tasering stuff about Lisa and how we're trying to have a relationship that doesn't follow all those shitty scripts about relationships, and Heather laughs and says fuck that, a left-wing orthodoxy is just as confining as a received orthodoxy if it's not giving you what you want. She's right. Fuck that.

I go to the toilets to swallow another Ativan to make up for the one that I threw up earlier and I wash it down with more strong lager. I tell Heather not to worry, that I'm fine, that I'll see her soon.

The chemicals are mixing nicely now, ethanol and lorazepam. I'm buoyant, warmly belligerent. It's a useful guide, the "avoid alcoholic drink" guide. Without it I wouldn't know which pills to drink on. It should be that an Ativan in the morning takes me through to lunchtime, and a couple of drinks at lunchtime should take me through to the athletics union opening its doors at teatime, and a couple of drinks at teatime should see me through to the evening, when I can take another Ativan. Thus inoculated against panic, I should be able to manage trips to the library, where I sit and write my essay on Milton, and why he seemed to think that Satan was more interesting than God.

Except it's not working out that way. The medication is filling my head with mashed potato. I need alcohol to bring myself back into focus. I need coffee to keep me awake. I need cigarettes to give my fingers a reason to touch my face. I need to eat because I remember promising Kath that I would eat. I need Lisa to not touch my cock but still be my nongirlfriend girlfriend. I need to stop wearing this spacesuit. And I need to figure out if it really was better to reign in Hell than to serve in Heaven.

I'm talking to Julie now about talking to Heather, then about how I used to talk about my drinking. She says that back in the eighties it was easier to have a drinking problem than it was to have an anxiety problem, and that because drinking also causes anxiety problems, it soon becomes impossible to tell if the problem is the drinking or the anxiety. She says drinking was the remedy that was also the poison.

I go into Coventry city center. I'm an agoraphobe who uses alcohol to control his agoraphobia.

Julie talks about dual diagnosis and says that she has worked with alcoholics and addicts for over twenty-five years and never fails to be astonished by the following fact: that she has never met an alcoholic yet who likes the taste of alcohol.

I live in fear of having a panic attack in an exposed place, or any place that exposes me. There are two places in Coventry where I go to feel safe.

She says, Addicts grow to love alcohol for taking away whatever it is that they want taken away: anxiety, depression, phobia, trauma.

The cinema and the cathedral.

They learn to trust alcohol. It will become the only thing they trust.

There's nothing on I want to watch, nothing I fancy. I wander across to St. Michael's.

They mistake the absence of pain for the presence of pleasure. Addiction is the love of any substance or activity that makes the pain go away. Pleasure is the absence of pain.

The new cathedral is built alongside the ruins of the old cathedral, the one destroyed during the Second World War. I remember the date from a book Jack got me from the library: November 14, 1940.

She says, Addiction has a life of its own, is an entity in itself. We can't just take it away and treat the "thing" that's left beneath, because the thing and the addiction have become entwined, inseparable.

It is vast and yet I am not fazed or threatened by its vastness. It is a space that can hold me, calm, noninvasive.

Drinking was the cure for anxiety and anxiety was a cure for abuse.

There is a huge seventy-five-foot-high tapestry called *Christ in Glory*, before which I sit and stare, patiently waiting for it to move. It's not a Christ I know from my childhood, not a pious or portentous Messiah. Here's a Christ perplexed by his own divinity, affronted by it even. He's a Christ who would be played by John Cazale in the biblical epic I direct inside my head.

There's the damage done to us, and then there's the damage we inflict on ourselves because of the damage that's been done to us.

There are columns which don't seem to touch the floor, but that just seem to float, suspended.

But the damage doesn't have to be terminal, or permanent.

Some of the stained glass looks like boiled sweets, other bits the colors you find in illuminated manuscripts.

I remember from somewhere that the code name for the bombing of Coventry was Moonlight Sonata.

I look out through the window at the ruins of the old cathedral. At least five hundred people were killed the night of the bombing.

There is a cross, a charred cross. Behind this cross is an altar.

Behind this altar is a wall on which are inscribed two words: Father Forgive.

I stand and look around me. My hands in my pockets feel numb with cold. I blow into my curled-up fist, raise the collar of my coat against the freezing night, and try to figure out where to go next.

AFTERWORD

Finally, the Church: speak with burning zeal about its self-righteousness, the narrow-mindedness of its bigots, indicate that all this can be murderous, hide none of the weaknesses of the faith. And then, *in extremis*, hint that the letter of the law, however unattractive, is a way to salvation for its very victims, and so justify moral austerity by the saintliness of those whom it crushes.

—Roland Barthes, "Operation Margarine," *Mythologies*

Did they let you choose where to go, give you a say in where you could have your "treatment"? America would be my guess, though the priest I spoke to later would neither confirm nor deny.

It's the States I imagine you in, when I imagine you in treatment. Boston or New York maybe, one of those cities with big turnouts on St. Patrick's Day and Pogues concerts. Do I imagine you there because I know how much the place annoyed you? I'm not imagining the therapy, though. The priest I spoke to was adamant that you were receiving therapy. There's an irony there. Ironic because you thought therapy was a way of man trying to short-circuit God, of trying to make himself whole rather than accept that he was incomplete.

So, sorry about that, for being the cause of them sending you to wherever it was they sent you. It was probably better than the treatment I received (and had to pay for, not having the funds of the Catholic Church to fall back on). The Church didn't offer to send me to America. Or anywhere. I told them about you and they said, Oh, and, You'll be pleased to know he admitted it (strange how it never occurred to me that you wouldn't). They said that the problem had been dealt with.

They didn't tell me about the retirement bash they were going to throw you. I learnt about that through Kath sending me a cutting from the *Lancashire Evening Telegraph* with a note saying, I thought this might interest you: You were always one of his favorites.

They told me about you getting Alzheimer's, and that you were living somewhere down in Sidcup, Kent, being looked after by the Marist Brothers. They said it as though that was going to be some kind of end to the story, as though I didn't have questions that I knew then were never going to be answered, that your wretchedly fading memory was taking away my story as well as your own.

I knew then that I'd never get to ask you my two key questions: What was it about me? And: Was I the first, the only?

It's a trickier question than you might imagine, this wondering if I was the only boy you'd fucked. I know that the stats would suggest not, that this stuff is compulsive, and that if I was the first I certainly wouldn't be the last. I'm not sure I believe it. Or if I want to believe it. You see, there's a bit of me that still believes I'm unique, that I really was your prime number, indivisible only by myself. I don't want to think of myself as part of a pattern, just another victim. It cheapens my own self-image which, as I'm sure you know after all that therapy, is pretty cheap anyway. Because of the being-fucked thing.

And so: What was it about me? You've left me with a pretty unappealing set of options. I've had plenty of time to think about them, all that time spent in psych wards, rehabs, therapists' offices. It's something like: a combination of narcissism and self-loathing, the belief that I must be the center of the world and a disgust with being so ill-equipped to be so. I fight against my own bitter self-regard, the voice that says, I must have been so very damned attractive, must have been some hot little number, to make you risk your vocation (both of them), your vows, your authority. How alluring I must have been; such *un homme fatal*.

And with a humorless smile I think, Yet what a disappointment I was. All those nights out, those don't-come-cheap seats at the theater, dinner and drinks: All for what? Some acne-scarred little ingrate who doesn't have the decency to come after you spend ten, fifteen, twenty minutes thrashing away at his cock. Such a letdown. I wasn't money well spent.

I don't remember the exact date when I reported you. I'd just had another suicide attempt and was sedated, so forgive me if the details are a little fuzzy. It's one of the problems of being abused, one of the occupational hazards. The abuse leads you to fuck up your life, and a fucked-up life means that you're a less credible witness to the abuse that fucked you up in the first place. It's an ironic trick of memory and survival: abuse makes you want to forget the abuse.

So it was late 1991 or early 1992 and I'd just slashed up my arms and I eventually told a priest called Father Phillip, who told his bishop, who told a friend of his in the Marists, who told his superior, and the superior confronted you and you said, It's true, and, But it takes two to tango. We okay thus far?

And so they sent you away to get therapy and you came back, presumably cured of your desire to fuck adolescent boys, and then you got ill and you got looked after and then, according to the printout in front of me from the *Lancashire Evening Telegraph*, you "died peacefully in the early hours of Sunday 20th of March 2011."

The college governor, one Father Noel Wynn, is quoted as saying: "Kevin was the life and soul of any party and found a great deal of enjoyment in life. He was a keen traveller and accompanied many parties of students abroad to Italy and Greece, a country he continued to visit on his own or with congenial confreres."

A solitary sentence about your time at the college says simply: "He left in 1993."

No mention of why you left, or time in therapy, or the admission of child fucking.

What there is a mention of is the following: "In 2008 a new £2.5 million performing arts centre—O'Neill Academy for Performing Arts—was named after the former principal."

Ever since I read this cutting I've been tormenting myself thinking of the various performances I'd like to perform in your performing arts center. There's one in which I sit on a dimly lit stage masturbating to a 3-D CGI avatar of Gloria Grahame whilst a voice offstage, say that of Father Noel Wynn, reads out the psychiatric sections of my medical history. It could be called "Congenial Confreres." Or maybe a more Buñuel-inspired one in which a group of bishops (a bench of?), in full clerical gear, spend a day binge drinking. It could be called "Two to Tango" and would culminate in them playing truth or dare with a select band of altar boys (collective noun: a temptation of?).

Not amused, Kevin? Sorry: it's just that there are certain levels of injustice that defeat my usual strategies of irony, and you having a performing arts center named after you is one of them.

How am I? Thanks for asking. The protection officer did say that you said you were worried about me, though presumably not worried enough to organize an apology or even a public admission of guilt.

But I'm doing better, these last six years. I've definitely quit the booze, and the drugs. Even the fags. I have therapy regularly, here in Nottingham, where I live. I pretty much fucked up my career. The opportunities were pretty limited for agoraphobes who medicated their condition with vodka and painkillers, even in academia and journalism.

And my parents are both dead: Jack in 1998, Kath four years later. Bowel cancer, both of them, cruel and undignified. Don't worry, I kept your secret. They loved you to the end, I made sure of it. They were both so proud of me having gone to your school, and so utterly entranced by the idea of me being taken up by you, that I couldn't tell them any other story. So I would sit and make monosyllabic noises in response to their inquiries about whether I'd heard from you or not, or did I ever think back to that time when you used to come and visit us, or wasn't it a wonderful experience to have gone to Greece with you? I made monosyllabic noises and I swallowed my resentment.

It's them that I can't forgive you for, the way in which you made their hopes and aspirations the tools of your own needs. It's them who spent their lives worrying if it was something they had done wrong to make their boy turn out the way he did. They had more trust in you than I ever did, more belief in what you represented. They were innocent, and it was them who got the blame. So rot in hell for that.

And I'll rot in hell for my own stuff, of which there is a depressingly large amount. Not child fucking though. I remember reading, years ago, about how most abusers had been abused and wondering if I would develop a taste for it, and planning how to kill myself if I started to find myself being sexually drawn to underage kids. Thankfully it's just not in me, whatever the "it" is. There's plenty of other stuff though: needy, manipulative, petty, vindictive, the familiar motifs of adults who have been abused as children (or just the familiar motifs of adults). I'm not good at being a survivor, at baring my wounds bravely or gently. I rely on kindness but am suspicious of it, suspicious of why I rely on it. And why it's being offered.

I'm getting better though. I no longer drink vodka for breakfast or carve up my arms to let the pressure out. I go to AA and tell my story. Or a story. I tell them about the booze and the blackouts and the regrets, and the adjustments to a life lived in sobriety. I don't tell them about how, some days, most nights, I can still taste your tongue at the back of my throat or how my stomach becomes a tsunami every time I encounter someone who I perceive as having power over me (which can be anyone). I say that I'm grateful for what I've got rather than bitter about what I've lost, and try to convince myself that I am. I say that I live my life one day at a time, which isn't true, and that I say the serenity prayer each morning, which is.

They talk in these meetings of a Higher Power, a phrase that at first sent me straight back to you and your boozy theological grooming. It's a measure of how desperate I was to stop drinking that I kept going to those meetings, kept showing up in those drafty church basements. Now I can conceive of a God who is nothing to do with you, a God who doesn't need my body to quell the loneliness of a middle-aged man.

On Sundays I go and sit with the Quakers. For an hour I sit and listen to the wind outside and the way it blends in with the sound of passing cars. I close my eyes and feel my breath go from my nostrils down into my chest, making its way to the soles of my feet. I feel the blood coursing through my veins, and sometimes I know what Quakers mean when they talk about "that of God" being in everyone.

We drink coffee afterwards and they tell me about their gardens or

ACKNOWLEDGMENTS

Thanks to: Ross Bradshaw and everyone at Five Leaves Bookshop; Caroline Hennigan and the staff at Nottingham Broadway; Janna Graham, Merce Santos, Alba Colomo, and all at Nottingham Contemporary.

Thanks also: Katherine Carroll, Hilary Cook, Russell Christie, Julie Crosby, Joel Davie, Jon Evans, Brendan Flanagan, Julianna Haubner, David Hesmondhalgh, Ian Kershaw, Rebecca Kidd, John "Mac" McClelland, Maggie MacLure, Brian McCormack, Deirdre O'Byrne, Tracey Potts, Emma Robertson, Mark Russell, Frank Rutten, Ira Silverberg, Nick Stevenson, Helen Steward, Matt Turpin, and Colin Wright.

Thanks to my agent, Tony Peake; my editors, Ravi Mirchandani, Nicholas Blake, and Ansa Khan Khattak. A special thanks to Jonathan Coe and Julie Hesmondhalgh, who conspired to get this book out in the first place.

Printed in the United States
By Bookmasters